Strategic Market Relationships
From Strategy to Implementation

Strategic Market Relationships
From Strategy to Implementation

BILL DONALDSON
University of Strathclyde

TOM O'TOOLE
Waterford Institute of Technology

JOHN WILEY & SONS, LTD

Other Wiley Editorial Offices

John Wiley & Sons, Inc., 605 Third Avenue,
New York, NY 10158-0012, USA

WILEY-VCH Verlag GmbH, Pappelallee 3,
D-69469 Weinheim, Germany

John Wiley & Sons Australia, Ltd, 33 Park Road, Milton,
Queensland 4064, Australia

John Wiley & Sons (Asia) Pte Ltd, 2 Clementi Loop #02-01,
Jin Xing Distripark, Singapore 129809

John Wiley & Sons (Canada) Ltd, 22 Worcester Road,
Rexdale, Ontario M9W 1L1, Canada

Library of Congress Cataloging-in-Publication Data

Donaldson, Bill, 1948–
Strategic market relationships from stategy to implementation / Bill Donaldson, Tom O'Toole.
   p. cm.
   Includes bibliographical references and index.
   ISBN 0-471-49443-7
   1. Relationship marketing. 2. Strategic alliances (Business).
   3. Business networks. 4. Industrial management. I. O'Toole, Tom. III. Title.

HF5415.55 .D66 2001
658.8′12–dc21   2001045658

British Library Cataloguing in Publication Data

A catalogue record for this book is available from the British Library

ISBN 0-471-49443-7

Typeset in Palatino by Deerpark Publishing Services Ltd, Shannon.
Printed and bound in Great Britain by Biddles Ltd, Guildford and King's Lynn
This book is printed on acid-free paper responsibly manufactured from sustainable forestry, in which at least two trees are planted for each one used for paper production.

To Caitlin
To Mary Shanley and Joe O'Toole

Contents

Preface

Relationships between independent business have always been part of our economic landscape. Relationships are becoming more and more intensive due to the interconnected nature of the global economy. An economic shock in one part of the world can spill over into the rest of the world because of the criss-cross connectivity of firms and finance on a global basis. Strategic alliances, joint ventures and research and development co-operation are commonplace in industries as diverse as electronic communications and hospitality. The power and prevalence of relationships means that they are at the centre of decision making in organisations. Deciding on the extent of co-operation has become a major strategic issue. Co-operating to compete is not only a feature of decisions concerning competitor and customer interaction but also supply chain, and managed relationships with other stakeholders such as employees, financial markets, government and interest groups. Even if a firm does not want to use relationships as a strategy for competing it still has to consider the complexity and connectedness of the market spaces in which it operates.

Organisations have to manage multiple and overlapping relationships. The multiplicity of networks any firm finds itself in requires a different strategic perspective. No one firm has all the knowledge and resources it needs to compete within its own control. Companies that can combine resources across organisations and accelerate learning across organisational boundaries are likely to have a winning strategy for the future. The disaggregation of the hierarchical organisation into a network of interdependent organisations has already happened. The challenge is how to hone our skills to manage this network and the wide variety of relationships in it. Close strategic market relationships require a managerial approach that seeks collaboration rather than confrontation, joint involvement rather than unilateral action and an acknowledgement of interdependence rather than independence. We believe that these relationships are complex but can be managed. This managerial activity is the focus of the text.

This is the first text that comprehensively addresses relationships as a strategic issue. It maps relationship choices from strategy to implementation. The text is divided into two equal parts: strategy and implementation. Considering relationships as strategic and as a basis for competition is central to this book. Strategic market relationships is the process of analysing, formulating and implementing a relationship strategy for an organisation. Ignoring relationships as a strategic issue would be a blind spot – missing a key economic reality. All firms must consider relationships strategically but not all firms have to use them as a strategy to compete.

The objectives of this book are:

- To present relationships as a strategic resource
- To chart a managerial approach to strategic relationships
- To complete the strategic market relationships cycle – from strategy to implementation
- To focus on close relationships as a benchmark for other types
- To present an integrated course of study in relationship strategy and implementation
- To act as a reference source for research in strategic market relationships

There are many unique features of this book. We have already mentioned that we take a strategic focus from strategy to implementation, take a managerial perspective, and provide an integrated course of study in relationships management. These in themselves make the book quite distinctive. However, in addition to these foci we cover many areas that are important to strategic market relationships but that are under researched at present. For example, relationship planning, relationships implementation (our 5-Ss of relationship implementation attempts to provide a managerial framework for relationship strategy implementation), and e-relationships. However, we own a debt to our colleagues everywhere who have provided a rich and diverse bedrock of theory and practice which we have integrated into strategic market relationships. The prime relationship nexus we concentrate on is the demand, competitive and supply relationships but do include examples and reference where appropriate to other stakeholder relationships, for example, to people especially in the implementation phase.

The book is aimed to be used as a textbook and source book. There are 13 chapters including the introduction and conclusion chapters to fit into a modular course design. Each chapter has learning objectives, chapter questions (including task-related questions), and ample examples including an application case at the beginning of each chapter. To reinforce the chapter learning, an end of chapter case is provided to enable the course to be thought using a case teaching method to complement the lectures. References can be found at the end of the book and each chapter includes further reading to facilitate research on the topic areas. The book is aimed at advanced undergraduate or at postgraduate/MBA courses. We would expect readers to have completed some courses in management or marketing before using this text. Management or marketing courses that have an element of strategy in them would be an advantage. Practising managers on MBA programmes may not need such background. We have structured the book as a stand-alone module in relationship strategy, management or marketing. Strategic market relationships are an exciting subject to study. Their multiplicity and variety make for interesting reading. Relationship theory has developed from many, and sometimes divergent sources. Therefore this book should challenge the widely held assumptions about how markets and businesses operate in a network economy.

Acknowledgements

The authors and publishers wish to thank the following for permission to use copyright material.

The American Marketing Association (AMA) for Figures 1.2, 4.2, 6.4 and 10.5, and Tables 2.1 and 6.1.

Butterworth Heinnemann for Figure 2.1 from Peck et al. (1999) and Table 2.2 from Gummesson (1999).

Dryden Press for Figures 6.3 and 7.1 from Turnbull and Zolkieweski (1997).

Harvard Business School for Table 2.4, Figures 8.3 and 8.6.

JAI Press for Table 5.1.

Jossey Bass for Figure 11.1.

Routledge for Figure 5.1 from Hakansson and Johansson (1992).

Prentice Hall for Figure 10.3 from Urban and Hauser (1993).

Naturally, in a work of this kind, the greatest acknowledgements must go to our colleagues and students whose ideas and, in some cases, content we have used extensively. In particular, we acknowledge the contribution of Michael Gaughan, Shaun Powell, Nikos Tzokas, Peter Jeffries, Stewart Laing, Yves Peeters and Alistair Calder.

CHAPTER 1

Introduction to strategic market relationships

Introduction and objectives

A change is taking place in the world of business and management. This change manifests itself in the way a firm interacts and deals with the demands of different stakeholders with whom the firm comes into contact. While some of these contacts are short and relatively unimportant, others are close and enduring. Key stakeholders in a firm are its customers and its investors. Managers have to meet, successfully, on the one hand, the demands from customers for greater value and satisfaction and on the other, the investors' demands for growth, profitability and enhanced shareholder value. Hence we can observe that making and selling is not sufficient to succeed in business. Instead it requires a different view of business – one that emphasises exchange and relationships, focuses on partnerships and accommodates the needs of different stakeholders. This represents a different and modified view therefore, in this chapter, we analyse reasons why this important trend in relationships has emerged, or re-emerged, and we compare traditional management, especially marketing management, with a relationship-based approach. Definitions of relationships and relationship marketing are considered and a claim is made for the need to study the subject in a new and different way based upon an analysis of the most important trends in today's markets. These trends are forcing businesses to re-think the markets in which they operate and the way they do business.

After reading the chapter you should understand:

- the reasons for the emergence of business based on a relationship approach;
- the comparison of transactional and relationship based exchange;
- the similarities and differences between traditional marketing management and strategic market relationships;
- the trends encouraging a relationship approach;
- the implications of relationships for the management of the firm.

The opening case illustration in this chapter highlights the need to develop close relationships with a range of different role partners to finance, develop and supply the market offer. In this business you have to be both quick and innovative. The capacity and risks associated with achieving market solutions can seldom be found in one company and the Formula One illustration that follows shows that new and improved products and services can no longer be handled by one firm or department. To compete in this arena, collaboration with partners in the supply chain, upstream and down-stream, is the most effective way to mobilise resources and overcome the disadvantages of scale. The illustration highlights that there are many different types of relationship that have to be managed and suggests that the manipulation of price, product, promotion and place are no longer enough to compete in today's markets. In the case of Jordan, if they did not operate in a relationship mode they would not have the new products and services and would not possibly be able to compete. This vignette also highlights that relationships with financial providers and others are vital to a business of this type and scale. Sometimes these relationships become more formal and hence, result in the creation of strategic alliances or joint ventures.

CASE ILLUSTRATION   **FORMULA ONE AND JORDAN GRAND PRIX LIMITED (JGP)**

In the highly charged atmosphere of Formula One the opportunities to innovate and increase the business are immense. Although there are a few dominant players such as Ferrari, Mecedes–McLaren and Jaguar–Ford, this is an industry characterised by co-operation among many participants in an effort to compete. One of these teams, JGP, was formed in 1992 by Eddie Jordan to manage and promote a Formula One racing team incorporating the design, development and manufacture of Formula One racing cars. The company has an annual turnover of £45 million and though it has not had the best season in 2000 it has previously ended third in the Formula One Manufacturer's League table.

The company's customers represent both sponsors and supporters. Sponsors contribute around £30 million per annum to the company and the supporters contribute around £2 million. The scale and expense of running a Formula One team means that relationships with sponsors are crucial and the company has recently worked with a new partner, Warburg Pincus, to continue to develop its relationships in competition with the 'big boys' in the sport. Relationships are increasingly important to the company as it attempts to overcome logistical and cultural barriers in what is now regarded as a truly global sport. The company's weak links with Eastern Europe and Asia put them at a disadvantage in this respect because they do not have a network of international partners. Further, their original sponsorship has been heavily tobacco-based and they now face the prospect of greatly reduced support from this area with an impending EU ban. Furthermore, the relationships that are vital to their future, particularly with engine and tyre manufacturers, are harder to manage as they are more difficult to gain any kind of exclusive deal.

In the space of 7 short years, JGP ranks in the top echelons of the sport, third only to the mighty Ferrari and Mercedes–McLaren teams. Jordan is based in Norfolk, UK in a high-tech purpose-built facility employing 170 people. The factory is not only home to the Jordan team but also home to representatives from various suppliers who work alongside Jordan engineers to develop and test new products and components. Such suppliers include Honda, Hewlett Packard and ESAT Digiphone. Revenue streams come from sponsorship, prize money, TV revenue, merchandise, the Formula One

Association and engineering and aerodynamic consultancy contracts. The owner's own philosophy comes straight from the sentiments expressed in much of this book "...for a team to succeed in Formula One it must be dedicated, innovative, flexible and fast to respond to the current market environment" (Bowen, 1999, p. 22). Part of the operation is through effective strategic alliances and relationships. These include relationships not only with sponsors but also with supporters who purchase merchandise, subscribe to the fan club and use JGP credit cards. New business is acquired through innovative market relationships and track performance. It uses IT to stay in touch with all role partners and some of the approaches are outlined in Table 1.1.

Table 1.1 JGP relationships

Sponsors	Supporters
Well managed and updated Web page communicating team news, views, etc.	Well-managed and updated Web page communicating news and views
Factory tours, sponsor days and evenings, newsletters	Competitions
Corporate entertainment at Grand Prix	VIP days at a Grand Prix, meet drivers, win merchandise
Drivers appearances and promotions	Jordan credit card with database of personal details and used for marketing
High profile brand exposure	Merchandise offers, competition details promotions and the like
Wide media coverage	Web page discussion forum
Strategic alliance with team sponsors	
Inter-sponsor sales opportunities	
Atmosphere – the fun team on the circuit	

The importance of the informal relationships should not be under-estimated even, or especially, in such a technically demanding and high profile business. JPG maintains a high media profile through its unorthodox and flamboyant approach to the sport. The team's impromptu post Grand Prix rock concerts have attained legendary status among the Grand Prix fraternity. Team members, including Eddie Jordan who plays drums; drivers, sponsors, commentators and media representatives are encouraged to join in, sing along and play with the 'band'. For media exposure, JGP offers great value for money compared with others, at only a fraction of the budget that Ferrari carries, because their stories are newsworthy, interesting and promote the fun element. Again, this is reflected by Eddie Jordan himself who declares "It is vital that customers (sponsors) feel part of the infrastructure of the company" (Allen, 2001, p. 22).

Significant revenue comes from Benson and Hedges and unfortunately for Jordan this revenue will be lost, although no fixed date has yet been agreed for the tobacco-advertising ban. New sponsors and global brands are pursued by many sports but this is increasingly difficult to achieve for a lower placed team. Venture capital is now in the sport and JGP sold a 45% stake to Warberg Pincus, a venture capital company at a cost of £70 million. They now own all the marketing rights to the Jordan name for the next 5 years and intend to gain further global exposure. Formula One has a global audience of 350 million and huge Internet potential (Edwards, 1999). The rise of pay-per-view TV will also influence the future direction of the sport. "There is only one winner and somebody has to come last. After a while people get fed up with coming last and pull out" according to Craig Pollock, BAR Limited (Allen, 2001, p. 22). Another threat is from the big players themselves. "I feel the flexibility of Formula One will be lost if teams are taken over by big companies" says Eddie Jordan (Allen, 2001, p. 22).

JGP competes with others for sponsorship, investors, media exposure and race position. These have an impact on TV revenues, top drivers and technicians and, of course, fans. Building relationships at the same time as competing is difficult to manage. Again, Table 1.2 shows the number of players involved and how difficult and complex relationship management can be.

Table 1.2   JGP sponsor relationships

Title sponsor Benson and Hedges 30% of revenue

MasterCard International[a]	EMC[a]
Hewlett–Packard[a]	European Aviation[a]
Lucent Technologies[a]	ESAT Digiphone[a]
Bridgestone Corporation[a]	Honda Direct Marketing[a]
NGK Spark Plug Co[a]	Imation[a]
Powermarque[a]	Scania[a]
Zepter	Keihin Laidlaw Colourgraphics[a]
Pearl Assurance	OS Integration
Diversey Lever	Serengeti Eyewear
Pilsner Urquell	Armour All
Intercond	Natwest Card Services
Playstation	

[a] Denotes a strategic alliance with agreed long-term commitment.

Sources: Bowen, 1999; Allen, 2001; Edwards, 1999; www.jordangp.com; www.itv-f1.co.uk

Structure and purpose of the book

The Formula One illustration places innovative activity in a relationship context that results in new ways to develop products and services and in finding new routes to market. It is our view that previous works on relationship marketing do not go far enough in the transition from the old order to the new. Relationships are not only a tactical weapon, but represent a different approach to buyer–seller exchange that is strategic. Therefore the new order suggests that you have to firstly select those with whom you have a relationship. Secondly, manage and sustain these relationships. Finally plan, organise, deploy and lead in relationship-based solutions across your business and its stakeholders. This implies:

- Re-configuring the business in terms of philosophy, organisation and management;
- Developing and maintaining partnerships with a range of stakeholders;
- Finding ways to secure competitive advantage and deliver superior added value.

This is a different view of business. It is not appropriate for everyone in every product/market situation but it is a vital way to operate and compete for many, and will produce superior business performance. Strategic market relationships is the process of analysis and formulation of a relationship strategy for a firm. Relationship management is the process of implementing it. Considering relationships as a strategic asset and as a basis for competition is central to this book. Strategic issues concern all in an organisation but these decisions are often seen as ones top management must ultimately make. Relationship decisions introduce a co-dependence on others and a co-involvement with them (managing partnership). A strategic market relationship approach is a risky strategy for organisations without the managerial capability to manage relationships. Therefore, a relationship orientation is a vital component to strategic success and a relationship strategy cannot be easily 'bolted-on' to existing methods. This is the first text to pursue a comprehensive assessment of relationships as strategy – from analysis to implementation. Many previous texts see relationships as a functional issue but we view them as an imperative for all functions but especially as a strategic function.

We argue that relationships are a strategic management issue and that the management of relationships is a core managerial task. Often relationships are seen as something the purchasing, customer service, or the salespeople do and relationship tactics are described for this level of implementation. However, if relationships are seen as a distinctive capability of a firm and can lead to its success, then active strategies should be pursued for a firm's key relationships with its suppliers, customers, and employees. Although we start from a marketing perspective, we develop ideas on relationship strategy and move on to specific implementation issues. We primarily concentrate on relationships between a company, its customers and the supply and distribution chain. Strategic market relationships are about analysis and planning for relationships in a co-dependent way – seeing relationships as a core organisational asset and being active in their management. We argue that managers need to put effort into relationships.

This book is divided into two parts. Part one addresses issues relating to the strategy of relationships in which we compare and contrast relationships with other approaches in management and consider the trends influencing relationship orientation. Following this introductory chapter we argue, in chapter 2, that relationships are strategic. Several different relationship domains are considered and we compare co-operation as a means of competing with traditional management approaches. We examine relationship value and issues concerned with the selection, positioning and competitive advantage opportunities afforded through relationships.

In chapter 3 we introduce theories underpinning relationships, dividing them into economic and behavioural-based theories. Further work by scholars should develop our understanding and we would advocate working towards a meta-theoretical perspective. Although students should study these theories in some detail, this chapter can be omitted by those keen to explore more pragmatic issues in relationships. Chapter 4 then applies the strategic planning process to relationships using a three-stage framework – analysis, formulation and selection, and implementation. In this chapter we introduce the core dimensions of relationship implementation in our 5-S framework of structure, staff, style, systems and schemes. In our view, this provides a planning methodology linking relationship strategy to implementation.

Chapter 5 on networks considers the connections, both strong and weak, between a range of companies and individuals providing insights into interactions between all actors in a network. In chapter 6 we attempt to classify relationships using our relationship classification matrix and examine relationship portfolios and how relationships might be developed. Using our 5-S framework, chapter 7 is concerned with how firms initiate, develop and retain profitable relationships. This extends, in a more specific way, in the following chapter where systems and schemes are considered in more detail. The main focus is on how a product or service is supplied in a relationship context and the emphasis is on the classic dyad between buyer and seller.

Subsequently, in chapter 9, implementation of E-relationships and the impact of IT on relationships are considered. Chapter 10 shows how relationships and the relationship based approach impact on innovation and, in particular, the New Product Development Process. In chapter 11 we consider how firms gain from relationships in their international activities. Chapter 12 assesses relationship performance and in chapter 13 some conclusions and further reflections on strategic market relationships are drawn.

The need to assess relationships from a strategic perspective was never greater. Perhaps this development just parallels a trend towards an economy where no individual can supply all the knowledge needed to deliver services and products that have some form of competitive advantage? This implies that combinations of unique assets of many participants may be needed. This type of economy requires a shift from the traditional hierarchical management and control systems to relationship management. Relationships are not a panacea to solve all organisational problems, but not to consider strategic market relationships and to decide how far an organisation wishes to go may leave significant opportunities to others. We believe relationships can be unique resources and deliver competitive advantage in some situations.

The emergence of strategic market relationships

The origins of a relationship-based approach to the management of a firm emerge from academics and practitioners in the fields of strategy, marketing and supply chain management. To some, such as Christopher et al. (1992), it appears to be a new way for marketing management to operate and is based on a managerial perspective that is part of a quest to make marketing effort more effective. In this context every customer is an individual, strong customer relationships are important for profitability, existing customers are more important than new ones and knowledge of the individual customer is paramount for the future direction of the business. To others, for example Gronroos (1994), relationships are strategic so that interactive marketing becomes a question of strategy – its origins, development and its continuation is a strategic focus for the firm. Yet another approach is to view relationships as part of the drive for a more efficient supply chain with the emphasis being on developing closer relationships between channel partners. This will take costs out of transactions, and by implication, the entire supply chain. This can also be strategic but is industry-specific.

Transactions versus relationships

A major distinguishing characteristic between types of exchange is to assess whether it is based on a market transaction or a relational exchange. The nature of these exchanges, their creation, maintenance and termination, is of crucial importance to the understanding of strategic market relationships. Suppliers can classify different types of customer relationships and must identify and manage their position on a spectrum between one-off sales and their important long-term relationships. This is shown in Figure 1.1.

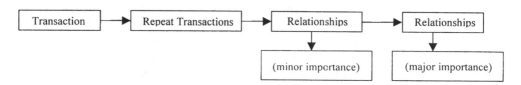

Figure 1.1   Behavioural spectrum of relationships (Source: adapted from Jackson, 1985).

At one end of the spectrum is the transaction-based approach where little or no joint involvement is necessary or desirable. Purchasing petrol for cash in a distant location one is unlikely to visit again is an example of a one-off transaction. Products normally associated with the 'hard sell' approach are more likely to be considered transactions or, if a relationship exists, of minor importance. Transaction-based marketing appeals for products which are to a standard specification, of low value and available under market-type conditions. These transactions command little customer integration between organisations and a buyer should check around between different suppliers to obtain the best price and availability. Suppliers may try to offer incentives but these are unlikely to sustain a differentiation and can be copied by competitors, hence they must expect to win and lose business mainly on price.

However, for most purchases, it would be normal for some form of relationship to develop such as buying your daily newspaper from the same retail outlet or visiting a local petrol station on a regular basis. Though this is a repeated transaction, in some cases, the relationship between buyer and supplier is of minor importance, while in other cases, the relationship, its longevity, quality and benefits are of major importance. Increasingly, we can observe businesses that fall into the latter category, with both buyer and seller finding it to their mutual benefit.

Industrial products and services, trade marketing and business-to-business selling are more typical of a relationship-based approach. Mutual success may depend on establishing and maintaining a sound relationship between supplier and customer. It is incumbent upon both parties in the relationship to assess the costs and benefits that are likely to accrue from a relationship based approach rather than one based on single discrete transactions. At the extreme right of the spectrum, relationships of major importance may formalise into partnerships, joint ventures or strategic alliances where significant co-operation and joint involvement is advocated and deemed necessary. The position on the spectrum will depend on a number of factors. First, on the basis of switching costs. If both parties have investments in the relationship in the form of stock, stock control systems, pricing and payment arrangements then there are likely to be substantial costs involved in transferring to other parties. Second, it is important to identify the position that is most appropriate along the behaviour spectrum. Excessive costs can be avoided in relationship building that may not be warranted by the volume of business between the parties. Third, arising from this, is the importance of identifying those partners with whom a relationship should be built and developed. Not all suppliers, from a buyer perspective, nor all customers from a supplier perspective, are worth investing heavily in relationship building. Finally, both parties should consider how the relationship would develop or possibly reduce and even terminate over time as market conditions and other circumstances change.

The classification developed by Jackson (1985) is a useful point of departure between a traditional transaction-based approach on the one hand and a strategic market-based approach on the other.

Table 1.3 highlights some of the key differences. The relationship model is more appropriate where there is a high degree of interaction, exchange of information, investments in stock and a resultant high cost to the buyer in switching suppliers. Where the buyer and seller are interdependent, very often satisfied with each other, a degree of inertia builds up. However, should the supplier fail to deliver and

Table 1.3   A comparison between the traditional and the strategic relationship approach

Traditional approach	Strategic market relationship
Transaction focus	Partnership focus
Competition	Collaboration
Firm-induced	Co-operation
Value to the firm	Value in partnership
Buyer passive	Buyer as active participant
Firm as focus for control	Firm as part of the process
Firm as boundary	Boundary-less
Short-term focus	Long-term focus
Independent	Dependence and network-led

perform as expected, the buyer may seek alternatives. In such a situation it will be difficult, if not impossible, to win the buyer back as high switching costs may have been incurred. Having decided to terminate the relationship the buyer will have no appetite for reviving it. The touchstone is whether the customer continues to do a single transaction at a time and needs short-term inducements to remain loyal or whether buyer and seller acknowledge their interdependent status. From a supplier's perspective, companies with both types of customers face great difficulty in a consistent strategy as they attempt to make optimum decisions over short-term (transaction) and long-term (relationship) horizons simultaneously. We will later consider how information technology has helped narrow the gap and make relationship building possible in even the most basic and impersonal of transactions.

As Figure 1.1 demonstrated, it is appropriate to view the transaction/relationship approach as a continuum with a variety of positions being tenable and even desirable. This means there are different types of relationships and we return to this issue throughout the book. In some cases, for example where there is integrated design or joint development activity in a project, then suppliers must develop a closer relationship with the customer, adopt a long-term perspective, be strategic and tactical and highly account-specific (Wilkstrom, 1996). This will involve significant up-front investment and consistently good performance. Other research has shown that those firms who have close relationships with their suppliers are subject to more frequent and detailed analyses than firms who may maintain a more distant transaction-based exchange (Donaldson, 1996). The challenge is clear; only invest in relationships where you are prepared to work, invest and promote continuing improvement or the business may be lost for good.

Traditional management and relationship management

Managing the various relationship types may place emphasis on managerial style and associated organisational culture. Companies using adversarial methods in dealing with one supplier might find it a challenge to change to a relationship approach. Organisations who pride themselves on their independence may find it difficult to pursue a strategy of co-involvement. The conventional approach, in an independent mode, involves adopting a proactive stance where the emphasis is placed on:

- Identifying customer needs and requirements;
- Anticipating future trends and monitoring environmental forces;
- Satisfying customers' existing and future requirements through managing the product or service package, optimising value for money pricing, maximising availability and delivery while promoting and selling benefits in the most effective way;
- Profit: ensuring that the company will be able to provide this process in the future.

We do not claim that this independent model of the way the world works is redundant but we do consider it will work only in certain situations and contexts.

In other contexts, the process can be too simple and too restrictive. Usually, a buying organisation will have an overall style which affects all relationships. One of the critical issues of managerial style is the need to match styles across organisations. Considerable pains need to be taken to select a partner that would be culturally compatible with one's own approach. Cultural compatibility should not be underestimated as many firms try to impose their culture on the partner firm (Sinclair et al., 1996). Indeed, the social structure of a relationship has been the focus of early social exchange theorists (Blau, 1964) and of the Industrial Marketing and Purchasing Group's research (Hakansson, 1982), especially the concept of relationship atmosphere. Perhaps the most helpful concepts with which to work on managerial behaviour are the process variables – trust and commitment. These variables have been found to be key mediators of the strength of a relationship (Morgan and Hunt, 1994). Different levels of trust and commitment can signal alternative stylistic approaches whether partnership, friendship, adversary or detachment (O'Toole and Donaldson, 2000).

From a buyer's perspective, the reputation and size of the supplier as well as the characteristics of the salesperson may be indicative of trust. In addition, the willingness to make adaptations and investments can also signal trust (Doney and Canon, 1997). Levels of trust (Sako, 1992) include contractual (keeping promises), competence (perform role competently), and goodwill (willingness to do more than is expected). These levels can be used to signal or withdraw trust or build a trustful reputation. Trusting behaviour is a potent tool of managerial intent and action.

With regard to commitment, this can be viewed as having two dimensions – input and continuance (Meyer and Allen, 1994; Gundlach et al., 1995). The committed input will vary with type of relationship. For example, some relationships may have idiosyncratic and dedicated resource investments and partners may share proprietary information. Continuance commitment is reflected in the temporal intentions of the parties. Long-term orientation is a key feature of certain relationship types.

Therefore, there has been a tendency for marketing to become a moral maxim based on empty rhetoric but lacking in substance as a means of operating the business. As a result, looking at strategic market relationships can offer alternative solutions more relevant to markets as they exist today. Strategic market relationships also offer the opportunity to create markets and new forms of exchange processes. Again, we will highlight some of these situations later in the text. Webster (1992) identified this trend from transaction marketing to strategic relationships and classified relationship types as shown in Figure 1.2.

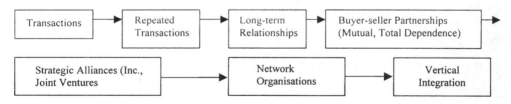

Figure 1.2   A classification of relationship types (Source: Webster, 1992).

As Figure 1.2 demonstrates there is a continuum from the one-off transaction to the vertically integrated organisation at the other end of the spectrum. To the left of this spectrum is the pure market where price is a given, competition is fierce and the role of marketing is to find buyers. In this situation there is no brand, no added service, no reason for customer loyalty and little or no differentiation in the product or service. Moving along the spectrum, the next situation is that of repeated transactions where loyalty is stimulated by branding or some aspect of performance. The aim, from a supplier perspective, is to provide 100% customer satisfaction, encourage repeat patronage and avoid losing customers. In a number of industrial goods and services, long-term relationships develop when buyer and seller are aware of each other and do business on a regular basis. In particular, where the proportion of bought-in goods and services is a substantial part of the cost price such as in motor manufacture, electronics and machine tools, more emphasis is given to developing, sustaining and enhancing these relationships. Based on models such as Toyota's lean supply concept (Womack et al., 1990) has stimulated other firms to work with fewer suppliers and distributors than had been the case in the past. A development of the long-term relationship is a situation of mutual, total dependence, where both supplier and distributors are limited to few in number and the relationship is formal and contractual. Based on the Japanese concept of *Keiretsu* (relationship structures) and *Canban* (continuous improvement) many western firms have adopted the ideas of TQM, JIT supply and closer relationships with their distributors.

Further along the spectrum are strategic alliances where companies, in order to achieve long-term strategic goals, agree to participate with role partners in order to be more effective in the supply and exploitation of a given market. The impetus for this is often to minimise transaction costs. In some case these strategic alliances will develop into formal joint ventures, where the aim is to proceed in perpetuity. In reality, many strategic alliances have been shown to be short-term and questions arise about the wisdom of choosing only a few suppliers with which to do business. Finally, at the extreme right of the spectrum are networks that are multi-faceted organisational structures leading to vertically integrated operations.

Definitions of relationship management reflect these changes in management and strategy. For example, one definition is that "relationship marketing refers to all marketing activities directed toward establishing, developing, and maintaining successful relational exchanges" (Morgan and Hunt, 1994). Such a definition embraces a variety of partners, not just customers and the term 'relationship' can mean a variety of things depending on how it is applied. It can be taken to mean any type of co-operation, from coercive supply relationship to strategic alliances (Webster, 1992). On the other hand, a more practical-based definition is that relationship marketing is how a company finds you; gets to know you; keeps in touch with you; tries to ensure you get what you want from them, not just in the product but in every aspect of their dealings with you; checks that you are getting what they promised you – all subject, of course, to it being mutually worthwhile to both parties (Stone and Woodcock, 1995). Currently, in consumer products and services, relationship marketing has been referred to as one-to-one marketing (Peppers and

Rogers, 1997), maxi-marketing (Rapp and Collins, 1994) and loyalty-based marketing (Reicheld, 1996).

Be aware that strategic market relationships are not biological but part of a management process whether buyer-initiated, seller-initiated or both. Our focus, in this book, is from a marketing perspective but we confess to seeing relationships as a management issue where functions become subservient to an integrated, holistic managerial perspective of the way a firm conducts its business.

As noted, definitions focus on relationship marketing rather than relationship management but the need for the organisation to satisfy a number of stakeholders renders such definitions obsolete. To explore this we consider stakeholders in the firm and assess what they are looking for in the relationship they have with the firm and compare this with the limited approach of some of the definitions of relationship marketing. A range of stakeholders are shown in Figure 1.3.

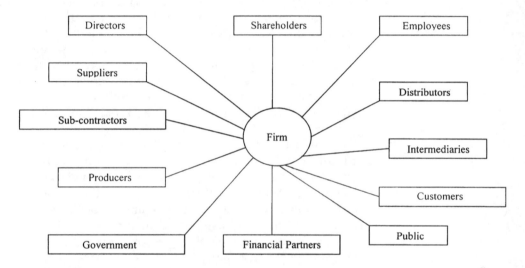

Figure 1.3   Stakeholding in the firm.

We consider relationships with stakeholders in different ways. First, on the left of the diagram is upstream with suppliers/sub-contractors and producers. The need to reduce transaction costs and enhance value for customers encourages, even necessitates, firms within a supply chain working together to achieve competitive advantage. A second group is the shareholders, directors and employees of the firm. A third group are those downstream in the supply chain who may be distributors, intermediaries and, we would argue most important of all, customers. Much of this book is concerned with these types of relationships. A fourth group is relationships with financial partners, not only shareholders in the firm but banks and other investors, perhaps credit brokers and other financial facilitators. Finally, relationships involving legal obligations or contracts such as local and national government authorities and with the public at large.

Trends driving relationships

The important trends driving a relationship agenda include the following:

Globalisation of markets and organisations that span them

In traditional business markets that were shaped by the industrial economy, opening new markets was difficult as it took years to conduct market research, construct and deploy physical assets, identify and deliver market-specific inventory and put production and sales capabilities in place. In the new economy, using e-commerce capability, markets can be opened overnight and virtual channels created to source, promote, sell, deliver and support goods and services. Established firms find new firms not only entering their market but also stealing market share as well. Organisations need to react to this threat, develop their own value propositions and enhance their brands to expand their global reach. Mass marketing has given way to mass customisation and organisations must be customer-centric on the one hand and have a global presence on the other. The answer is to access information in real time and leverage knowledge and understanding of customers and markets. Customers need to know not where you are but who you are and what you can do?

Firms must adapt and change to reflect this global imperative. They have to operate across geographical boundaries and, thus, manage intra-organisational relationships. The quickening pace of competition on a global basis creates new market opportunities but also threatens existing market structures. To learn to be global is a smart move for independent companies but can only be achieved, in most situations, by cross-organisational learning that reduces risk and overcomes cultural barriers.

Falling world growth rates

Many markets are consolidating and the players who operate in these markets find the size of the cake shrinking. This necessitates a re-focus on delivering value and building up entrepreneurial skills since physical assets are less important. Yet the new global model is culturally diverse and organisationally complex. For example, in Europe, car manufacturing capacity in 1999 was operating at 73% utilisation despite sales growth of 25% since 1995 (Lofthouse, 2000). In the UK grocery market, there were approximately 1500 buying points for 60% of the market in 1970, an already concentrated market. By 1980 this had reduced to 625 buying points. In 1999, 60% of the market is represented by just seven buying points (IGD Research, 2000). Given these market scenarios in times of falling growth or market rationalisation, companies must co-operate to compete.

Merger and acquisition activity

As many industries will testify, e.g. pharmaceuticals, financial services, electronics and telecommunications, in times of rapid environmental change and increasing uncertainty, firms take refuge, or seek protection from uncertainty, in mergers and acquisitions. Greater productivity can come from acquiring knowledge, skills and resources than from developing these internally. It is also likely to be gained from activity between organisations than from within organisations. Therefore, coupled with increased mergers and acquisitions, we can observe a greater readiness to outsource. Whatever the reason, companies need to collaborate more widely and more deeply with other organisations to deliver superior customer value. Skoda is a good example of a company with limited routes to market yet in combination with Volkswagen they have gained considerable market share and reputation. In other industries, such as retailing, the ability to reduce transaction costs through efficient supply relationships has been a major factor in the success of Tesco to emerge as market leader.

The need for strategic supply chain management

In most markets, business-to-business markets in particular, firms are aware of the need to improve efficiency in their exchange relationships. Many firms are limiting the number of suppliers with which they do business while working more closely with those they can retain. This trend has been led by the Japanese such as Toyota who introduced lean manufacturing, a process by which they work very closely with a very limited number of suppliers. In other cases, firms are seeking to develop markets in collaboration with suppliers and customers rather than in conflict, which existed hitherto. Such arrangements, whether formalised in joint ventures or operating informally, are characterised by increased levels of customer support and closer collaboration. The role of management in the establishment, maintenance and adaptation of relationships between seller and buyer is therefore important. Yet, the global model is culturally diverse and organisationally complex. International logistics, price processes and information flows create new problems in organisational complexity. The winners will be those who can integrate logistics and inventory management, forecast demand accurately and can still be flexible and responsive – value creation with cost efficiency.

Organisational complexity and the impact of information technology on business efficiency and the rapid development of electronic commerce

In order to meet these demands organisations have to be efficient, yet responsive. In traditional business markets, high collaboration and interaction costs drove high levels of vertical integration. Therefore organisations found it easier and more cost-effective to own many pieces of the value chain. In the new economy, communication and IT has made the virtual organisation possible. By assembling a network of best in class partners that specialise and excel at various links in the value chain, new levels of quality, cost savings and service can be achieved. In this situation niche players can co-exist with industry leaders.

Research carried out by the Boston Consulting Group (BCG, 1999; BCG, 2001) suggests that one-fourth of all US business-to-business purchasing will be done on-line by 2003. BCG estimate that between 1998 and 2003 business-to-business e-commerce will grow 33% per year and reach $2.8 trillion in transactional value. This research also showed that the business-to-business e-commerce market is greater than normally reported because private electronic data interchange (EDI) represents the largest share of volume (86%) and most additional volume will be based on internet transaction (90% by 2003). However, it is not only the technology that drives a relationship agenda. The importance of human capital and knowledge is being recognised as an important strategic resource. The increasing specialisation of knowledge means that firms have to co-ordinate activities to gain access to each other's unique human capital.

What do strategic relationships imply for management?

The consequences of this difference in approach to strategic market relationships manifests itself in the degree of adaptability by the seller to the particular needs of individual customers. In industrial markets, where the buyers are relatively few and some of who will be crucially important to the well being of suppliers, the idea of relationship management has existed for some time. For example, Unilever (customer) and ICI (supplier) work together to compete more effectively in the European market. In some instances, closer relationships are instigated by suppliers in an effort to protect their interests and defend their position in competitive markets.

In other situations, closer working relationships may develop from buyer initiatives where the need for continuity of supply, just in time operating programmes or economies of scale are likely to be vital in the supply chain. Chungwa, a Taiwanese VDU producer led to a number of suppliers building facilities around their European plant in Lanarkshire is an example of this approach. Joint awareness or mutual dependence is important from both buyers' and suppliers' perspectives. This also means recognising mutual participation in areas of product design and modification, pricing, distribution and promotion. The focus therefore is on customer relationships where the supplier in the exchange process should be flexible, adaptable and interactive.

The characteristics of organisations operating in a relationship mode include:

- Developing new opportunities via partnerships and strategic alliances;
- Outsourcing of non-core activities;
- Using product development teams to turn ideas winning products and services;
- Open relationships with their employees;
- Using IT to serve customers better and gain competitive advantage;
- Employing customer satisfaction measurement linked to the company's compensation and reward structure;
- A focus on being market-driven and customer-led.

The relationship approach can be differentiated from any other business based on certain criteria such as:

(a) its belief in not only satisfying or even delighting customers but involving customers as the number one priority;

(b) by investing resources to research markets and customers on a one-to-one basis;

(c) by taking a planned and joint approach towards delivering customer satisfaction.

Firms must not only choose their partners carefully but structure and manage these partnerships thereby allowing time for the relationship to grow and develop. It implies a corporate culture based on trust, open communication and a lack of opportunistic behaviour.

It is necessary for a firm to show their belief and commitment in their relationship with stakeholders. Action needs to be taken not only for change to occur but also for the development of a relationship with particular parties. For example, beliefs about the relationship can be signalled through long-term contracts, fair price dealings and, in short, developing the social structure of the relationship. Specific action can be taken to signal this change such as helping in emergencies, by being responsive and adaptable to requests and by investing in the relationship. Managers should consider actions to demonstrate this investment, for instance in supplier training, provision of managerial assistance and financial support for their customers. Other ways to enhance relationships include providing information on production planning, preferred supply arrangements and specialised supply management structures. Such joint cost-reduction programmes confirm realisable benefits in relationship structures. The need to mobilise resources behind customer-based solutions in an appropriate context is central to relationship enhancement.

Developing a relationship orientation and implementing it in practice may place a strain on managerial style and associated organisational culture. Companies used to more adversarial methods of dealing with suppliers or customers may find it a challenge to change to a relationship approach. Organisations who pride themselves on their independence may find it difficult to pursue a strategy of co-involvement. For managers there are opportunities in taking a closer look at relationships and dividing them into types. Potential gains and losses could be attributed to each type. A firm may be over-committed to certain types of relationships and could improve productivity by a change in focus and mode of co-operation.

Chapter summary

In an effort to anticipate, react and adapt to change, firms are being forced to move from the traditional management activity to a new relationship approach based upon new forms of exchange. This has been characterised by a movement away from seller initiated effort focused on manipulating resources in an independent and prescribed fashion to one of increased understanding of the exchange process, where the buyer is more pro-active. This exchange is based on the joint efforts of the various buyers and sellers in the supply chain. In this new order, exchange is characterised by collaboration and co-operation rather than conflict and confrontation, by joint involvement of participants rather than unilateral action, and by interdependence rather than independence. This leads to a focus that takes as its unit of analysis the exchange process, with the transaction at its focal point, seeking both to understand and manage these relationships. This is in contrast to the traditional approach which focuses on orientation, concepts and techniques more appropriate to the selling organisation, which at worst neglects the customer and at best treats the customer as a passive component in the exchange process.

CASE FOR DISCUSSION

FIRST DIRECT

First Direct was one of the first telephone banks in the UK. Midland Bank, after conducting market research, found that many customers did not use branches and the level of satisfaction amongst others was relatively poor. As a result, First Direct was launched as an independent bank by Midland in October 1989 and provided a phone only service 24 hours per day, 7 days a week. When launched it had no direct competitors and with an improved speed and service for their customers they rapidly expanded. By 1998 they employed 4100 people at three sites in Leeds, Birmingham and Hamilton. Their customer base is more than 1 million and they aim to double this within 10 years (Mazur, 2001). They were awarded the Management Today/Unisys Service Excellence Award in 1998.

Their initial strategy was based on the following:
- Service channel – conventional banks had very limited opening hours especially for those people with non-flexible working hours. The any time, any place solution met a real customer need.
- Brand name – due to the absence of the physical premises, the company invested heavily in its brand name to create the image and reliability necessary for this type of operation. Consequently, advertising was an essential aspect of its marketing strategy.
- Service quality – in 1989 long queues, slow service and poor communication between teller and customer was the standard for this industry. Constant personal, relevant communication, albeit a relationship on the telephone, established a rapport between company and customer.

A good database is an essential part of the process since it enables a dialogue between customer and company and vice-versa. The result was the creation of cross-selling opportunities for investment plans and other savings schemes. Most calls are handled without any need to transfer to a specialised department and investment in training for call handlers paid off for the company.

At the time of launch, although they did not disguise their connection to Midland, only 20% of customers were from Midland. Seventy percent were aged 25–44 and 38% lived in households with an income greater than £35 000. These customers had higher average balances but tended to use services more often than the average bank customer. The company also used extensive marketing research through internal and external surveys and by feedback mechanisms through their call-handlers. Customer satisfaction levels are well above the industry average and 33% of new customers join because of personal recommendation. As a recent Keynote report highlighted, the companies most likely to succeed in the changing world of personal banking are those able to build lasting relationships with their customers (Keynote, 2000).

However, the market continues to change. In 1994, fewer than 2 million people in the

UK had telephone bank accounts but within 3 years this has quadrupled to over 9 million. First Direct has now introduced a PC based service. In 1997, 6% had used an on-line service but this will increase to 15% by 2003. Today, First Direct is facing competition from High Street Banks, Supermarkets, Building Societies, Insurance companies and Electronic Delivery providers. For example, Virgin Direct have attracted over 250 000 customers within 3 years, Egg.com has taken £100 million pounds in savings and many new competitors seem to be entering the market such as Intelligent Finance, a Halifax-backed, internet bank.

Questions

1. Use a SWOT analysis and collect new information to analyse the current position of the business.
2. What aspects of the service experience would you focus on to develop and grow the business?
3. How would you classify the nature of the relationship between an individual customer and the bank?
4. Although using the telephone, First Direct was very much a relationship-based operation, how can this relationship be sustained and developed in the face of increasing competition?
5. Can First Direct make a transition from personal banking to business customer banking?

Sources: Keynote, 2000; Mazur 2001: www.firstdirect.co.uk

Further reading

Achrol, R.S. and Kotler, P. (1999), Marketing in a network economy, *Journal of Marketing*, 63 (Special Issue), pp. 146–163.

Barringer, B.R. and Harrison, J.S. (2000), Walking a tightrope, *Journal of Management*, 26 (5), pp. 367–403.

Berry, L.L. (1983), Relationship marketing, in *Emerging Perspectives on Services Marketing* eds. Berry, L.L., Shostack, G.L. and Upah, G. AMA, Chicago, IL.

Christy, R., Oliver, G. and Penn, J. (1996), Relationships marketing in consumer markets, *Journal of Marketing Management*, 12 (1–3), pp. 175–187.

Egan, J. (2001), *Relationship marketing, exploring relational strategies in marketing*, Financial Times, Prentice Hall: Harolow.

Futrell, C.M. (1998), *Sales Management: Teamwork, Leadership and Technology*, 5th edition, Dryden Press, Orlando, FL.

Grönroos, C. (2000). *Service management and marketing, a customer relationship management approach*, 2nd edition, John Wiley & Sons: Chichester.

Gummesson, E. (1996), Relationship marketing and imaginary organisations: a synthesis, *European Journal of Marketing*, 30 (2), pp. 31–44.

Gummesson, E. (1999), *Total Relationship Marketing*, Butterworth Heinemann, Oxford.

Moller, K. and Halinen, A. (2000), Relationship marketing theory: its roots and direction, *Journal of Marketing Management*, 16 (1–3), pp. 29–54.

O'Malley, L. and Tynan, C. (2000), Relationship Marketing in Consumer Markets: rhetoric or reality? *European Journal of Marketing*, 34 (7), pp. 797–819.

Sheth, J. and Paravatiyara, A. (1995), The Evolution of Relationship Marketing, *International Business Review* 4 (4), pp. 397–408.

Chapter questions

1. Identify a product or service where the relationship of minor importance and one where it is of major importance. Select variables in the marketing of this product and explain how they can be used differently in each relationship context.
2. According to Webster (1992), customer relationships are a key strategic resource of the business. How can such a resource be exploited and managed from a supplier perspective?
3. The monadic paradigm views the buyer and seller as independent rather than interdependent, emphasise their separate analysis rather than appreciating the similarity of their task, and assumes that a single discrete purchase rather than purchases in the context of an ongoing relationship. Discuss the view that this paradigm is no longer an adequate representation of marketing exchange.
4. Explain how an understanding of the differences between transaction-based marketing and relationship-based marketing can assist the firm in its marketing strategy.
5. To what extent do you agree that the conditions in which customer relationships are more likely to develop and prosper or deteriorate reflects internal organisational factors or external market factors?
6. In this chapter, several trends have been identified as driving a relationship approach to business. Are there other trends/influences you feel should be included and, if so, why?
7. What characteristics and specific actions might represent high/low levels of trust between buyer and seller?
8. Selecting a business or organisation, elaborate on the relationship that the organisation has with either financial stakeholders or public/government stakeholders.

CHAPTER 2

Relationships are strategic

Introduction and objectives

Relationships between a company and its employees, customers, and other interested stakeholders are strategic. Certain decisions made about these relationships form part of the strategic management of a company. These decisions set the parameters for implementing a relationship strategy at lower levels in an organisation. Often, relationship decisions are made without due consideration of their strategic value. In this chapter, we map out the strategic domain of relationships and the decisions about relationships that we believe are strategic. Comparing co-operative approaches to competing with competitive ones is also addressed. This is not to suggest that a relational approach to competition fits every situation, but that it is an option and that relationships are a strategic tool of major importance. The chapter also addresses key relationship strategy issues such as relationship value, selection, positioning and the competitive advantage opportunities afforded through relationships. After reading this chapter you should know:

- the different domains in which relationships can be applied;
- the strategic dimensions of relationship thinking;
- the difference between competitive and collaborative approaches to competition;
- have gained insights into strategic relationship issues such as relationship value, selection and positioning;
- whether relationships afford competitive advantage opportunities that are sustainable.

The case illustration presents us with a view of competitor alliances in the airline industry. This industry is still highly regulated and protected by many national governments but the key players have found ways around these prohibitions through partnership. The scope and depth of these partnerships varies widely between the core alliance groups listed in the case illustration. Often it also varies among the individual partners in the alliance. Strategic alliances have a history notable for their failures. The co-operation does not work out for many reasons including partner incompatibility, little benefit from the alliance, few, if any, attempts to implement an alliance programme that cuts across both organisations and binds them together. Simply, having an alliance does not mean it is strategic. The strategy should be visible in the overall intent but also in the actions taken to implement the alliance agreement by managers. Recently, we have seen airline alliance partners shift between alliances. While this may be as a result of a new strategy, it implies that the past partnership was strategic only in name. The real challenge for an airline alliance is to move past the rhetoric and into a real alliance with tangible strategic benefits.

CASE ILLUSTRATION   **AIRLINE INDUSTRY**

The airline industry now comprises up to 500 independent carriers, many of whom are tied together to share each others resources. Yet they are all competitors. However, these competitors often have different territories and have grown out of state-owned companies. In fact, deregulation has been one of the factors driving the closer co-operation between potential competitors. In the past, two airline alliances were the norm but were notoriously unstable. Currently, super alliances have been emerging. These alliances are in place of consolidation which is hindered by regulatory and legalistic mechanisms put in place by governments. The current shape of these super alliances are:

Oneworld (18% of world traffic; www.oneworld.com; www.star-alliance.com; www.skyteam.com; www.nwa.com/alliance)
American Airlines, British Airways, Cathay Pacific, Quantas, Iberia, Finnair, Lan Chile, Air Lingus. This alliance was launched in 1999.

Star (16% of world traffic)
United Airlines, Lufthansa, SAS, Thai Airways, Air Canada, Singapore Airlines, Austrian Airlines, Air New Zealand, British Midland, Mexicana, Tyrolean, Lauda-Air, Varig, Ansett, ANA

Delta (12% of world traffic)
Delta Air Lines, Air France, Aeromexico, Czech Airlines, Korean Air

KLM/North West (6% of world traffic)
KLM, Northwest Airlines

Note: Market traffic figures are estimate.

The type of co-operation between the partners varies enormously between the alliances. First is the consumer side to the alliances. A necessary question, at least in the short-term, is which brand? The airlines are selling their own brand but also that of an alliance. Until these alliances settle down and their brands begin to be known by consumers, a good deal of confusion will remain in the marketplace. Customer alliance benefits include seamless travel with attendant better connections, sharing of airport lounges, cross-use of frequent flier programmes (provided a passenger stays within the alliance partners), and, above all, lower average fares. The latter open-skies model of alliance has facilitated the reduction in fairs through co-operative pricing which gives a certain amount of benefit to each partner. Some of the alliances harmonise fares among the partners. Most alliances share routes (code share – you could buy a ticket for one airline and can end up on a plane of one of the other partners), with fewer sharing the other consumer marketing benefits, although frequent flier programme sharing is getting very common. Outside the consumer marketing benefits, alliances are also seeking mechanisms to pool other resources to reduce each carriers' costs.

Inside the boundaries of each alliance partner the potential for sharing is endless. Sharing of facilities in catering, cleaning, ground crew, engineering, maintenance, ticketing, on-site presence, and aircraft buying all offer scope for sharing and significant cost saving. The potential in this area depends on the strategy of each carrier and what it believes its core competencies are. It may be unwilling to share in an area where it has made much investment and where it estimates its advantage lies. The more alliances move into internal areas the higher the alliance exit barriers will be for any one potential carrier. Individual airlines specialise in many parts of the business from catering to reservation systems; for example, Lufthansa is a world leader in aircraft maintenance.

Alliances have varying policies on cross-share holding in the other alliance members. Some alliances make this a requirement while others do not. Cross-share holding may create a stability but, of course, unless the shares are preference or are required to be held, they can be easily sold if a partner wishes.

The strategic domain of relationships

Relationships with key stakeholders are strategic. Managing relationships is a key strategic issue. Obviously, the external company–customer–supplier–competitor nexus is important but so, too, is the internal network between people and across functions and divisions. Also, macro networks with agencies, government and shareholders play a role in strategy formulation. In this text relationship theory and management are given central focus – viewing relationships as a critical platform for building strategy and sustaining advantage.

Strategy is concerned with the direction and scope of a business into the future. Strategy has been described as being about winning (Grant, 1998). This means delivering sustained value to key stakeholders. These stakeholders may range from employees to share markets (Kay, 1993a). When an organisation stops producing value its rationale for existence ceases. We argue that relationships can deliver sustained value. It is not a strategy for all firms but can work for some. However, without consideration of relationships as a strategic issue, a firm may miss opportunities or face unforeseen threats in its competitive environment.

The dominant approach to strategy is a rational model in which a business is positioned and its direction decided by that company's management after a review of the fit between the business and its environment. It is a planned approach that views the business as an independent actor. We label this view as the traditional approach to strategy. The strategic management of relationships falls outside this view and requires an organisation and its management to accept the idea that the organisation is embedded in layers of connected networks and that many stakeholders are active, or potentially active, in the formulation of company strategy by their actions. It is within an interdependence and co-operative spectrum that relationship strategy is developed. Consideration of a firm's resources and their linkage to partnering organisations and individuals becomes a key determinant of strategy.

Relationship strategy emerges from organisational–partner interdependencies in contrast to the deliberate single organisation independence model of traditional strategy.

The strategic domain of relationships can be easily seen through approaches that categorise overall relational exchanges. In particular, Morgan and Hunt's (1994) relational exchange categories, Peck et al.'s (1999) six markets model and Gummesson's (1994, 1999) 30Rs of relationship marketing. Each of these authors' categorisations demonstrate the strategic potential of market relationships. Morgan and Hunt's (1994) model of 10 discrete relationships is presented in Table 2.1. It describes relationships from a focal firm perspective and divides them into 10 types which are further grouped into four generic categories: supplier partnerships, lateral partnerships, internal partnerships, and buyer relationships. Clearly, choices about partnership can be strategic. Senior management has to decide how close these relationships are to be. Are they to become part of the firm's competitive advantage? If so, how are resources and competencies to be used and developed to deliver such value? These questions are strategic ones. The domain of relationships presented in Table 2.1 and in the subsequent table and figure can therefore be strategic.

Table 2.1 Relational exchange categories (Source: adapted from Morgan et al., 1994)

Category	Description
Supplier partnerships	
1. Goods suppliers	Partnerships between manufacturers and their goods' suppliers
2. Services suppliers	Relational exchanges between service providers and their respective clients, for example, advertising agency-client relationship
Lateral partnerships	
3. Competitors	Strategic alliances between firms and their competitors
4. Non-profit organisations	Alliances between a firm and non-profit organisations, for example, public-private partnership
5. Governments	Partnerships for joint research and development between the state and private organisations
Buyer partnerships	
6. Ultimate customers	Long-term relationships between firms and ultimate customers
7. Intermediate customers	Relational exchanges of working partnerships in distribution
Internal partnerships	
8. Functional departments	Exchanges involving functional departments
9. Employees	Exchanges between a firm and its employees, as in internal marketing
10. Business units	Within firm relational exchanges involving such business units as subsidiaries, divisions, or strategic business units

Figure 2.1   Six market domains (Source: Peck et al., 1999).

Figure 2.1 presents Peck et al.'s (1999) six markets model. Each of the six markets provides a domain for analysing the strategy potential of relationships. Each market can be identified, analysed and planned for. Customer markets are at the core of the six market framework. Developing customer loyalty and building relationships with customers or buyers represent a central theme in managing customer markets. Referrals from users or from knowledgeable parties often represent a critical source of revenue for a firm. This is especially true for markets for professional services such as doctors and lawyers. Internal relationships with employees contribute to overall organisational harmony and efficiency. Employee satisfaction and retention are often drivers of successful relationships elsewhere. Indeed, in services businesses retaining employees can foster stability in links with customers. For example, in personal banking we often like to deal with the same person repeatedly. Employees, whether managers or staff, act as relational interfaces and have a crucial advocacy and relationship building role. Recruitment markets for current and potential employees represent another key market with which to manage relationships. Markets which have an influence over the organisation are external to it and can impact both on its operation and status. Media, governments, investors and pressure groups are all influence markets. For example, in the mid to late 1990s, press reports and coverage of how retail banks seemed tougher on the smaller account holders in terms of payment and charges than they were on wealthy personal borrowers, undermined a certain amount of personal banking trust among the general public. Some argue that it allowed other new bank brands to enter the market such as supermarkets. A similar scenario happened in the insurance market. Relationships are easily damaged and may be difficult to recover when expectations held over long periods of time are suddenly upset. Supplier and alliance markets also feature in a firm's value creation network. They often have a determining input into the quality of the service delivery process of another company. We provided the case example of airline alliances at the start of the chapter.

Gummesson (1994, 1999) takes a macro view of potential relationship categories. While some of his 30Rs may be beyond the planning needs of an individual firm, they show the potential domain of relationship strategy application. Implicitly, his model has parallels with the concept of a stakeholder partnership of strategic management (Freeman and Reed, 1983; Kay, 1993b). Recognition of key organisational interest groups – employees, shareholders, customers, suppliers, community – and how these interests should be balanced? and what happens if an interest group becomes dominant? – are all core strategic issues. Gummesson's (1994) 30Rs of relationships, reproduced in Table 2.2 shows the potential domain of relationships but also the multilayered, overlapping nature of relationships. For example, a company can be a supplier, customer, competitor and part-owner of another firm. By now the strategic domain of relationships should be obvious. This text provides a generic set of tools and principles for the study of a range of different relationships rather than focusing on any particular categories.

Table 2.2   30Rs of relationship marketing (Source: Gummesson, 1999)

Classic market relationships

R1	The classic dyad – the relationship between supplier and the customer
R2	The classic triad – the drama of the customer-supplier-competitor triangle
R3	The classic network – distribution channels

Special market relationships

R4	Relationships via full-time and part-time marketers – marketing and sales department and all others who influence the customer relationship directly or indirectly
R5	The service encounter – interaction between the customer and service provider
R6	The many-headed customer and the many-headed supplier – all contact personnel involved in the relationship
R7	The relationship to the customer's customer – help your customer sell more through and understanding of its customer
R8	The close versus the distant relationship
R9	The relationship to the dissatisfied customer
R10	The monopoly relationship: the customer or supplier as prisoners

Table 2.2 (*continued*)

R11	The customer as 'member' – enlisted as member through loyalty programme
R12	The electronic relationship
R13	Parasocial relationships – relationships to mental images and symbols, for example, to brand names and corporate identities
R14	The non-commercial relationship – the non-commercial sector
R15	The green relationship – environment and health issues
R16	The law-based relationship – relationship based on legal contracts
R17	The criminal network

Mega relationships

R18	Personal and social networks – often influence business
R19	Mega marketing – seeking relationships with governments, legislators, influence individuals and others to make operations feasible
R20	Alliances change the market mechanism – sometimes alliances are necessary to make the market work
R21	The knowledge relationship – knowledge acquisition drives many alliances
R22	Mega alliances change the basic conditions for marketing – for example, the European Union (EU), or the North American Free Trade Organisation (NAFTA), or the World Trade Organisation (WTO)
R23	The mass media relationship

Nano relationships

R24	Market mechanisms are brought inside a company – for example, profit centres inside a company
R25	Internal customer – relationships between internal customers and suppliers
R26	Quality provides a bridge between operations management and marketing
R27	Internal marketing – relationships with the 'employee market'
R28	The two-dimensional matrix relationship - inter-relationships caused by new ways of organising, for example, product management and sales will have overlapping reporting responsibilities
R29	The relationship to external providers of marketing services
R30	The owner and financier relationship

Translating the strategic domains identified into a set of strategic questions is another way of demonstrating the high-level importance of relationships. These questions are:

- decisions concerning collaboration or competition as a strategy - whether or not to pursue relationships as a strategy. Overall vision and direction for relationships set by top management;
- choices about which relationships to develop – deciding which relationships to develop or new ones that might be developed;

- choices about levels of relationship benefits to provide - allocation of resources to relationships. Levels of product/service to each relationship, investment and adaptation patterns;
- choices about how benefits are delivered – organisation structures to relate to each of a firm's relationships.

These strategic questions will determine the shape of a firm's relationships with its stakeholders. If a company decides to pursue a competitive or 'go it alone' strategy then it will minimise its relational actions. If a closer strategy is pursued then some key decisions may be made on a joint basis, for example, joint new product development or cross-shareholding. Making decisions about which relationship to develop or, indeed, divest, form part of a portfolio choice. For example, a higher value may be put on a percentage of customers based on the amount they spend and these customers may then be given more benefits. Customer clubs often operate in this way to provide incentives to make further purchases. This makes the decision to form clubs a strategic one as it concerns the allocation of organisational resources and a direction the marketing function has to take. Organisation for relationships to deliver value is another key strategic issue. Despite the growth of relational organisation systems, for example, key account management, it is still a major challenge to organise in a cost-effective way for relationships. Often organisations put in place the front end customer support but fail to deliver behind the scenes. Organising around processes that deliver value to a relationship remains a strategic challenge.

Running in parallel to the core strategic decisions are implementation plans which represent the day-to-day delivery of relational promises. These plans can be identified in each business function but are often multifuctional. For example, involving users in new product development will require co-operation among users and, at least, the research and development and marketing departments. Using relationships as a strategy requires, like all strategic decision, choice-making by managers. Some of these choices are the focus of the remainder of this chapter.

Strategic relationship issues

Collaboration as a competitive strategy

The traditional approach to competing in a marketplace is competitive that is a 'survival of the fittest' philosophy. One of the key contributors to modern thinking on competition is Porter (1980, 1985) whose seminal ideas on industry structure, competitive advantage, and the value chain have gained widespread application. Porter recognised a collaborative type of advantage in his 1990 work on the competitive advantage of nations (Porter, 1990). Groups of firms located close by, that have built up a tradition supported by home government and other organisations, seem to have developed unique advantages. Examples of these types of advantage include the Finnish advantage in mobile telephony which has produced the global giant, Nokia, the silicon value cluster of high-tech firms in the US, the small entre-preneurial network that characterises the knitware industry in Modena, Italy. To visualise strategy in a co-operative way, an organisation must not only recognise the possibility of collaboration but must also plan and analyse strategy from the perspective of its relationship. Relationship planning is the subject of chapter 4, but suffice to note that often strategy is formulated and selected from the preserve of one firm acting alone (independence mode of strategy development – the tradi-tional view). The relational view is more complex, requiring strategists to take on board the notion that organisations are embedded in a network of relationships. This interdependence can directly affect an individual firm's strategy (the relational mode of strategy development). Table 2.3 provides a comparison of traditional competitive strategy with a co-operative one at the main levels of strategic deci-sion-making.

Table 2.3 **Comparing and explaining the relational and traditional strategy view (Source: Authors)**

Strategic dimension	Relational view	Traditional perspective
Structure	Bilateral – close mutual relationships	Relationships managed by the market
Strategy formulation	A two party dyad or network interconnection	Firm induced – firm as independent actor
Organisation-environment	Embedded in a social	Firm has control over
Relationship	System – layers of connections influence choices that can be made	Choices and makes them in a rational, independent way
Study of the customer relationship	Customer as active/ interactive participants in a firm's marketing	Customer as external, passive respondents to a firm's marketing effort
Resource allocation	Allocation and effect of resources on the relationship	Control of resources and risk of sharing are major concerns
Co-ordination mechanism	Parties trust each other and act equitably	Power is advantage and gives control
Nature of the exchange	Long-term view permits committed action	Short-term view minimises investment in the relationship

Table 2.3 implies a relational strategy view as being distinct from a traditional strategy perspective. However, there are probably gradations in between the two positions. Strategy is often presented in the traditional way through a firm formu-lating and implementing its choices, independent of considerations as to how its partners might affect or respond to its strategy (Johnson and Scholes, 1997; Hill and

Jones, 1999). A relational approach questions the traditional view of strategy. Formulation and selection of strategy is influenced by relationships and this insight may enable other strategy alternatives to emerge. The case at the end of the chapter concerns the shift in strategy to a relationship approach by Wal-Mart and Procter and Gamble. Table 2.3 compares a relational strategy with a traditional adversarial approach to managing relationships. This contrast is analogous to the one in Table 2.4. Table 2.4 presents the power and trust game that often characterises the relationship between a manufacturer and a retailer. While in any relationship, power and trust are core processes, Table 2.4 facilitates the reader to reflect on traditional modes of competition (the power game) with the relational one (the trust game). This contrast is developed in the end of chapter case. A framework for relationship planning which includes strategy formulation and selection as well as analysis and implementation is presented in chapter 4 of this text.

Table 2.4   The power versus trust game (Source: Kumer, 1996)

	The power game	*The trust game*
Modus operandi	Create fear	Create trust
Guiding principle	Pursue self-interest	Pursue what's fair
Negotiating strategy	Avoid dependence by playing multiple partners off against each other	Create interdependence by limiting the numbers of partnerships
	Retain flexibility for self but lock in partners by raising their switching costs	Both parties signal commitment through specialised investments, which lock them in
Communication	Primarily unilateral	Bilateral
Influence	Through coercion	Through expertise
Contracts	'Closed', or formal, detailed, and short-term	'Open', or informal and long-term
	Use competitive bidding frequently	Check market prices occasionally
Conflict management	Reduce conflict potential through detailed contracts	Reduce conflict potential by selecting partners with similar values and by increasing mutual understanding
	Resolve conflict through the legal system	Resolve conflicts through procedures such as mediation or arbitration

Relationship value

Value added in a relationship or by a relationship is central when considering relationships as strategic (Johnson and Lawerence, 1988; Wilkstrom and Normann, 1994; Ramirez, 1999). If an activity does not add value then is it worth pursuing? Is the sum of a relationship greater than its parts? In a later chapter we link relationships to performance which is a measure of value produced. A close relationship with a customer, supplier, and even competitor can represent an asset (Madhavan et al., 1988; Johnson, 1999). Zajac and Olsen (1993) and Wilson (1995) see relationship value coming from the learning and knowledge generated and maximised when partners repeatedly interact. Relationships allow the gains available from joint value creation to be exploited. With two or more partners working together, value can be maximised in relational routines and processes. Value created in a relationship or in a broader network is referred to in many ways but the reader might think in terms of 'value co-production or co-creation' to represent additional value created in a relationship. Practically, this can come about through the creation of intangible and tangible value.

Intangible value can be difficult to identify. This is particularly true in consumer market relationships. Intangible value can be based on a perception of the overall costs and benefits of the relationship (Ravald and Gronroos, 1996). Often this is related to emotive values, for example, value embodied in the brand and its personality. The Body Shop may have close relationships to its consumers because of the ethical values that make up the brand. These values may cement the relationship and retain the consumer. Relationship value can be linked into intangible emotions and preferences developed over time from the actions of a firm, for example, superior customer service can deliver this type of value. Intangible value has been measured by concepts such as loyalty and retention, for example, the lifetime value of a customer (Haskett et al., 1997). Symbolic value can be advantageous as it may be difficult to copy and where tangible value is not possible it may be the only avenue for relationship building. Even in Internet markets, firms are looking to the symbolic value of brands to create relationships, yet they have a one-to-one with their consumers! Intangible value is often reflected in the brand. This type of value is often individualised in people as consumers, in people as buyer-seller, in people in competitor organisations. It provides a social structure to the relationships and helps its functioning. It creates additional value-added as it is difficult to quantify and identify. Managing it is also difficult. Management of this value is linked to organisational culture and managerial acts. A relationship orientation must pervade the entire company if this approach is to be successful. Other forms of intangible value include personal relationships and historical ties. These can create trust and loyalty which can be very difficult to break.

Value is also tangible represented in actions taken in a relationship (Wilkinson and Young, 1994; Ford and McDowell, 1999), or as outcomes of a relationship. An investment in a relationship creates a tangible value attached to it. Some examples would be investment in an information technology link, in supplier training, shareholding in a customer company. This type of value creation may create relationship specific investments or assets. These assets must be managed and have attendant risks and rewards. In close relationships they are viewed as positive, mutually reinforcing assets. In more distant relationships they represent risks which need to be safeguarded against. The clearest manifestation of value is as an outcome – a new product created in a relationship, a higher level of customer loyalty, employees going that extra mile, investor trust in management. Creating value in relationships might be viewed as effort minus returns. If the resources put into relationships were put to an alternative use would a higher return be generated? Not all relationships will pass the test but if they are strategic they should. Much of relationship management is about value creation through visible and invisible ties.

Relationship selection and positioning

By now, readers should see that strategy is about choice. The choice of relationship can determine many outcomes. If you are in a supply relationship with a powerful partner who controls much of your output then your margins and return will be more or less determined, particularly if you have few alternatives. Choice is a complex problem – witness our airline industry introduction – which global alliances? Now we could also ask – which alliance will add value? Choice is closely related to position. How your company is positioned vis-à-vis other competitors is important. To have the best set of relational connections is advantageous. This set moves over time as you should. Therefore, position in the network of relationships becomes a strategic issue. How does an organisation make the selection and positioning decision? This text provides the tools and techniques needed. Network analysis is given a chapter as is a relational planning approach. Also, the relationship classification chapter provides tools for analysing relationship types and developing relationships. Selection and positioning choices are made through analysis. This is a ongoing task for the relational strategists.

Competitive advantage from relationships

Many authors have argued that competitive advantage can be obtained from relationships (Kanter, 1994; Kay, 1995; Huxham, 1996; Stone and Mason, 1997). However, sustainable relational competitive advantage may be difficult to achieve and impossible in many types of relationship. Competitive advantage is usually demonstrated in higher than average performance outcomes. Competitive advantage can be generated by superiority in skills/resources. Relationships, while often sold as a panacea, offer limited competitive advantage possibilities. Competitive advantage that is located in the unique resources which tie companies together is often argued to be sustainable (Hunt and Morgan, 1995; Lorenzoni and Lipperini, 1999). Developing knowledge and management capability, built-up over time in a relationship can be difficult to copy and therefore argued to last or be sustainable. Barney and Hansen (1994) found certain types of trust had competitive advantage potential. High levels of mutual trust such as that involved in goodwill or willingness to take action over and above the minimum necessary may have advantage potential but contractual (doing what you signed up to) and competency trust (ability to do the job) may not. Mutual trust and unique assets seem to be two possibilities for competitive advantage in relationships. It is important to distinguish between advantage obtainable in a relationship with that which is driven by environmental forces such as globalisation. Just because firms are driven to co-operate – the co-operate to compete hypothesis (Bleeke and Ernst, 1993; Beckett-Camarata et al., 1998) – this may not yield sustained advantage. The airline industry groups in the commencement case illustration may be a case in point.

Dyer and Singh (1998), in a comprehensive review of relational competitive advantage, delineate the realm of advantage available through relationships and its sustainability. Competitive advantage from relationships emerges from:

- Relationship-specific assets – investment and adaptation unique to the relationship;
- Knowledge routines – joint learning as a focus for higher order value, for example, ideas from another firm may define a new product;
- Combining complementary resources and capability – often lead to the joint creation of new products, services and technology. For example, Nestle combined with Coca-Cola to distribute hot canned drinks. This partnership combines Coca-Cola's distribution networks with Nestle's soluble tea and coffee capability;
- Lower transaction costs than competitors – trust creates a atmosphere where costly safeguards and checks are not needed.

Dyer and Singh (1998) argue that if advantage is to be maintained or sustained some of the following criteria should be present in the relationship:

- Difficult to identify what generates the advantage (its causes are ambiguous);
- Causes can be identified but there is not enough time to copy (time to market can be significant in many sectors, for example, electronics);
- Interconnectedness between the parties to the relationship may have created a unique asset;
- Partner scarcity – just as relationships with advantage potential are scarce the corollary that partners of this type are also scarce holds;
- The relationship is unique in total that is difficult to divide into component parts and is governed by rules and regulations unique to the parties.

Can the conditions set out by Dyer and Singh (1998) be met? It is our position that these conditions are rare. Otherwise, everyone could imitate and erode advantage. Partnership advantage is another source of competitive advantage and complements advantages available from other sources such as having unique industry conditions in your favour or being a unique firm. Relational advantage requires another individual or organisation to be in on the game. Examples of these type of advantage are not replete in the literature. At the end of this chapter, the case discussion of Wal-Mart and Procter and Gamble may represent relational advantage. IBM co-operates with dozens of firms even with its rivals such as Apple, for example, in the joint development of a common operating system. Does this mean relational competitive advantage is present? Probably, as IBM has built up an impressive relationship management and co-operative capability which it can leverage across its organisation to produce relational competitive advantage.

Chapter summary

This chapter began by presenting a range of relationship domains. These ranged from supplier partnerships to strategic alliances. Due to the range of domains and their potential impact on the firm, relationships were argued to be a strategic issue for the firm. Obviously, not all relationships are strategic, and not all firms use relationships as a strategy, but they must be considered as a strategic alternative. Competing using relationships was compared to the traditional independent mode of competition. The comparison was affected at all levels of strategic decision-making, again demonstrating the strategic power of relationships. A retail trust-based strategy was compared to a power one. This comparison is extended in the end of chapter case discussion of Wal-Mart and Procter and Gamble's relationship. The strategic issue of relationship value was also addressed. A relationship is only worth managing if it adds value of some type to a firm. Value is often seen as an outcome of a relationship but here the intangible and tangible parts of process value were also outlined. Intangible value is often represented in emotive bonds whereas tangible value is visible in unique assets in a relationship. The final strategic issue presented was that of relationship selection and positioning. Choosing the 'right' partner and positioning your organisation in a web of relationships are crucial issues which will be returned to in other chapters of this text. If relationships are to be strategic then they should have the potential to create competitive advantage. We argued that the competitive advantage possibilities of a relationship are limited and rare. The criteria for evaluating sustained advantage were also delineated. Competitive advantage might be created in unique assets in a relationship and in certain forms of trust.

CASE FOR DISCUSSION   **WAL-MART & PROCTER AND GAMBLE**

Wal-Mart is the world's largest retailer and a US company. Its main business is the operation of discount stores. It is pursuing aggressive international expansion plans, for example, it bought Asda in the UK in 1999 and in the same year launched an on-line partnership with AOL (America On-Line), the Internet service provider. The AOL joint venture will involve a co-branded site providing access to Wal-Mart customers (some 90 million people per annum at the time of case writing) to its products on a customised version of AOL's basic service. Wal-Mart was founded by Sam Walton, to save himself a few dollars. His desire to drive down costs is legendary illustrated by the corporate story that the name of the group was changed from Sam Walton Stores to Wal-Mart to save money on signs! Wal-Mart's commercial decisions follow a simple rule: drive down the cost to your business to drive up the volume of sales. Traditionally, this cost-driven philosophy was the building block for its relationships with its suppliers. An aggressive price-based strategy was followed – supplying organisations were forced to drive down their prices or face de-listing. Wal-mart followed a classic adversarial approach to procurement. However, a small group of people changed this strategy to a co-operative approach with certain major suppliers to achieve the same objectives but with benefits for both parties.

Since the mid 1980s Wal-Mart and Procter & Gamble have been developing their channel partnership. Procter & Gamble is the world's largest consumer products group with in the region of 300 brands and over 100 000 employees. Well known brands include Pampers disposable nappies, Always sanitary towels, and Ariel detergent. Obviously, Wal-Mart needs Procter & Gamble's brands and P&G needs Wal-Mart's access to customers. The partnership is based on mutual need of two large and successful companies. Even so it has become a benchmark for manufacturer-retailer relationships. The re-orientation of the relationship took time to develop and Kumar (1996) argued that a major foundation of this development was trust. Up to the point of change in the relationship, the key characteristics of the two company's exchanges have a parallel in the power game described in Table 2.4. Wal-Mart would dictate to P&G how much it would sell and at what prices and if it did not comply threaten to drop its products or give them poor self-space. No sharing of information, very little contact between the organisations except price negotiations, the absence of joint planning and integration of systems were a feature of the old relationship.

The relationship began to take a different shape in the mid 1980s when Sam Walton meet the vice president for sales at P&G. They examined the relationship between the two companies and set in place a process of investigation of co-operative potential. They assembled a team across both organisations to examine exact costs and benefits of co-operation. It proved dramatic both in terms of direct tangible benefits but also set about creating a social structure for the relationships. Both types of benefits were key to unleashing a new co-operative spirit. Over time a close co-operative relationship was developed. The two companies found that a collaborative approach could deliver higher value than a traditional adversarial competitive approach to competing.

The co-operation started in the information technology area with P&G taking over responsibility for managing Wal-Mart's stock for its products. This ensured there were very few periods when there were no stocks of P&G's product in any of the Wal-Mart stores. Periods of no stock (stock-outs) were a feature of the past relationship. P&G could now determine the stock levels, distribute the product to individual stores and get paid quicker through electronic invoicing. This process lowered costs for both partners and delivered benefits to the final consumer who found the most popular brands of Pampers, for example, always in stock. Of course this began a further process of adding increased value. The companies started to exchange information on sales, costs and customer data. The information system now co-ordinates online the production and delivery of the goods with the sales in the shops. The relationship became future orientated as well as being efficient in the present. To succeed, both partners had to share the benefits of collaboration. Reducing stocks for the retailer and on-time delivery by the manufacture meant that P&G also needed benefit which came through quicker payment and higher sales. Sharing of sensitive information about sales and consumers brought further benefits. P&G's and Wal-Mart's partnership is not exclusive. They have partnership with other companies. While many of the same benefits can be achieved, these other partnerships are not always the same. Some will involve risks to Wal-Mart and P&G's relationship, in particular where competitors are involved and each party then must be assured that no sensitive information is leaked. This confidentiality can only exist where this is a strong corporate trust and interaction between the two partners. In addition to the strong social relationship, P&G has used separate teams to manage other close retailer strategic collaborations.

Source: authors' research and includes: Walton and Huey (1992); Kumar (1996).

Questions

1. Compare and contrast the benefits available through a collaborative versus an adversarial approach to competition for Wal-Mart and P&G.
2. Examine the risks of a collaborative approach for each of the partners.
3. Evaluate the sustainable competitive advantage of the relationship between Wal-Mart and P&G.
4. Examine the possibilities for the type of collaboration described in the case to apply to a smaller supplier to Wal-Mart or another retail group with which you are familiar (for example, Tesco or Marks and Spencer). How much of the partnership success would you attribute to company size in this case? (current sales data is available from the websites of both companies: www. walmart.com; www. procter-gamble.com).
5. Develop a implementation programme for changing a relationship from one based on competition to collaboration over a specified time frame, e.g. 1 year, using the material in the case as a framework. Detail what would be done in the first month through to what would be achievable at the end of year 1.

Further reading

Axelrod, R. (1984), *The Evolution of Co-operation*, Basic Books, New York.

Baum, J.A.C. and Korn, H.J. (1999), Dynamics of dyadic competitive interaction, *Strategic Management Journal*, 20 (3), pp. 251–278.

Dill, W.R. (1975), Public participation in corporate planning – strategic management in a Kibitzer's World, *Long Range Planning*, February, pp. 57–63.

Morgan, R.M. and Hunt, S. (1999), Relationship-based competitive advantage: the role of relationship marketing in marketing strategy, *Journal of Business Research*, 46 (3), pp. 281–290.

Payne, A., Christopher, M., Clark, M. and Peck, H. (1995), *Relationship Marketing for Competitive Advantage: Winning and Keeping Customers*, Butterworth Heinemann, Oxford.

Riley, F.D.O. and de Chernatony, L. (2000), The service brand as relationships builder, *British Journal of Management*, 11 (2), pp. 137–150.

Weber, J.A. (2001), Partnering with resellers in business markets, *Industrial Marketing Management*, Vol. 30, No. 2, pp. 87–99.

Wilson, T.H. (1992), *Value-Added Marketing: Marketing for Superior Results*, McGraw Hill, London.

Chapter questions

1. Using the airline alliance case vignette in the introduction, or another alliance, review the current state of a particular alliance. Is it really strategic in nature? On which criteria did you base your evaluation?
2. Examine the argument concerning the strategic nature of relationships. In your opinion, can relationship be considered within the domain of strategy?

3. Questions such as whether to use collaboration as a strategy? Which relationships to develop? what level of benefit to provide? How to deliver these benefits? Are presented as strategic issue for the firm. Examine the rationale for this and indicate your level of agreement.

4. Are all stakeholder relationships strategic? Are some more important than others? Is it possible to build strategic relationships with consumers when your firm is operating in the mass market?

5. Competing using a collaborative strategy would seem a cosy way for a firm to exist when compared to the hard world of head-to-head competition. Discuss.

6. Develop an hypothetical situation, or use the text cases, or your own experience, of a firm using a competitive and relational approach to competing. How would they differ? Would the outcomes of the two modes vary?

7. Relationships can have both tangible and intangible value. In what way can this value add-up to something that differentiates a partnership from that of another competing set?

8. Evaluate the competitive advantage potential of relationships as a strategy. When can a relational approach be sustained?

CHAPTER 3

Relationship-based theories

Introduction and objectives

In the previous chapter we identified certain drivers adding impetus to the strategic importance of relationships, and to the multifaceted characteristics of marketing exchange, in an inter-organisational context. Predominant among these characteristics is the complex nature of individual, group and organisational influences on business relationships. In this chapter, we explore theoretical principles relating to, primarily, buyers and sellers, who take part in mutual exchange for profit. We see that strategic market relationships are a different way for many firms to organise and manage their businesses. Assessment of these relationships, based on the complexity of organisational buying and selling, requires an evaluation of organisational exchange theory as a basis for the explanation of decision-making and for prescriptive managerial guidelines. Five theoretical streams relevant to strategic market relationships are described, considered and evaluated prior to the more managerial-based concepts introduced in subsequent chapters. These theories are either economic or behaviour-based reflecting the discipline from which they emerge.

Economic-based theories cover agency theory, transaction cost economics and resource-dependency theories of the firm. Agency theory can provide unique, realistic, and empirically testable propositions relative to co-operative efforts between two parties and would suggest itself relevant to buyer-seller exchange. The transaction cost economics theory suggests what conditions are necessary for bilateral or hierarchical structures to develop rather than competitive market forces. Tentative propositions of relevance to strategic market relationships emerge from this theory. Finally, resource-dependency theory based upon concepts of power and conflict provide additional propositions relative to inter-organisational exchange behaviour.

Behavioural-based theories include social exchange theory and the interaction approach. Social exchange theory, originated from the work of Blau (1964); Macneil (1980) and others draw attention to the set of norms that govern contractual relationships as well as emphasising the importance of trust and commitment in relationships. Interaction and networks is a theoretical stream developed from the work of the European International Marketing and Purchasing Group (Hakansson et al., 1982) and from idiosyncratic case studies (e.g. Easton, 1998) that have provided a rich vein of ideas, concepts and insights into relationships.

By the end of this chapter you should:

- have understood the key theoretical ideas that influence strategic market relationships;
- assess the implications of the economics school represented by agency theory, transaction cost economics and power-dependency theories;
- identify the contribution from the behavioural school as represented by the interaction and social exchange theoretical stream of thought;
- be able to decide on the worth of a meta-theoretical approach to strategic market relationships.

CASE ILLUSTRATION   **THE ELECTRONICS INDUSTRY AND THE SEMI-CONDUCTOR MARKET**

According to Dataquest (1999) the electronic equipment market has an annual turnover in excess of $931 billion. Of this, the semi-conductor industry is, by value, approximately 20%. The total value of the semi-conductor market is predicted to be close to $250 billion by the end of 2002. Approximately 75% of this are split amongst the top 20 suppliers with Intel dominant followed by companies such as NEC, Motorola, Toshiba, Texas and others.

The industry has been characterised by increasing consolidation with a trend to the large players becoming even bigger and with greater economies of scale creating barriers to entry. Semi-conductors fall into different product categories and in the commodity memory market, which is heavily DRAM (Dynamic Random Access Memory) centric and includes players such as NEC, Hitachi and Samsung. In the current and future market, the competition tends to divide between two main forms. First, system level integration with companies such as Cadence where the system is on a SOC (Silicon Chip) or, alternatively, systems software, which is usually bundled with standard products and has been the approach favoured by Microsoft and Intel from the 1980s onwards.

Nowadays, it can be observed that there is less profit in electronic equipment or in semi-conductor equipment products and materials and increasing value in terms of add-on software solutions. The result is that some companies are pulling out of manufacture to concentrate on the added value from solutions software. The market clearly divides into those companies which are highly capital intensive and who pursue Moore's law approach to competitive advantage in the market. Moore's law states that the capacity of a semi-conductor device will double every 18 months and systems developers are continually searching for the 'killer' applications that can make efficient use of this capacity improvement.

The semi-conductor vendors value proposition has therefore moved from being manufacturing and technology centric to systems knowledge driven. This has put greater emphasis on the intellectual property to provide the systems knowledge. For example, Intel and Texas Instruments have spent over $2 billion acquiring such key competencies by buying recognised systems engineering companies world-wide. Other companies have based their growth on licensing core technology to companies who have the capability for integration and manufacture. Some traditional semi-conductor manufacturing companies have also begun the process of out-sourcing standard manufacturing to foundries. Motorola, for example, have recently announced that, by the end of 2000, almost 50% of all manufacturing will be out-sourced.

Therefore, in the future, semi-conductor vendors, OEM's (original equipment manufacturers), foundry and package and test design will all be allied in partnership agreements between firms who were once strict competitors. The industry is one that cannot sustain the phenomenal growth rates of recent years, yet there is still a constant evolutionary process that is fuelling growth. The future seems to lie in system level integration between manufacturing solutions and routes to market, which comply with cost and performance requirements of today's customers. As Andy Groves of Intel suggested in his speech in San Francisco in February 1999, the electronics industry has reached 'inflection' point. The winners are likely to be those companies who grasp the concept of efficient use of new technology and can provide a value proposition to their customers, which competitors cannot match.

Sources: Dataquest, 1999; www.motorola.com; www.intel.com

Relationship theories – an overview

The vignette for this chapter highlights the costs and risks involved in hightech, fast changing industries. Traditional managerial approaches seem incapable of providing the speed and degree of change required to compete. Yet any developments involve a risk. This risk can be reduced by developing closer relationships upstream and down-stream in the supply chain. For example, developing closer relationships with sub-contractors enables superior products to be developed and more efficient cost of supply. Developing appropriate software or solutions in this business demands that you are both quick and innovative. The capacity and risks associated with achieving customer solutions can seldom be found in one company no matter its size or resources.

The information age is creating something of a revolution in business. New technology will lead to greater precision with which to observe marketing phenomena and greater technical power to plan and implement strategy (Timmers, 2000). New business models, reflecting the organisation of product, service and information flows and the sources of revenues and benefits for suppliers and customers, are required. Developments such as electronic scanning data, telemetry, the Internet and e-commerce are and will continue to change the nature of buyer-seller interaction in most industries, albeit for some products and services more than others. In the context of market relationships, two significant observations can be made. Consumers, on one hand, using call centres and Internet based technology will self-serve for many products and services. Organisational buyers on the other hand will improve their own information systems, taking a more proactive approach to purchasing and their choice of suppliers. They can also change the balance in their relationships in their own favour. The result, increased choice for customers and consumers and, by implication, a need for revised theories of buyer behaviour. Secondly, marketing is not uniform across contexts where the necessity of time, changed circumstances and different situations need to be examined carefully before making general hypotheses about the nature of marketing phenomena. Today's most successful businesses like Cisco, Amazon and Microsoft did not exist 20 years ago and cannot attribute their success to conventional marketing wisdom. The lack of stability in the marketing environment and in observing marketing phenomena necessitates theories, which take account of the adaptability and responsiveness of both parties in the exchange process. This confirms our view that market relationships are strategic.

In the search for relevant theories in strategic market relationships we will consider five theoretical streams, two economic-based and three behavioural-based. There should be advantages in this approach in that much has been written in recent years extolling the virtues of a relationship approach but too much of this has been empty rhetoric. We therefore need to assess relationships in a more objective, rational and rigorous manner. For example, all customers would like to have better service, higher quality, lower prices, speedier delivery and greater availability – this becomes mere truism. To be competitive, firms must control costs and restrict the benefits provided to customers. Otherwise losses may occur no matter how customer friendly or socially desirable the relationship might be.

The theories we have selected to aid our understanding of strategic market relationships are shown in Table 3.1.

Table 3.1   Theoretical concepts that can be applied to strategic market relationships

Theory	Basic concept	Examples of authors
Agency	Exchange risk	Eisenhardt
Transaction cost economics	Economies of transactions	Williamson
Resource dependency	Power conflict	Reve
Social exchange	Social embeddedness	Macneil
Interaction	Interaction	Hakansson

Agency theory – dealing with risk

> Overall the domain of agency theory is relationships that mirror the basic agency structure of a principal and an agent who are engaged in co-operative behaviour, but have differing goals and differing attitudes toward risk.
>
> (Eisenhardt, 1989, p. 59)

Given this domain, it is not unreasonable to adapt agency theory to buyer/seller relationships. The key ideas in agency theory are as follows:

1. That there is a trade-off between two parties, the seller and the buyer. In a legal sense there is an important difference in that an agent does not normally take title to the goods but acts in different capacities as an intermediary.

2. The Principal would be expected to assume a position of self-interest and expect that others will take advantage. In response control mechanisms will be established. Thus we can observe complex legal contracts between buyers and sellers, between employers and employees and different ways to monitor the behaviour of the other party.

3. In the economic sense, agency theory is applicable in that both parties are interested in the efficient organisation of information and reduction in risk-bearing costs. The unit of analysis can be taken as the contract between buyer and seller and the degree of formality in such contracts will vary from highly informal or market based to highly formal, hierarchical and legal. The position adopted will reflect the following characteristics of contracts:

   – authority of each party. Who controls the contract, principal or agent?
   – incentive system. To act in the interest of the other party then it may be necessary to offer incentives. Example of this is some form of loyalty rebate or in the case of an employee some form of bonus.
   – standard operating procedures. It may be necessary and prudent to write out the rules of the contract to avoid exploitation and to be explicit what each party requires.
   – dispute resolution. In the event of discrepancy about who should have done what, then procedures for resolving these difference will be required.
   – non-market pricing. To offset potential losses both parties may build in non-market pricing to offset losses.

4. The key assumptions reflect both those of the individual person and those of organisations. The personal includes self-interest and risk aversion. The organisational assumptions include goal conflict among participants, efficient contract governance between one party and the other and information asymmetry between buyer and seller. Information is a purchasable commodity that has a value for each party.

5. The theoretical ideas have implication for relationship management. These include:

   – co-operative behaviour – to what extent are buyers and sellers likely to co-operate?
   – goal conflict – what are the effects of self-interest at the individual level and goal conflict at the organisational level?
   – information asymmetry – can the positions be identified by the power of participants within and between organisations? (bargaining, negotiating, coalitions)
   – bounded rationality – that is logical given certain assumptions
   – uncertainty – are the outcomes measurable? time? task programmable? What level of risk is acceptable? Close relationships accept a lot of risk but if the cost of building in safeguards or the costs in monitoring the 'fairness' in the relationship are high then it would be appropriate to finds alternative governing mechanisms.

Agency theory therefore uses the metaphor of a contract to describe the relationship between principal and agent, buyer and seller, and is primarily about reducing risk and managing uncertainty. The possible contribution of agency theory may be in explaining the type and level of relationship interaction that exists between the two parties. For example, agency theory could be applied to the customer service problem to explain the provision of information by the seller to reduce uncertainty for the buyer. In addition, it can be applicable to incentives open to both, in developing closer relationships and enhancing the co-operation between them, in an effort to minimise joint risks. Conversely, where a product is widely available to a specification in a known market, i.e. low uncertainty, low risk and adequate information, buyers do not require elaborate relationship interaction and sellers should not increase their costs by providing higher levels of support than the market requires. Put simply, if markets are governed by market forces then relationship building will be less important, whereas if there is high uncertainty, increased risk and inadequate information, then relationships will be relatively more important, represented by co-operation rather than conflict between them.

The weaknesses of the agency theory include the restrictive nature of the assumption that the contract between buyer and seller can be likened to that between principal and agent. Specific rules of transactions governing triadic relationships cannot embrace the vagaries of a wide range of buyer seller transactions and relationships. To be useful, this theory requires careful specification of assumptions followed by logical deduction to predict certain outcomes. We can use this theory to understand the nature of risk. However, the theory is limited when buyers and sellers have similar attitudes to risk, share information and co-operate. In such circumstances, where a range of possible outcomes is possible, the agency theory combined with other theoretical perspectives can prove useful. One of these perspectives is transaction cost economics.

Transaction cost economics (TCE) – assessing costs

Transaction cost economics (TCE) is an explicit theory of the mechanics governing inter organisational transactions. The theory is founded on twin concepts. It incorporates certain behavioural assumptions of individuals and organisations and the attributes of transactions. The aim is to economise on transaction costs by assigning them to governance structures in a discriminating way (Williamson, 1985). An overview of TCE suggests the following key issues:

1. The transaction is the basic unit of analysis and that any contracting problem can be investigated in TCE terms.
2. Transactions (classified by attributes) are assigned to governance structures by incentives and adaptations. These structures vary from market to market and hierarchical patterns.
3. It combines behavioural actions (bounded rationality and opportunism) with economic ones (asset specificity) and in the presence of uncertainty it provides helpful explanation of economic phenomena.

4. One core theme of TCE is that "the idiosyncratic attributes of transactions have large and systematic organisational ramifications" (Williamson, 1985, p. 53). Behavioural assumptions centre on the idea of bounded rationality (intended rational) and opportunism (self-interest seeking with guile). Transactions are linked to these behavioural assumptions by institutional arrangements or governance structures. These governance structures range from a formal hierarchical structure within a firm to a market-based system between firms with bilateral governance structures representing intermediate positions.

5. Individual behaviour can be characterised as strong (maximise), mixed (bounded) or weak (organic). Their orientation can be opportunistic (strong), simple self-interest (mixed), or obedient (weak). It is likely, except in very few cases, for example one-off purchases or monopolistic transactions, that ongoing buyer/seller transactions and relationships will be characterised by bounded rationality and opportunistic behaviour.

6. The reasons for the differences in transactions will relate to three particular factors - asset specificity, uncertainty and frequency. Asset specificity, or the extent to which specialised or unique assets are needed to support the exchange, is the most critical dimension for describing transactions. As Williamson states "Parties engaged in a trade that is supported by non-trivial investments in transaction-specific assets are effectively operating in a bilateral trading relation with one another. Harmonising the contractual interface that joins the parties, thereby to effect adaptability and promote continuity, becomes the source of real economic value". (Williamson, 1985, p. 30). For example, transactions that depend on high and relatively fixed investments and are committed to a particular customer or market, require more complex governance structures in the form of future guaranteed orders or higher prices, as incentives to risk taking behaviour. The notion of fixed versus variable costs can still apply but a more important issue is whether costs (fixed or variable) are specific (locked-in) or non-specific. Depending on the degree of specificity, a classification of transactions can be made. Specificity can refer to site, physical assets, human assets and other dedicated assets.

Therefore TCE theory can go some way to explaining differences in types of transactions and to what extent integration takes place. Our concern here is not with formal integration but with loose forms of integration and in particular co-operation. Traditionally, formal integration was the result of anticipated economies of scale that achieved significant cost savings. The extent of such formal integration would be limited by the economies of scope, for example forward integration by consumer goods companies is limited by the need to stock a wide range of produce in a retail outlet. The effects of technology does not by itself lead to greater integration but will arise from the need to protect specific investments in the face of uncertainty. "…decisions to integrate are rarely due to technological determinism but are more often explained by the fact that integration is the source of transaction cost economies" (Williamson, 1985, p. 87). Finally, externalities such as reputation and competition may necessitate closer integration in the form of more formalised hierarchical structures.

TCE offers a general model with potential managerial solutions. In essence it is about learning related to cost structures and finding ways to minimise transaction costs over both short run and the longer term. However, buyer and seller relationships operate on many dimensions, not all of which are explicit. In organisational markets, an important factor limiting entry to markets is the existence of close cooperation between existing players. This is especially the case with existing re-buy products where customers consider themselves satisfied and there is no propensity to change. In these situations strong, lasting relationships are common. In other cases technological dependency, formal contracts or the costs involved in changing suppliers, reinforce the relationship. The result is closer co-operation and a concomitant increase in activities that can be classified as relationship enhancing.

According to TCE, firms operate most efficiently under market conditions. Firms are aware that price competition is insufficiently profitable for the business enterprise and an attempt is made to differentiate the product in order to gain monopolistic profits. This can be achieved by investing in research and development. For instance, finding superior products, through market segmentation or other forms of closely aligning to specific customer needs and by superior promotional and sales programmes. These approaches can be both costly and risky. For instance, the continuing high failure rates for new products. As a result of specific investments and market uncertainty firms will attempt to form closer links with customers and their own suppliers (hierarchy). This is not only cost-efficient but it also reduces uncertainty thereby helping to form bilateral structures. Conditions of bilateral dependency exist but will be under strain because of the threat from new entrants with technically superior products or competing for lower prices. The system would be characterised by instability and firms will either merge forming a unilateral structure or fragment into a market-based system.

Market factors alone may not be sufficient to explain some relationships because of influences such as power and domination. For example in the UK, former public utilities such as Royal Mail, British Gas, British Telecom and Scottish Power, although now privatised and operating in competitive markets, clearly enjoyed market power and domination. What can be observed is an enigma in that firms may be forming closer ties with customers at the same time as they sub-contract periphery tasks to outside contractors. In other words, replacing hierarchical structures with more market-based systems with suppliers at the same time as they are forming various alliances with customers. BP is an example of this as it sub-contracts accounting and audit services (to Anderson Consulting) while forming alliances with customers and competitors (e.g. ICI and CIBA-Geigy). TCE offers an explanation here in that market-based systems operate more effectively for some transactions but not others, and the specificity of assets and uncertainty over risk help determine whether market or hierarchy is preferred. It could therefore be hypothesised that on the one hand, for branded consumable goods there is little benefit of closer ties between manufacturer and customer. On the other hand, for consumer durables such as motor cars where technical complexity is high there is some benefit. There is also some benefit between manufacturers and wholesalers or retailers as a result of investments in stockholding, joint promotions, etc. but these will be restricted by economies of scope in product, market and information. In organisational relationships where such economies are negligible, asset specificity is high and externalities such as reputation are important then relationship building will be important and is characterised by closer links between the parties.

Closer relationships may be formed as surrogates for market monopoly power and/or technical innovation. Do firms invest in closer relationships because they lack genuine superior new products and lack market power? Closeness can be related to restraint on competition where the cost of capital is expensive (R & D unprofitable), where technological skill is unavailable, weak or lacking or where routes to market in terms of distribution may be limited. If technology is lacking or held constant, organisational innovation may be a source of competitive advantage by the nature of the customer relationship and closeness of buyer and seller.

Resource dependency theory – power and control

One reason for entering into relationships is to gain access to and make full use of the resources of other parties. In the retailing sector in the UK, seven large chains dominate the packaged grocery market and power is largely in the hands of the bigger retailers. Manufacturers and suppliers have to meet the needs of these customers by co-operating with each other. General Motors and Ford, fierce competitors, have combined resources to exercise purchasing power over automobile suppliers. The use of Internet portals with similar motivations will create new chains of supply within different industries. Often the aim is to exercise power over price, supply or access to markets. Resource theory may explain this type of behaviour although the perspective is from a focal firm perspective rather than a relationship or network one. This view is often concerned with the issue of gaining resource or other control over a partner organisation. Control of critical resources and a focus on the power-dependence continuum are key factors in deciding governance (Pfeffer and Salancik, 1978; Heide, 1994). This can be contrasted with a social exchange perspective that supports the mutual value potential of inter-organisational exchange. The point of departure is different and our concern is the governance mechanisms affecting such relationships. The exchange relationship is limited by the perceived value/need for the resources and by the potential use of power. The key features of the resource-dependency school of thought are as follows:

1. Exchange happens in order to gain access to needed resources. Firms, in general, do not have access to all the resources they need to carry out their business objectives. One response to this access problem is to build an internal hierarchy to produce the resource. This is seen as an increasingly inefficient and risky strategy in a changing, somewhat turbulent, global environment. Therefore, there is a growing need to gain access to critical resources of other parties. From a resource-dependency view, this is seen as a control problem and the key question is the degree of control one can exert over a partner on whom

one is dependent? The loss of autonomy is a central concern of the resource-dependency school.

2. One approach is to assess governance scenarios arising out of resource-dependency as a response to uncertainty and dependence (Heide, 1994). In common with transaction cost analysis, firms are presumed to co-operate in conditions of high uncertainty. Thus, dependence is a response to uncertainty. This is one interpretation but it can be argued that dependence can also be a response to choice or opportunity. For example, adaptations have been found to develop out of the social structure of a relationship in response to reciprocation or to be unilaterally based on the power-dependence position of a partner (Hallen et al., 1991).

3. Dependence on partner firms is one of the main results of a resource view. Being dependent is not seen as a positive outcome of the resource-dependency school and should be avoided if at all possible. Indeed, building in safeguards has been suggested as a balancing mechanism in the exchange relationship (Heide and John, 1988).

4. The key process driving this approach is power-conflict assessment. Nowhere is this focus more evident than in the channel literature where this concern has been demonstrated (Stern and Reve, 1980). This view has been supported with the suggestion that the channel literature should broaden its scope to include a more socio-political perspective (Frazier, 1983). Social exchange would reduce the likelihood of negative power use and facilitate conflict reduction through open communication. Power use is most likely under conditions of highly substitutable exchange relationships or relations of a recurrent nature (Yamaguchi, 1996). It is also likely to be strongly present in a relationship in which one partner dominates and uses its power (Gassenheimer and Calantone, 1994).

5. Switching costs is one of the key elements in the analysis of resource-dependence theory. Building-in or avoiding switching cost is a core dilemma in buyer/seller relationships (Jackson, 1985). However, from a social exchange perspective, bilateral firms would have an objective to make them more interdependent, the opposite of the approach suggested in resource-dependency theory.

6. A contribution of resource-dependency to the understanding of a relationship is that it can be conceptualised as an asset or a resource. It is a resource because much of what goes on in a relationship can generate returns to the parties. This is where social exchange and resource views meet. Where resources are seen in terms of their interactive rather than focal firm perspective they correspond to a social exchange view. This has been extended based on knowledge competencies in relationships and interactions (Wikstrom and Normann, 1994). However, much resource-dependency based work is still focused on the ability of an individual firm to exploit its resource environments. This focus has its roots in classical economic theory of the firm and is illustrated in Prahalad and Hamel's classic competence article (Prahalad and Hamel, 1990). Although resource-based work can make an important contribution to the study of relationships, much of the literature is likely to continue to focus on the activities of a single actor (Wernerfelt, 1995).

Work in the literature on channels of distribution suggests that it is important to distinguish between the possession of power and the use of power (Frazier, 1999). For example, a seller may not exercise power in order to develop the relationship over a long term or discourage the buyer from actively seeking alternative sources. In situations where the seller has high power but considers it wise to pursue a long-term relationship, the approach will be service-based rather than overt and coercive. In situations where the seller has high power but long term co-operation is not considered essential, the approach is likely to be more pressurised and the level of service less. Since the influence and use of power will relate to market dominance, the buyer, with limited options, may have difficulty in evaluating the benefits of a relationship since no, or limited alternatives, will be available. The only relevant measure of this relationship would be based on the expectations of the buyer rather than the intent of the seller. Power, and the use of power, is likely to reflect factors such as market size, market growth, market volatility, the threat of competition in the future and technological uncertainty.

The second dimension in the equation is the notion of conflict. Conflict, defined as tension between social entities and the frequency of disagreements over salient issues, will be influential in decisions about relationships. Indeed, the reason for investing in relationship enhancing activities is to reduce the level of conflict between the parties and increase the level of co-operation to the benefit of both. Further, conflict can explain why a seller will invest in a relationship in excess of that which a buyer may demand. This is because the seller will reach maximum efficiency at quite a low level of conflict handling intensity whereas a buyer will reach maximum efficiency at a higher level (Gemunden, 1985).

The idea of matching of firms and resources to customers and markets is a uniquely marketing concept. Thus, the extent to which firms undertake closer ties with their customers reflects both internal organisational and external market factors. For example, IBM's concept of partnership is a strategic core in which the company attempts to offer the highest service, forms close alliances but incurs high costs in doing so. This has moved the company from supplying products to focusing on offering consultancy services and solutions to their customers.

Social exchange theory – relationships as social entities

Social exchange theory views inter-organisational governance in the context of a social structure where firms are inter-dependent and rely on reciprocation. Trust and equity are key variables in this approach. Self-interest is best maximised by the returns available through co-operation in a relationship (Blau, 1964). In this approach, the analysis of interfirm relationships moves from the focal firm to the dyad or network level in an effort to understand inter-organisational relationships (Cook and Emerson, 1978; Bradach and Eccles, 1989; Husted (1994). The method of governance using social exchange is relational contracting, based on a bilateral mechanism of co-ordination. The main features of social exchange theory are as follows:

1. Social exchange concentrates on the relationship rather than the transaction. The core element of this approach is the study of interaction between parties in a relationship. This assumption is central to the Industrial Marketing and Purchasing Group (IMP) of researchers (Hakansson, 1982; Ford, 1990).
2. Relationships are embedded in a social structure (Granovetter, 1985). Over time, a complex personal and organisational structure evolves between firms. There is a social structure present in many types of relationships but in terms of governance when social structure dominates, a bilateral one is in operation. In other words, a positive effect of social exchange occurs. If this were not the case, an alternative form of governance based on the economic model would be in place.
3. Social exchange accepts the self-interest motivation but adds that this is best achieved when actors behave equitably and in the best interests of the partnership. This form of high motivation category of relationship exchange captures the essential self interest but intense nature of bilateral relationships (Dwyer et al., 1987). The rational economic decision unit is bounded by the social context of decision making and by the expectation that the relationship will endure over time. Benefits and burdens will be equalised in the longer term.
4. The essential nature of relational contracting as social exchange has been well documented (Macneil, 1980; Dore, 1983). Dore developed the concept using Japanese business to explain its key characteristics. This moves us beyond Macneil's notion that bilateral contracting is just a set of norms that govern relationships and sees it as a management structure with the norm of mutuality facilitating specific business advantages, for example, joint product development or cost reduction.
5. Under a social exchange view, boundaries between firms become blurred as vertical disaggregation is facilitated and enhanced. Firms become linked in a chain with other firms within a network context (Anderson et al., 1994).
6. The key processes driving social exchange are trust and commitment. These processes moderate the impact of power and determine the perception of fairness in an exchange relationship. One of the earliest studies that demonstrated this was a study of individual network position and the effect of social structure on power, equity and commitment (Cook and Emerson, 1978).

The interaction approach – co-operation and networking

The traditional organisational theorist's approach would be to examine the problem from a management perspective, usually top-down or from a worker's satisfaction or behavioural perspective. The focus on the customer is neglected. Researchers in marketing have also failed to take into account the context and processes in which exchanges take place between buyer and seller (Miettila and Moller, 1990). These would include:

- co-ordination processes;
- exchange processes;
- adaptation processes;

- evolving bonds that can be classed as lower order (economic, technical, legal, social planning), or higher order (attraction, trust, commitment);
- perceived outcomes - satisfaction, indifference, dissatisfaction;
- competitors;
- agencies and intermediaries;
- environment;
- tasks such as technical complex services, joint ventures or turnkey projects;
- personal contacts, competence, motivation, relative size, importance, specialisation and experience of the players.

The fundamental activity in marketing is the transaction, i.e. the exchange between two parties. The focus is the inter-organisational system defined in terms of transactions that take place between social actors. This compels research to take a dyadic perspective in which the relationship between the two transacting parties is highlighted. Some writers have called for a new paradigm away from the monadic towards the relational nature of inter-organisational exchange "...the monadic paradigm views the buyer and seller as independent rather than inter-dependent, emphasises their separate analysis rather than appreciating the similarity of their task, and assumes that a single, discrete purchase rather than purchases in the context of an ongoing relationship is representative of inter-organisational exchange." (Dant and Wilson, 1988, p. 91). The dyadic approach treats the buyer and seller together but is limited to viewing the exchange process as a one time discrete event rather than viewing it as one transaction in an ongoing relationship. The outcome is for researchers to examine the relational approach to enhance understanding of buyer seller relationships. This is an aggregation of individual, interpersonal and organisational dyads and networks (Moller and Halinen, 2000).

The primary interest is in how and why different transactions are created, sustained or avoided between parties. As a result, it is possible to build on dyads to groups of dyads or networks as the starting point for studies of aggregates of organisations. Thus, it is appropriate to start with the dyad and look for further linkages. The focal point is the dyad that can be considered to operate within a primary task environment of suppliers and customers. Embracing this is a secondary task environment of other suppliers to suppliers, customer's customers, regulatory agencies and others. Finally, there is the macro environment of general economic, social, political and technological factors. The proper field of research should be conducted across a sample of specific or unique dyads.

In the context of industrial marketing two approaches have particular significance. First, the interaction model developed by Hakansson and others in the International Marketing and Purchasing Group (IMP) (Hakansson, 1982) and secondly, the work of Jackson at the Harvard Business School (Jackson, 1985) already referred to in chapter 1. We will explore the IMP model in more detail in chapter 4. This is because the interaction approach is related but separate from relationship theory because of its idiosyncratic and highly descriptive approach. In fact, it is not a theory at all since it describes individual situations, albeit in a highly complex way, and does not meet the criteria of law-like generalisations required by theory (Hunt, 1983). Nevertheless, it represents the most significant contribution to relationship thinking and application.

The origins of the interaction approach appear to have evolved from dissatisfaction with the 4Ps paradigm as an inadequate managerial framework when applied in an industrial marketing context and as a result of a series of empirical studies in a variety of industrial international situations. The main arguments against the traditional view centre on the idea that buying is not a single discrete purchase, that marketing management consists of more than the manipulation of the marketing mix to a generalised passive market operating in an autonomic way, and that marketing and purchasing do not operate in separate and discrete ways. In industrial exchange the relationship is more likely to be characterised by small numbers of buyers and sellers who are both active participants in the process, whose actions are identifiable by others and which have long term effects (interaction rather than transaction). There are likely to be specific investments in technical and organisational routines that result in a relationship characterised by stability, source loyalty and inertia. To explain marketing activity requires an understanding of the differences between relationships as they apply in concentrated and diverse markets. The IMP group refers to this as the interaction approach. Their focus is on the relationship rather than the buyer or supplier.

Meta approaches to researching into relationships

The theories presented in this chapter should add to our knowledge and understanding of relationships and be useful for those interested in researching relationships that need a theoretical understanding before starting. While it may be easier to start with a focal relationship, much of the best work on relationships utilises a case-based approach (Easton, 1998). There is a need to research both sides of a dyad (much research is one-sided) but, at the same time, a focus on dyads alone can lose the larger perspective of a network. Analysing networks presents high levels of complexity due to its potential size and some would argue taking, as a minimum, a triad. That is a focal relationship and another significant connection.

Our view is that the main theoretical schools on relationships pursue rather narrow definitions of relationships with few exceptions. The narrow definition is based on the rigid adherence to theoretical assumptions about how organisations and markets work. By putting aside these assumptions and testing a wider definition of relationships, research can develop and expand the relational domain. Transaction cost economics (Williamson, 1979, 1985) assumes performance is optimised in transactional efficiency, and through the performance maximisation efforts of a firm acting alone. Agency theory, like transaction cost, examines the outcomes of relationships between principals and agents in terms of economic costs, particularly, the cost of potential relational abuses and the monitoring of a partnership (Bergen et al., 1992). The channel literature also sees economic benefits as the main outcomes of relationships with a particular focus on costs and profits of relationships (Heide and John, 1988). In particular, it concentrates on the power-dependency relationship and the outcome balance of any change in this relationship.

Again, performance is viewed from the perspective of the individual firm. While these benefits are important, other schools see more behavioural approaches as being beneficial. The social exchange school of relationships (Cook and Emerson, 1978; Macneil, 1980) includes wider benefits of relational co-operation. Areas such as flexibility, and satisfaction become key outcomes of interfirm relationships. Also, the motivation for relationships that emerges is different from the economic schools. Joint outcomes are included as a beneficial starting point for the assessment of relational effectiveness.

Therefore, assessment of relationships can be seen to vary widely among the main theoretical schools. It is possible to categorise their views into behavioural and economic dimensions of relationships, and on the basis of their assumption of how firms analyse relational performance. Indeed, both these facets may be helpful to the initial development of a more comprehensive explanation of relationships. The literature on relationships is beginning to support this argument. For example, Granovetter (1992) supports combining economic and behavioural dimensions as both these motivations are found side-by-side in organisations. Zajac and Olsen (1993) argue that a single party emphasis may neglect important interdependencies between organisations and thus, the possibility of joint value maximisation. Gassenheimer et al. (1994) argue for a blending of economic and behaviour measures from a channel perspective, and in general marketing theory.

Including both behaviour and economic dimensions and recognising the motivation behind the relationship assessment may provide a basis for a comprehensive definition of relationships including economic and behaviour dimensions, and recognition of the motivation for performance assessment. In addition, strategy research has supported the expansion of relationship performance measures outside the traditional financial management or economic domain (Eccles, 1991; Kaplan and Norton, 1996).

A conceptualisation of the relationship construct should recognise the inherent motivation behind relationships and the behaviour and economic dimensions of relationship performance. Relationship research has a unique opportunity to do what related fields are now pursuing: an integrated assessment recognising the multifaceted nature of the area. If a firm is motivated solely by its own goals then it will exclude certain elements from its relational assessment and may be happy to do so, for example, it may be unwilling to commit itself to joint product development or invest in other committed actions, thereby deciding to exclude itself from the performance these could generate. However, the importance of strategic market relationships will vary and possess different characteristics depending upon which type of exchange is appropriate. An approach based on recognition of their mutual interdependence is characteristic of many organisational marketing situations where building and maintaining strong, lasting relationships is vital for long term prosperity. We develop our own model of relationships in chapter 6, reflecting both the economic and behavioural aspects of relationships.

Chapter summary

This chapter reviewed five main streams of exchange theory in order to develop an appropriate perspective to study strategic market relationships. These streams were agency theory, transaction cost economics and resource-dependency theories essentially from an economic perspective and the interaction approach and social exchange theory which are primarily behaviour-based. Agency theory suggested certain circumstances in which service and co-operation may be preferred to conflict and bargaining, particularly when faced with uncertainty and risk. Similarly, transaction theory suggests that the greater the investment in non-trivial assets, coupled with market uncertainty and regular transactions will result in sellers and buyers reducing their total costs by joint activity and service aspects rather than conducting market based exchange. Power-dependency theory leads to some ambiguity in relationships since power is not always exercised, especially by sellers in advantageous market positions who may prefer to take a longer-term view of their opportunities. Nevertheless, relationships are influenced by the relative resources of both parties, constraints on their behaviour and opportunities in end markets. Finally, the work on relationships in industrial marketing and the interaction school plus the social exchange theorists suggest further testable propositions relating both to the nature of transactions and the characteristics of the relationships. Our conclusion is that a meta theoretical perspective incorporating behaviour and economic dimensions may yield more useful criteria for evaluating strategic market relationships than any one single theoretical approach.

CASE FOR DISCUSSION   **MERIAL**

Merial was formed in 1997 by the merger of two pharmaceutical companies, MERCK and Rhone-Poulenc, combining their animal health and poultry genetics businesses. In a market of increasing cost and intense competition, Merial is a research driven company operating on a global basis and its livestock business group operates in the UK selling a range of animal health products to end users through a selective distribution chain as shown in Figure 3.1.

Operating within UK and European rules and regulations, products are sold under licence in one of the following categories:
– General sales list
– Pharmacy and merchants list
– Pharmacy medicine
– Prescription only medicine
– Controlled drug

The pharmaceutical industry over the last decade has been characterised by a number of acquisitions, mergers and joint ventures. Veterinary product manufacturers have reduced from 26 in 1987 to 17 in 1998 of which only nine invest in R&D (NOAH Compendium). Merial currently invest 8.5% of turnover in R&D. To remain competitive, duplication of products and staff must be kept to a minimum but at the same time they need to work more closely with the distributor partners and end users.

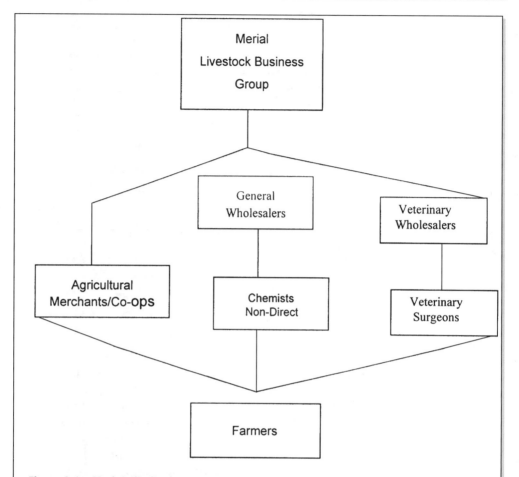

Figure 3.1   Merial distribution structure.

In the last few years agriculture in the UK has been in recession with strong sterling, a ban on British exports of beef, reduced meat consumption and poor climatic conditions. The problems with BSE and the Foot and Mouth expidemic in 2001 have created even greater uncertainty in the farming community. At the same time there has been increased pressure from government and consumer groups to ensure the welfare of animals and safer controls in the food supply chain. Subsidies are being reduced and the main supermarkets and becoming even more dominant. To keep costs down, yet record all aspects of food supplies such as feedstuffs, medicines and animal welfare, partnerships between key influencers and providers in the supply chain will have to be nurtured and managed. This means a link between farmers, vets, agricultural advisors, meat processors, supermarkets and others.

Merial assist in this process to help the farmers with good husbandry, farm management practices and with innovative new products. Yet there are less farmers so it is vital to form partnerships with the remaining farmers, veterinary surgeons and distributors to ensure market coverage. The only way to grow the business is through added value products and relationship marketing with customer support centres replacing some of the high cost of the traditional sales person. The new role for sales people is therefore more advisory than product selling in which help with their customers market planning, training staff and managing customer contacts is very time consuming and demanding (see Figure 3.2).

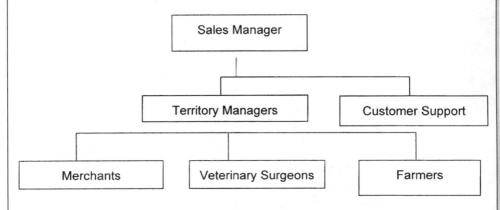

Figure 3.2 Merial sales structure.

Questions

1. Identify the factors that appear to be driving this business from a transaction to a more relationship-based exchange approach.
2. Critically assess the approach that Merial have taken so far and identify what else the company might be doing to position themselves competitively in the future.
3. Identify general and specific actions that you would recommend for Merial to compete successfully in the future.
4. Given that relationships with intermediaries and vets are all important to the company suggest measures to control costs and evaluate relationship performance.
5. To what extent should the company develop one-to-one relationships with farmers and what value can the company add for their group?

Further reading

Aoki, M., Gustafsson, B. and Williamson, O.E. (1990), *The Firm as a Nexus of Treaties*, Sage, London.

Axelrod, R. (1984), *The Evolution of Cooperation*, Basic Books, New York.

Barringer, B.R. and Harrison, J.S. (2000), Walking a tightrope: creating value through interorganisational relationships, *Journal of Management*, 26 (3), pp. 367–403.

Ford, D. (1998), *Managing Business Relationships*, Wiley, Chichester.

Ford, D. (1997), *Understanding Business Markets*, 2nd Edition, Thomson Press, London.

Ghoshal, S. and Moran, P. (1996), Bad for practice: a critique of the transaction cost theory, *Academy of Management Review*, 21 (1), pp. 13–47.

Lincoln, J.R. (1984), Analysing relations in dyads, *Sociological Methods and Research*, 13 (1), pp. 45–76.

Moran, P. and Ghoshal, S. (1996), Theories of economic organisation: the case for realism and balance, *Academy of Management Review*, 21 (1), pp. 58–72.

Nooteboom, B., Berger, H. and Noorderhaven, N.G. (1997), The effects of trust and governance on relational risk, *Academy of Management Journal*, 40 (2), pp. 308-338.

Robicheaux, R.A. and Coleman, J.E. (1994), The structure of marketing channel relationships, *Journal of the Academy of Marketing Sciences*, 22 (1), pp. 38–51.

Seth, A. and Thomas, H. (1994), Theories of the firm: implications for strategy researchers, *Journal of Management Studies*, 31, pp. 165–191.

Sheth, J.N. and Garrett, D.E. (1986), *Marketing Theory: Classic and Contemporary Readings*, South Western Publishing, Cincinnati, OH.

Chapter questions

1. Select examples of relationships, one of which where economic aspects are most important and one where behavioural aspects are more important.
2. Show how transaction cost economics may be helpful in deciding the type of relationship between a supplier and a retail customer.
3. To what extent do you agree that the assumptions which condition agency theory are too restrictive to be applied to relationships in practice? Give examples.
4. Try to be specific on the variables that represent the nature of trust between buyer and seller. Which of these are most important and why?
5. Defend the IMP model against criticisms that it is too descriptive to be considered a theory.
6. How might Jackson's lost for good model assist in deciding what investments to make in buyer-seller relationships?
7. To what extent do you consider the traditional model of marketing management is redundant in the new age of information technology?
8. The motivation to enter into or sustain a relationship is often not explicitly stated. Choosing your own context try to be explicit from the perspective to one to the parties involved.

CHAPTER 4

Relationship planning

Introduction and objectives

In chapter 2 we argued that relationships were strategic. Strategic market relationships must be planned for so that their maximum value can be tapped. We apply the strategic planning process to relationships using a three-stage framework – analysis, formulation and selection, and implementation. Relationship planning is dynamic and requires top managers to be continuously involved in focusing resources and mobilising people to reach long-term goals. Once the relationship planning process and the assumptions and principles that underlie it are outlined we detail the dimensions of relationship analysis. The formulation and selection of a relationship strategy has been presented in chapter 2. Formulation and selection of strategy is aided by many tools presented in this text, especially those in chapter 7 on relationship classification and development. In addition, we detail a relationship strength assessment tool that can help guide the relationship choices of managers. Finally, the authors address the importance of strategic relationship implementation. Many important implementation issues run throughout this text but this chapter provides an introduction to the social and structural tools and tactics needed to implement relationship strategy. These tools and tactics are summarised using a 5-S relationship implementation framework.

After reading this chapter you should know:

- how the strategic planning process can apply to relationships: analysis - formulation - implementation;
- the key principles of relationship planning;
- the critical dimensions of relational analysis;
- recapped on how relationship strategies are formulated and implemented;
- how to assess the strength of a relationship;
- the linkage between relationship strategy and implementation;
- the core elements of an implementation plan.

The hotel industry provides us with an introductory case illustration. We draw examples from the industry to illustrate best relationship practice and to demonstrate core relationship planning principles. These core principles are detailed further into the chapter: interdependence, longer-term horizons, analysing interaction, values and images, people and process, and networks.

HOTEL INDUSTRY

There are many different types of hotels, hotel chains and independent operators (see footnote[1] for useful web resources). This illustration concentrates on the luxury and upper end of the market but managing relationships is not limited to this market. In fact, many of the groups mentioned have offerings in many different market types. Not all guests require or want a relationship when they stay at an hotel. They expect to be satisfied and indeed this satisfaction may lead to repeat visits. A repeat visit on its own may not indicate a relationship but could be a precursor to it. Recognising the inter-dependence of an hotel on its employee and customer markets is easy on face value. Putting it into action is more difficult. Designing systems that will allow an active customer means bringing them into the process. When you visit an hotel many elements of service can be set-up and rigid, not facilitating customers to participate as they are only designed around the management systems of the hotel. For example, check-in and -out and meal times can be strictly regulated. Failure to meet an hotel's deadlines can mean extra charges. However, some hotels have improved their processes to fit customers' rather than managements' schedules. The Sheraton Group[2] has re-worked some of its housekeeping systems to allow check-out as late as 4pm.

Many hotel industry practices are short-term in nature. For example, how some hotels in the industry practice yield management can be short-term. Yield management aims to maximise room occupancy and price per room. Sometimes this practice can involve opportunistic behaviour with very high rates at particular times. This can hit loyal customer's trust hard, who can then find themselves paying over the odds on one particular night. Maybe yield management should only be practised on customers with whom an hotel does not want to build a relationship. Ritz-Carlton were among the first to evaluate the value of a loyal customer which in the early 1990s was estimated at $100 000.

Customers who want a relationship will respond in an interactive way to the offer-ings of an hotel. They will go out of their way to act as advocates for the hotel's products and services and are themselves committed users of the hotel's services. This interactivity characterises a relationship. However, very little is known about what might characterise a high-level interaction between an hotel and its client. Some examples of high-level trust might include: keeping a block of rooms for a corporate booker even though they could be sold today at a higher price, demonstrat-ing that the hotel trusts its staff by letting them make decisions without referring to a manager, high trust customers may tell at least 10 or more people about their stay, and committed users spend more per stay than other types. The hotel industry is also attempting to bring in users at the design stage to differentiate and customise its service from the beginning as the inside of hotels are becoming more and more stan-dardised (see, Bowen and Shoemaker (1988), for a further discussion on how to involve users).

The Hilton Hotel group[3] (also owners of the Stakis group in the UK) epitomises another relational planning principle: the importance of values and images. The Hilton

[1] www.hotelschool.cornell.edu; www.hotelresource.com
[2] www.sheraton.com
[3] www.hilton.com

Group has a set of core values that emphasise its core stakeholder groups called the Hilton Pride (Huckestein and Duboff, 1999). The core values are delighting the customers, loyal team members, satisfied owners and shareholders, successful strategic partners, and involved community. These broad values encompass all key relationships but specific objectives for each of these are set. Value statements for each stakeholder group are a benchmark for these groups' perceptions of the company. Hilton is an hotel standard in the luxury market. Its brand image conveys a status and expectation to all its core stakeholder groups. The Hilton image is particularly important in developing relationships with the holiday traveller as an individual relationship with each of these customers is difficult considering the number of hotels and beds the company has to offer. Yet, of course, each hotel is local and can establish a presence on this basis.

The Marriott Hotel Group[4] is in the same competitive set as the Hilton. The Marriott group owns the Ritz-Carlton – a by-word for luxury hotels. Marriott is viewed as a good company to work for. Training is a corporate philosophy at Marriott. It has also a highly rated management training programme for building leaders from within the organisation. Accor[5], a French company that incorporates Sofitel, Novotel, Mercure and Ibis, has its own training institute which is so highly regarded it is used by other companies. Up to 10% of its graduates work for other firms. People are a central principle of relationship planning as implementation of a relationship can only happen through them. The hotel industry is often associated with low wages and a military-type command structure. These often work against employee flexibility and retention which are key elements in relationship management.

Wider network connections are a feature in understanding and applying relationship planning to the hotel industry. For example, Choice Hotels is an international franchise group[6] incorporating such brands as Comfort, Quality, Clarion, Sleep, Rodeway, Econo Lodge and Friendship. These brands are tied together by a central reservation system and strict operational procedures for each category. Forte Hotels[7] (group also includes Le Meridien hotels and resorts, and the Posthouse and Heritage brands) in common with many groups, is part of a wider network of connections. It is linked to its parent Granada Group PLC which gives it access to a large media and entertainment group, and to its suppliers for the provision of value added services for its customers. In addition, it has a range of travel partners such as the airlines: American, Delta and TWA (you can earn airline miles for these airlines when you stay at a Forte hotel). A set of partners beyond the simple confines of running a business can provide important opportunities for differentiation and sharing of resources with these partners

Note: The hotel groups selected represent a sample and readers are encouraged to research other groups and independents. In researching this illustration we found interesting relational practices in many hotels.

[4] *www.marriott.com*
[5] *www.accor.com*
[6] *www.choicehotels.com*
[7] *www.forte-hotels.com*

Strategic relationship planning process

The application of the strategic planning process to relationship is made apparent by our argument in chapter 2 that relationships are strategic. Relationships conceived as such should be part of the strategic planning process. In our application of the process we will concentrate only on relationships. In practice, many other business choices are part of the planning process. Indeed, relationship issues may impact other business choices and vice versa. Readers who wish to review the total range of business choices put through the rigour of the planning process can review initial chapters in strategic management texts by authors such as Johnson and Scholes (1997), Grant (1998), Hill and Jones (1998) and Mintzberg et al. (1998). Using a planning framework is merely an aid to choice making but necessary as the risks and rewards can be great. If we think about the impact of strategic relationship alignments in telecommunications, computing and entertainment businesses, we can readily understand the importance of using a planning approach to making choices about relationships.

There is no agreed strategic planning process in the texts cited earlier on strategic management. We chose, for simplicity of presentation and to concentrate on the issues, the 'rational' planning model that is analysis followed by formulation followed by implementation. These three phases are linked and iterative. However, the criticism of this type of planning approach is that, in practice, decision-making does not follow these neat stages and that planning happens in an evolutionary organic way emerging from organisations and their interactions over time. Whilst we agree with this view, for ease of presentation and to organise all the material we needed to present we choose the alternative (for an interesting revision of a variety of planning approaches the reader is referred to Wittington, 1993). Relationships are often a product of a long history (Keep et al., 1998) and are shaped by repeated interaction (Hakansson and Wootz, 1979). Our presentation fully captures this dynamic. Often managerial instinct and tacit knowledge are used to make choices without resort to any planning approach. However, as a means of organising this text and to facilitate learning we present relational planning using a rational/ sequential model. The strategic planning process is presented in Figure 4.1.

It comprises three core elements: analysis, formulation and selection of strategy, and strategic implementation. Analysis provides the input for strategic choices. In analysing relationships we evaluate each relational stakeholder. Obviously, more emphasis may be placed on areas considered more important. Relationships with customers, suppliers, competitors and the interconnectedness of these relationships must be analysed. Analytical tools and techniques are provided throughout this text. Later in this chapter the key dimensions of relationship analysis are provided.

Formulation and selection of a strategy involves making choices about which direction a company should take. A company should be able to decide its overall competitive methods and goals, its position in its main product-markets, and the guiding management principles for each of its key resource areas – human, financial, physical, technical, and market. Organisation size and scope will influence the level of detail of a strategy by top managers. All the key choices should be inte-

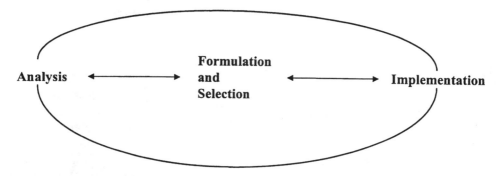

Figure 4.1   Strategic planning process.

grated and act as a clear signal of intent by the company. Formulation and selection of a relationship strategy means making the choices outlined in chapter 2: should we pursue a collaborative approach? which relationships should be developed? what benefits should be offered? how does a company deliver on these benefits? how are we positioned vis-à-vis the network of relationships we compete within? what relationships development strategy should we pursue? what organisation structures should be developed to manage relationships?

Finally, all plans must be implemented. Poor execution has repeatedly been found to dilute good strategy and good implementation has also been found to mask ill-considered strategy (Bonoma, 1985; Colgate and Danaher, 2000). Implementing relationship strategy is a key feature of many of the chapters of this text. In this chapter we outline the core relationship strategy implementation issues such as investments and adaptations, organising for relationships, monitoring relationships, building relationships through brands, and service process and systems. Many of the relationship implementation tools and tactics aim to lock-in a partner to a relationship but if not accompanied by a fundamental belief in relationships as a strategy ,this lock-in may not work. Many loyalty programmes fall into this trap. They can be designed to promote loyalty but can end up being used by consumers to gain maximum benefits from a range of different providers. In this case no loyalty is added only costs, unless the information benefits of the database outweigh any costs. This approach to loyalty may not then be strategic which is one reason, if any are needed, to include implementation as part of the planning process.

Strategic relationship planning: some key principles

The very notion of planning strategy for relationships requires an outward orientation – examining the resources and competencies of your partner when developing strategy and the impact of these on your business. Even if an involved relationship strategy is not chosen it can be beneficial to analyse relationships. In the discussion of relational planning principles a co-operative strategy is assumed. In the introductory case illustration, practice examples of each principle are given. The key principles are:

Interdependence

In the relational planning view, all stages of the process are influenced by the interdependence of parties for successful outcomes. Where the traditional model of planning sees planning as an independent act precipitated by a focal firm for maximising its short-term outcomes, a relationship planning scenario means working on partner outcomes and sometimes involving them in the planning process. For example, a firm might involve investors in decisions about company finances for new ventures not just to maintain goodwill but also to benefit from external advice on any move. The relationship planning model incorporates partners as an active component. The dual role of planning for self and others brings a unique dimension to the planning process.

Longer-term horizons

Co-operative relationships are characterised by long-term rather than single transactions. This means that firms can maximise value over repeated interactions rather than in a single one. The temporal horizon permits organisations to take risks with other partners that they would otherwise not do. For example, a buyer might pay a slightly higher price today for a benefit or deal in the future with a particular supplier. A decision like this is possible as it is informed by a history of past behaviour which is expected to continue into the future.

Analysing interaction

An added dimension to strategic planning by taking a relationship position is the need to analyse interaction. The interaction between a firm and its customers, suppliers and other partners. The assumption is that our success is predicated on theirs. The key dimensions in this analysis are provided in the next section of this chapter and many tools of analysis presented in other chapters of this text.

Values and images

Mass consumer markets have always posed a significant challenge for relationship proponents. How does a company have a relationship with the mass market? The Internet retailer, Amazon.com is the subject of the end of chapter case. Dell computers individualises each of its personal computers through its Internet ordering system: you can build your own computer. The hurdle of mass customisation is also been met by companies such as Hewlett Packard who push the task of differentiating a product for a specific customer to the last possible point in the supply network. They do this through modular design which can be combined at the last possible point in the value chain. Consumer markets are highlighted here as often it may be beyond the scope of a firm to develop an individual relationship with all consumers. Of course, they may also not want one. Therefore, relationships depend on values, often ethical, with which partners can identify and on which they can make trusting decisions. A consumer may shop at a certain store, or bank at a particular branch because they identify with the values of a company. Designing a set of values for partner relationships becomes critical in relationships where you cannot take direct action. However, they also are important to other relational types. Values should reflect the assumptions and intent of a company's dealings with a particular partner set. Values are clearly related to the images of a company and its brands. A company's image and brands are evaluated by its market. These evaluations stem from partners' evaluations of past activities and behaviour of the firm which then comprise the perceived values attributed to that company by its partners. Relationship planning has to consider the 'invisible' part of the relationship and plan for it. A sound way to start is with a value statement that is followed. Some of our best loved companies seem to be able to do this.

People and process

People and process are two key elements in strategic relationship planning. Relationships are socially constructed – people interact with others across organisations and with consumers. Planning for an individual company's human capital in a relationship and the value it adds is part of relationship planning. The people side of relationships include managerial intent and action. So often organisational culture and managerial willingness dictate the pace and intensity of relationship development. The 'people factor' is deemed critical in service businesses but is central to all relationships. In addition to people, exchanges between an organisation and its relationships happen through processes, particularly in the supply and demand chains of a company. Relationships are about processes which are combinations of products, services and other interactions. When analysing relationships, an organisation must examine all aspects of interaction between it and its relationships. These interactions do not comprise single events but chains of linked events or processes. Relationship process examples include those of developing trust and commitment, the relationship orientation of a firm, sales and customer support in customer relationship, employee satisfaction and retention, media and financial market communication processes.

Networks

The final principle of relational planning is the network. A firm is embedded in a series of connected relationship which in turn are connected to other relationships. Analysing the total network to which a firm is part is a task in strategic relationship planning. We devote a chapter in this text to the system of wider connections and linkage that form part of a firm's relationship infrastructure. Often network connections are visible through alliances such as those in the global telecommunications or airline markets but more often the strength of network ties are represented in patterns of trading consummated over long periods which are usually indivisible from the structure of the industry itself. The network dimension of relationship planning is its most complex level. An understanding of your organisation's relationships must be met by an understanding of connections between the other players.

The six key dimensions of relationship planning form tenants of understanding of much of the material in this text. The authors aim to help the reader and student of relationships to get into the detail of each principle which are different to those normally underlying a strategy course because relationships are unique and need distinct tools, techniques and practices to maximise their business value. The remainder of the chapter will delve further into issues within the three elements of the strategic relationship planning process.

The dimensions of relationship analysis

This section will present the dimensions of relationship analysis. It is built on the principles of relational planning outlined earlier. A collaborative view is taken. The model can be applied to industrial, consumer and other inter-organisational relationships. Obviously, the focus for the analysis of any market relationship will be different. That is the depth of analysis into each variable will be different. We will use the seminal framework of the IMP's (International Marketing and Purchasing Group) interaction model as a basis for relational analysis (Hakansson, 1982). This framework is adapted to suit the broad relationship perspective of this text as the model was developed for industrial relationships. The foundation for relationship analysis is the interaction pattern between a firm and its relational partner. The model is presented in Figure 4.2. It has four basic dimensions within which a set of variables for analysing a relationship are presented.

The interaction process

The interaction process is how the parties to the relationship interact. This interaction tends to be of two types: the shorter-term episodic exchange, for example, one transaction, and the series of interactions built up into a longer-term pattern of norms and expectations of both parties. The analysis of episodes and longer-term interaction involves a consideration of the following dimensions:

- product and service components exchanged;
- information exchange patterns;
- money transfers;
- communication exchanges (interpersonal bonds and emotive bonds built through brands);
- long-term institutionalisation (expectations built up over time, for example, levels of service expected, or typical responses to problem solving);
- adaptations made (mutual adaptation in products and processes made by firms

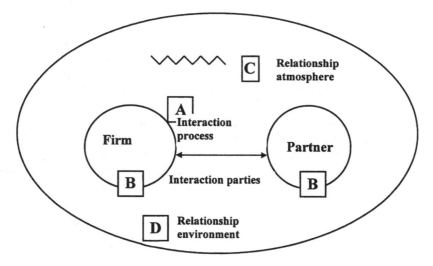

Figure 4.2   Interaction model (Source: Hakansson, 1982).

typically in industrial markets but also a feature of the attempts at mass customisation in consumer markets);
- analysis of repeated interaction value (loyalty and retention effects) and partners
  as advocates for your business.

Interaction parties

Understanding the interacting parties be they organisations or individuals is a
central dimension of relationship analysis. When two organisations are interacting
we must be familiar with our own organisation but also the people and processes
(how business is done) in another organisation. The analysis of interaction parties
consists of the following:

- understanding individuals (behaviours, attitudes and opinions of those
  involved. In consumer markets this element of analysis is a major component
  and may lead to a segmentation of consumers);
- history of relationship management;
- resources and competencies of each party and resources used in the exchange
  (the nature of the resources and competencies that can be accessed in a relationship gives you a good idea of benefits in the relationship);
- for inter-organisational relationships understanding company size, strategy and
  structure is crucial.

Relationship atmosphere

The relationship atmosphere pervades the exchange. It is characterised by an 'electricity' symbol in Figure 4.2. The atmosphere between individuals affects the relationships and is a mediator of it. In a consumer-organisation, relationship atmosphere is fuelled by the perception of a company and how it operates, whereas in organisation-organisation relationships atmosphere is perhaps more a feature of the actions taken. Elements of atmosphere analysis such as power is beyond the scope of any single text such as this and requires considerable managerial skill to unravel and understand, yet insights into power bases provides clues to understanding the total relationship. For example, a firm that uses its power can obtain better deals from its partners but this in turn may make the partners unwilling to co-operate in other areas such as new product development. The areas to be analysed in relationship atmosphere include:

- an understanding of how power is used and the interdependence of the parties;
- an analysis of the trust among the partners;
- an analysis of loyalty towards company and products;
- analysing closeness and co-operation;
- expectations and norms in the relationship;
- analysing commitment in the relationship.

The relationship environment

Perhaps this dimension of relationship analysis is the easiest to understand as we all are familiar with the analysis of environmental forces. In relationship analysis, the environment is that which effects the relationship rather than the broader environmental analysis conducted for formulating general company strategy. However, it is analogous to the political, social, technological, and economic analysis that is part of a general strategic environmental analysis. The elements which comprises relationship environmental analysis are:

- the pace and direction of environmental change affecting the relationship;
- the degree of internationalisation of the relationship and market (the global market and cultural dimension of relational analysis);
- position in the channel structure of a relationship;
- connectedness of the relationship to other relationships (the network dimension of relational analysis).

Just by reading through this section should give a picture of how relationship analysis is different to other types of strategy analysis. A lot of tools and techniques are presented in this text which help analyse each of these dimensions. But the relationship student should also note that there are plenty of research avenues in each of the dimensions presented. In the referencing section at the end of the chapter further selected reading is available on some of the dimensions presented. Variables such as power, trust and commitment are critical to understand and analysing relationship interaction. Many insights can be gained by applying the relevant dimension of the interaction model in Figure 4.2 to a relationship of your choice. Each of the dimensions are connected to each other but, in total, provide a framework for building a picture of a relationship between partners. The ties that bind can be seen to be very complex and difficult to break in this context. Also, the ways ties can be built are indicated in each dimension.

Chapter 2 dealt with strategy formulation and selection. Once analysis is complete the strategist must begin to make choices about the strategies to pursue. This is the role of the formulation and selection phase of relationship planing.

Relationship strength in formulating and selecting strategy

As already outlined, formulation and selecting relationship strategy is about choice making. The bases on which choices are made, the alternative courses of action, and the selection of a strategy are all part of the formulation and selection process. In this section a relationship strength tool is developed to aid in strategic choice making.

To aid in choice making some method of taking a 'snap-shot' of a relationship is needed. The relationship strength tool provides such a picture. Relationship strength measures the underlying motivation or assumptions guiding the relationship and the intensity of interaction between the parties (O' Toole and Donaldson, 1999). The level of strength found in any relationship is an indicator of an actor's focus or motivational engagement which is captured in beliefs and actions taken in a relationship. Assessing a relationship using the relationship strength comprises a social (belief) and economic (action) element. If the assessment was based on only one of these dimensions then significant potential might be missed. For example, a relationship may be very co-operative and open but may not have strong economic ties, or a relationship may have strong economic ties through dependency and be very uncooperative and forced. Capturing both the economic and social dimensions of a relationship avoids missing key actions or beliefs that are essential in any assessment tool. The relationship strength tool brings together two ideas kernel in assessing the nature of a relationship: economic action and social belief. Close relationships exhibit a high score on both dimensions – significant economic action unique to the relationship has been taken by the partners and the bonds between the partners are intense and binding. Many relationships will have elements of economic action and social belief but the level of each will vary widely. Strong relationship strength is a strategic resource for a company that may be difficult to copy by other firms as, at this level, unique action and bonds are a feature of the relationship.

Turnbull and Wilson's (1989) discussion of social and structural bonding is analogous to the idea of relationship strength outlined here. Lincoln (1982) defines strength as one of the relationship properties in a similar manner to this text. Indeed, Dwyer et al.'s (1987) concept 'motivational investment' and Whetten and Leung's (1979) concept 'instrumental value' have many parallels to the relationship strength concept defined here. In a buyer-supplier relationship the assessment of economic relational commitments rests with the extent partners have invested and adapted to each other in the past or may do so in the future. In other words, the partners have taken specific actions in the relationship or are willing to do so. These actions represent an economic commitment to the relationship. Investment and adaptation patterns have been found to influence the structure of a relationship (Hakansson, 1982; Hallen et al., 1991). Making an assessment of the strength of a relationship must involve an evaluation of economic actions taken in a relationship. Relationships are said to be weak or strong depending on the level of economic action taken in the relationship. These actions are very often reflected in committed action patterns such as investment and adaptation.

Blau (1964) viewed the development of relationships as a social process. Social bonds tend to cement relationships and tie partners together. Presence or absence of these bonds can influence other elements of a relationship and drive a relationship. For example, belief about a partner's use of power, or whether or not a relationship will be reciprocal, will influence the strength of a relationship. Many relationships could not operate without a certain amount of social bonding taking place and it may be necessary for a relationship to develop. Macneil (1980) referred to the bonds that develop between organisations as a 'social contract'. In assessing relationship strength, a case can be made for including a behavioural component in its evaluation: an assessment of the belief (social orientation) in the relationship by the partners.

In chapter 6, we link the concept of relationship strength with relational classification. Different relationship types require varying levels of belief and action. For example, from a buyer-supplier relationship perspective, it may be to a buyer's advantage to invest heavily in supplier training, provision of managerial assistance, provide information on production planning, and utilise specialist supply management structures in very close relationships when compared to more distant types. The specific dimensions of relationship strength will vary with the type of relationship under consideration. Different beliefs and action sets will be considered important in the range of relationships possible for a company.

Strategic relationship implementation

A relationship strategy will ultimately be implemented in each of a firm's functional areas, for example, in marketing and human resource management practice. How is a relationship strategy implemented? Much of this text concentrates on the implementation issue, for example, relationship innovation, relationship management, sales and customer service, e-relationships and measuring relationships are all part of relational implementation.

Relational implementation is associated with processes that link an organisation to its partner. Adding to or subtracting from these processes is the day-to-day task of relationship implementation. For example, it might be a relational strategy decision to involve customers and suppliers in the new product development process but implementation will set the structures and systems in place to make this happen. We introduce a 5-S framework to help plan for relationship implementa-

Table 4.1   The core dimensions of relationship implementation

Dimension	Description
1. Structure	Organisation structure for relationships, for example, team-based structures such as key account management
2. Staff	People dimension of a relationship. Managing the social structure of a relationship. From engineers to customer service personnel. Training is critical here
3. Style	Everything managers say and do. Beliefs and actions of managers determine the overall philosophy and direction of a relationship
4. Systems	Setting-up relational systems such as sales and service process, supply chain management system, relationship performance scorecards, order fulfilment system
5. Schemes	Programmes that support relationship implementation, for example, investment and adaptation patterns, loyalty and retention programmes, relational communication

tion. The aim of the 5-S framework is to link strategy to the implementation of social and structural ties in the relationship. Relationship implementation is about developing the social bonds and structural ties in a relationship. When detailing the relationship strength assessment tool we highlighted the belief and action component of a relationship. Relationship strength happens at an implementation level by bonding people, organisational systems, and processes together. We provide an implementation framework for doing just that in this section.

The key dimensions of relationship implementation are presented in Table 4.1. We summarise these in a 5-S framework: structure, staff, style, systems, and schemes. Each of these has a role to play in the day-to-day or operational management of relationship strategies. Implementing relationship management strategies is under-researched. The 5-S framework in Table 4.1 provides a planning methodology for linking relationship strategy to implementation.

A *structure* must be put in place to manage a relationship. This can be difficult to visualise when we are dealing with connections between physically separate organisations (Davidow and Malone, 1992, refer to this as the virtual organisation). Managing an entity that is boundary-less requires considerable skill. The structure challenge in close relationship is involvement of partners in the decision making process. For example, Xerox corporation has made major advances in involving users in the new product development process. There are many other exemplars including IBM's development of the key account management system where teams of people manage key customer relationships. The main difficulty with the structure issue is the need to combine skills from a variety of functions, for example, marketing, finance, and operations. It has always been difficult to implement team-based organisational structures. Relationship ties are process driven which does not suit a functional approach to structure (see, for example, of a process structure Cardozo et al. (1992), discussion of a customer-linked strategy). We revisit the issue of structure in chapter 7. However, at this stage, the reader might wish to reflect on organisational systems such as Quinn's (1992) spider's web organisational type which transcends all key functional areas, or in a federation structures (Provan, 1983) as useful ideas in seeing a current set of relationships. These structures concentrate on connections between activities. Spider web organisations have a focal centre with waves of connecting and inter-linked bonds, and a federation is a set of independent but linked organisations such as franchisers-franchisees, or the independent retailer's relationship to a symbol group (wholesaler) to which it is a voluntary member.

Staff or *people* cement bonds and are communication channels in a relationship. In close relationships, bonds can be at many levels in the organisation which requires careful planning as they can personalise a relationship and create meaningful social interaction. People always have been a central tenant in managing services businesses due to their front line role. This role is epitomised in Kanter's (1989) metaphor *'teaching a giant to dance'* (creating innovative and service responsiveness in large organisations), or in Gronroos's (1990) moments of truth (encounters between service personnel and customers that make or break a relationship). The human factor is emphasised in relationship management. Training and support and, of course, openness and flexibility of people to allow them to make policy changes is important in developing relationships. For example, employees must have flexibility to make decisions to suit individual customers not just retort 'sorry, it is against company policy', or 'they do not allow that here'. Any staff member in contact with the relationship becomes an asset in managing it.

Much relationship policy becomes the rhetoric of managers who are not committed to it. Managerial *style* in relationships at all levels of management, especially, middle management is vital to the successful implementation of relationship strategy (Kathandaraman and Wilson, 2000). Ricard and Perrien (1999) found that developing a relationship oriented culture by banks was a key facet in implementing relationships with their commercial clients. The role of managers in banks is crucial to the shaping of perspectives by industrial clients in their purchase of bank services. Therefore, all of a company's programmes and policies including how they reward managers has to be geared towards relationships. Everything managers say and do about their relationships is infused into the organisation as other employees take their cues from managers' beliefs and actions. This is why it is often difficult to change a relationship strategy or to copy another organisation. Managers' beliefs and actions are resistant to change. For example, changing from adversarial modes of buying to more co-operative ones is rarely achieved except on paper by being called something else like partnership which means little more than the old regime (see Matthyssens and Van den Bulte (1994), for the managerial implications of such a shift). Researchers in relationships must be careful to spot this kind of difference.

As referred to in structure, relationships are processes which require *systems* to be designed around their structure. From a marketing perspective the sales and customer service systems must be built around relationships. From an operations management or logistics perspective the system of supply chain management is another area with relationship management implications. Financial systems can also support relationships – the type of information revealed to investors can affect their trust in the organisation – a key indicator of relationalism. How an investor perceives a company's performance may be indicative of how he/she is signalled to by that company. The management of relationship performance and incentives for relationship performance also provide support and direct backing to a relationship strategy.

Finally, *schemes* or tactical relationship acts are often used as tools in the relationship implementation phase. Tesco's success with its clubcard which had 10 million members after 2 years in operation, is an example of using a loyalty tool in relationship management. Investment in schemes should be designed to create meaningful switching costs that is making it difficult to switch to another relationship but because the parties want to rather than have to stay in the relationship. Loyalty and retention programmes like the use of loyalty cards are now staple parts of most organisation's relationship programmes. They often include a financial incentive but should be also rooted in value sets deeply held within the organisation and in the relationship to offer real benefits as opposed to adding additional costs to the company. Adaptation patterns can be strong indicators of action at an implementation level. Adaptation can include modifying a product or process, for example, buying a personal computer from Dell direct can be modified to your specification through the Internet. We have added communication here as how an organisation communicates to its relationships including marketing promotions can impact on how it is perceived in the marketplace. For example, sales people and buyers communicate in relationships on a daily basis. What they say and offer can signify an organisation's buying or selling approach.

Each of the 5-Ss are covered in more detail in the implementation chapters of the text where further material is presented which will provide more analytical support to aid in planning for relationship strategy implementation.

Chapter summary

In chapter 2 we argued that relationships were strategic. In this chapter the strategic planning process was applied to relationships. A three-stage relationship planning process was presented consisting of analysis moving to formulation and finally, to implementation. Six core principles of relationship planning were also outlined which were given practical application in the hotel industry introductory case illustration.

A framework for relationship analysis was presented based on the International Marketing and Purchasing Group's (IMP) interaction model. The diversity and range of variables that comprises relationship analysis were grouped using the IMP's interaction framework. The essential elements of the framework are the interaction process, the interaction parties, relationship atmosphere, and relationship environment. Relationship analysis includes assessments of relationship capability, power, and trust in the partnership. Relationship strategy formulation, or making relationship strategy choices, was mainly covered in chapter 2. An additional technique is introduced in this chapter that of relationship strength. Relationship strength assessment is an aid to choice making and measures the assumptions guiding the relationship and the intensity of interaction between the parties. It can be used to develop a 'snap-shot' of the nature of the relationship. The final stage of relationship strategy is implementation. A 5-S framework for relationship implementation was presented to aid in the diagnosis of implementation challenges and planning for relationship implementation. The 5-Ss are structure, staff, style, systems and schemes. Many chapters of this text cover these implementation issues in more depth. Linking relationship strategy to implementation is vital and may inform and change the relationship strategy approach intended.

CASE FOR DISCUSSION   **AMAZON.COM**

According to Jeff Bezos, founder and CEO of Amazon.com

...our customers are loyal right up to the point somebody offers them a better service. That's the dimension on which we compete. The goal of Amazon.com has to be to make sure that we are the pre-eminent brand name associated with on-line bookselling in the year 2000. I think we have a huge opportunity to build an interactive retailing company beyond books.

(Seattle Times, January 5th 1997).

Amazon.com continues to be the biggest provider of on-line books but now offers a range of other services. The quote serves to illustrate the difficulty in building customer relationships in a market where there is direct one-to-one communication between the customer and the company. A virtual relationship is not a panacea for managing and implementing a relationship strategy. To complete this case study we encourage the reader to visit the Amazon site[8]. This should help assess how the company develops and maintains its relationship with individual customers. It should also provide the opportunity for comparison to other similar Internet retailers and store retailers who have a significant Internet presence. Competing Internet book retailers include Barnes and Noble, the US chain, WH Smith in the UK, and booxtra and Bertelsmann's bol.com in Germany[9].

The first page of the Amazon.com web site shows the current diversity and range of Amazon's products and services. The company has moved on many fronts to satisfy a broad range of customer's needs using the Amazon brand as an integrative factor. The company was founded in 1994 and is based in Seattle in the US. The Amazon.com name has become one of the most recognised e-commerce brands in the World and is the most recognised in the biggest e-commerce market: the USA. In a survey by Interbrand, of the World's most valued brands, Amazon is ranked 57th. In January 2000 the company changed its logo to communicate its belief that it is one of the most customer-centric firms in the world. It currently is estimated to have 16 million customers. The new logo (see web site) depicts a smile replacing the existing downward curve. The

[8] *www.amazon.com*
[9] *barnesandnoble.com; whsmith.co.uk; booxtra.de; bol.com*

smile starts under the A and ends under the Z emphasising Amazon's new A–Z retail offering.

The company has grown from selling primarily books to selling CDs, toys, electronics, videos, DVDs, software, video games, auctions, e-cards, drugs amongst its products. To deliver on this variety the company has linked into a range of other suppliers and brands. Through Amazon.com's zShops, any business or individual can sell virtually anything to Amazon.com's more than 16 million customers and with Amazon's payments system can accept credit card transactions, thus avoiding the hassle of off-line payments and Internet security worries. Amazon has become an e-tailing (electronic retailing) hub. In addition to its own site it offers a search engine for the web as a whole to expand its service to its customers (All Product Search). Amazon has a book retailing site in the UK (amazon.co.uk) and one in Germany (amazon.de). Amazon is aiming to be an Internet shopping destination for everything. It is the number one Internet book retailer, the number 1 music retailer, the number 1 DVD and video retailer. As an example of its strategy to become a destination site, in 2000 it joined with drugstore.com, the leading drug e-tailer, in which drugstore.com became a permanent part of Amazon's web structure. It is part of Bezos' strategy of making Amazon.com the only place where you can find anything and everything you might want to buy online. Drugstore.com is an online source for retail and information on health, beauty, wellness, personal care and pharmacy. Amazon.com has many other partnership with e-tailers such as Pets.com, HomeGrocer.com, Gear.com (luxury sports ware) and Ashford.com (watches and jewellery). Amazon.com's relationships with its partners can include equity stakes.

Customers at Amazon's web site can chose the type of relationship they want. Regardless of the depth and duration of the relationship, Amazon's basic customer service process is user friendly and up-front about its promises. This starts without the elaborate graphics and clutter that so many of us are familiar with on the web. Each customer is guaranteed privacy, can un-subscribe at any time, plus if you avail of Amazon's information services via email you are under no obligation to buy. You can choose to give a lot of detail and engage in user feedback, for example, through joining specialist groups with similar interests, and receive ongoing notices from Amazon and its partners. If you chose to be a visible user you could be engaged in conversations with other users while you shop. At a minimum, you will receive a customised account which can be accessed easily at another time. Amazon's service will automatically customise your searches to your geographic location without prompting and provide a related product list as well as reviews in an unobtrusive way. These reviews may come from other customers, critical reviews by journalists taken from newspapers and magazines, and from Amazon's own staff. Even though the product offering is massive you will never notice this and the search time is short. A lot easier than the physical shopping cart alternative! Once you've ordered, confirmation and other communication is automated by e-mail. Besides the advantages of convenience, selection and service, Amazon are cheap. However, handling and order charges reduce the price differential when compared to traditional physical retailers. Repeat business is running at around 50% according to the company. The company pushes service options as mentioned and has special registers of interests which allow them to e-mail their customers with, for example, information on when a new book is published by a favourite author. This service is referred to as 'eyes'. Keeping satisfied customers is a priority as they can tell a lot of people if they are not happy by posting a note on the Internet. Amazon.com is developing specialist programmes by linking with other specialist web sites or to use the Amazon term 'Associates', for example, a industry group will use Amazon as a referral site for books and publications thus developing a specialist book market for Amazon. In return, Amazon gives these sites referral fees. In early 2000 there were estimates that Amazon's associates programme had 300 000 registered associations.

One key feature of the Amazon set-up is its logistics system. This starts when a customer searches. Amazon have always been a software development operation. One of their unique advantages to date has been to keep ahead of the competition in developing Internet software tools, for example, it takes less time to search at Amazon's site when compared to its competitors. The sophistication of Amazon's systems might equate it to its physical cousin Wal-Mart in being the web's equivalent by offering such a variety of products and services. The key difference is that Amazon's technology allows it to customise to everyone through its information provision. Specialist editorial information is organised and provided for most products: the information you want is at your fingertips. Once your order is made a computer takes charge signalling it to the nearest distribution centre which is mainly automated. Once shipped you are e-mailed to say your purchase is on its way. Obviously, Amazon uses distribution partners for postal and parcel deliveries. Although the Internet is invisible, the behind the scenes logistical operation is similar to that used by physical companies: Amazon's warehouses are literally huge (one is 800 000 sq.ft.). This operation allows Amazon to deliver in 1–7 days. Often its delivery dates are closer to 1 day in the US.

The staff at Amazon are very driven due to the entrepreneurial nature of the business reflected in the fact that the founder still runs the company. The structure of the company is lean. Amazon is open 24 hours a day and has a strong customer service (mainly through e-mail) and marketing focus. Another key part of the company is software development which allows Amazon.com to offer even more services to its customer and partner companies. In fact, Amazon pump what ever resources they have into their customers and developing relationships with them rather than into elaborate corporate offices or facilities. It is not uncommon to find the founder still staying over night at the company and for the employees to work 12–14-hour days. They are motivated by the nature of the business and by the remuneration packages available which include stock options. How Amazon.com will develop in the future is a matter of debate. Delivery on promises to its relational partners is what keeps it ahead.

Questions

1. Examine the core relationship implementation issues covered by the case using the 5-S framework.
2. From the information provided in the case evaluate the level of integration between each implementation area. Could this integration be further strengthened?
3. Comment and evaluate the strength of a relationship with Amazon and one of its partners as presented in the case and with web site research.
4. Discuss the extent, to which you believe Amazon is implementing a close relationship strategy or a strategy in which relationships are not its core mode of competing.
5. Using the material in the case as a reference base, analyse the interaction process and atmosphere of an Amazon-customer relationship. What does your analysis reveal about the character and duration of such a relationship? Examine the implications for a virtual relationship.

Further reading

Anderson, J.C. and Narus, J.A. (1990), A model of distributor firm and manufacturing firm working partnership, *Journal of Marketing*, 54 (5), pp. 42–58.

Cannon, J.P. and Perreault Jr., W.D. (1999), Buyer-seller relationships in business markets, *Journal of Marketing Research*, 36 (4), pp. 439–460.

Cook, K.S. and Emerson, R.M. (1978), Power, equity and commitment in exchange networks, *American Sociological Review*, 43 (October), pp. 721–739.

Doney, P.M. and Cannon, J.P. (1997), An examination of the nature of trust in buyer-seller relationships, *Journal of Marketing*, 52 (2), pp. 11–27.

Frazier, G.L. and Rody, R.C. (1991), The use of influence strategies in interfirm relationships in industrial product channels, *Journal of Marketing*, 55, pp. 52–69.

Gundlach, G.T., Achrol, R.S. and Mentzer, J.T. (1995), The structure of commitment in exchange, *Journal of Marketing*, 59 (1), pp. 78–92.

Hallen, L, Johanson, J. and Seyed-Mohamed, N. (1987), Relationship strength and stability in international industrial marketing, *Industrial Marketing and Purchasing*, 2 (3), pp. 22–37.

Husted, B.W. (1994), Transaction costs, norms and social networks, *Business and Society*, 33 (1), pp. 30–57.

Meyer, J.P. and Allen, N.J. (1994), Testing the 'side-bet theory' of organisational commitment: some methodological considerations, *Journal of Applied Psychology*, 69 (3), pp. 372–378.

Michell, P., Reast, J. and Lynch, J. (1998), exploring the foundations of trust, *Journal of Marketing Management*, 14, pp. 159–172.

Oliver, C. (1990), Determinants of interorganisational relationships: integration and future directions, *Academy of Management Review*, 15 (2), pp. 241–265.

Peters, T.J. and Waterman, R.H. (1982), *In Search of Excellence: lessons from America's best run companies*, Harpers and Row, New York.

Turnbull, P.W. and Valla, J.-P. (1987), Strategic planning in industrial marketing – an interaction approach, *European Journal of Marketing*, 121 (5), pp. 5–20.

Zaheer, A. and Venkatraman, N. (1995), Relational governance as an interorganisational strategy: an empirical test of the role of trust in economic exchange, *Strategic Management Journal*, 37 (2), pp. 77–88.

Chapter questions

1. Debate the extent to which you subscribe to the idea that relationships can or should be planned. Do you believe the material in this chapter would be more beneficial for some firms rather than for others?
2. Outline a strategic planning process for relationships? Compare this process to a planning process with which you are familiar? Outline your main criticisms of the process presented in this text.
3. Apply the core dimensions of relationship analysis to a company of your choice. What picture does it give you of the relationship? Could you use your analysis to change the nature of the relationship (how the parties interact)?]
4. In a group discussion setting, use the principles of relationship planning to challenge the way you think about how business is conducted. In what way do the principles of relationship planning conflict with your normal

response to decisions on such issues as resource allocation, training, and pricing.

5. Develop a relationship assessment tool for a relationship of your choice using the definition of relationship strength presented here. Does the combination of an assessment of beliefs and actions give you the 'snapshot' needed?

6. Examine the core dimensions of relationship implementation? Evaluate the 5-S framework presented – does it improve relationship planning to assess the dynamic of implementation, and if so, in what way?

7. Make a relationship strategy choice and follow it through to implementation. What implementation challenges does the 5-S framework reveal? How might these challenges be overcome?

8. Based on the relationship planning framework presented, and using the case material or an organisation with which you are familiar, conduct an audit of the relationship planning process? What type of recommendations would you make? What insights has the planning framework given you?

CHAPTER 5

Networks

Introduction and objectives

The rationale for forming relationships is also applicable to networks. Closer co-ordination in the supply chain, government and public policy interventions in markets, electronic linkages, technology complexity and change, and globalisation are all forces fostering increasing interdependence and connectedness between firms, their customers and the wider economic environment. The study of the connection between all these actors is the study of networks. The structural, social and economic bonds between businesses, between them and other public and private organisations and between the technology, resources and people of all these organisations are the ties of networks. Often a reader may think of networks as networking or interpersonal connections that one might use to get a job, or a contract, or to sell goods and services, but this networking is only one small part of networks. Strategic alliances, franchising are visible networks but these are not the most common networks. Every industry is characterised by connections, both strong and weak, between a range of companies and individuals. Network analysis provides us with insights into the interaction between all the actors in a network.

The chapter begins with a case study illustrating network analysis applied to industrial districts. The definition of networks as overlapping connections between a host of actors in a particular group is explored as is the wider implications of using networks to study interorganisational relationships. Network analysis is presented in detail. A micro and macro approach to analysing networks is described. A micro approach starts with an individual firm to begin its analysis. This method is of most direct appeal to practitioners and business strategists. A micro view is broader and begins with an industry or economic system. It is a broader economic systems context understanding. The chapter continues with an appreciation of the key elements of network strategy, especially, network position and changing position in a network. A variety of network forms are presented and two applications of a network approach examined in more detail – the strategic alliance and innovative network. The chapter concludes with a case study on networks in biotechnology and pharmaceuticals.

After reading this chapter you should know:

- what networks are and their composition;
- how network analysis is applied to the firm;

- how networks are applied at a macro level, for example, to an industry;
- the strategic potential of networks;
- the variety of different network forms;
- how networks have been applied to enhance innovation and to manage strategic alliances.

The introductory case study demonstrates the power of networks when applied to industrial districts. It shows how companies, governments and agencies can co-operate to develop an industrial success model in a particular region. The power of fostering the interaction and strengthening the connection between all interested, both private and public, parties in a given geographic area can add significant development momentum to the district.

CASE ILLUSTRATION   **INDUSTRIAL DISTRICTS**

The Italian industrial district of Modena is noted for its networks of small firms employing less than 50 people. These firms are usually grouped according to their product and have a low degree of vertical integration. Production is conducted through collaborative subcontracting arrangements. Firms grow through subcontracting rather than through expansion or integration. Modena has a high rate of these firm types relative to the rest of Italy. The maintenance of a small, usually, family owned firm is paramount to the success of the network. Some of the network sectors include knitware, clothes, motorcycles, shoes, bio-medicines and machine tools. The survival of these networks is due to many factors including: the power of unions in larger firms pushing up costs and thus the flexibility of smaller firms to employ people (and family members) on more flexible wage rates; the demand for more customisation and the development of flexible technology which makes small firms quite efficient; the protection and administrative support for the system by local authorities; and the culture of an extended family provides a personal contact network and employment source for the firms. Also, many specialist firms create diversity and creativity that acts as a spur to the network. Some larger entities have formed in the region in response to international competitive pressures that resemble a hub and spoke structure with a central firm co-ordinating the network. The specialisation of firms has maintained an excellence, difficult to copy outside the district. However, the willingness to change as trends and technology adapts is the key to survival.

Baden-Wurttemberg is cited as one of Germany's strongest industrial districts. The state of Baden-Wurttemberg has as its capital Stuttgart. The industrial sectors of electronic engineering, automotive engineering and machine building account for the major growth in the region's manufacturing since World War II. Large firms dominate some of the networks whereas others are centred on smaller firms. Obviously, larger firms are key in automotive and electronic engineering including American and Japanese firms such as IBM and Sony, attracted to the region due to its specialist expertise in the area. However, many large German firms also feature such as Audi and Bosch. State and industrial associations have contributed to the success of this region. State government has been active in supporting industry since its development in the 1950s including in technology transfer, training and strong linkages to third level applied institutes (Fachhochschule). In addition, support given to research and development is intense with state supported research institutions. Whilst not all firms participate actively or intensely in networks, the combination of industry, government and the firms has acted to benefit all. Support factors are often linked. The presence of a cluster of firms attracts specialised labour, research facilities develop around these, and local government acts to support local clusters. Layers are developed on layers that tend to build the network. However, it would be a mistake to assume that all players were collaborative or participated centrally. Highly specialised small firms may not find partners with which they can collaborate locally and may be reluctant to use co-operation because of the independence mentality of the owner-manager. Certain links with customers are outside the district and are global.

Silicon Valley in the US is another industrial district often compared to a network form of organisation and is interesting, in that at first glance, culture is not an important variable explaining network structure. That is, local government and economic organisation are more traditionally seen as supportive of free-market rather than network structures. However, Silicon Valley is arguable a world centre for the development of semiconductor and computer technologies. Therefore, a study of industrial districts beyond the limited scope of specific culture areas is a worthwhile endeavour. Much of the success of Silicon Valley is attributable to the skills available in the region such as design, research, people, venture capital, and marketing. These supporting technical and institutional infrastructures form a cluster with associated spin-off effects to the extent to which success is predicted by locating in the region. It is said that if your company wants to become a global player in software then a presence in Silicon Valley is a necessary prerequisite. Participation in industry associations and personal professional ties across organisations is a key element in the success of the district. Sharing of information has helped continued technology innovation as has the preponderance of small firms and the entrepreneurial activity characteristic of the region. The latter has meant the region has survived in very uncertain and changing technology environments. The professional nature of industrial organisations in the district around people rather than organisational hierarchy, and this extended professional contact network across organisations has facilitated the development of the region.

Defining networks

It might be useful for the reader to use the image of a spider's web to visualise a network. Although networks might not have such a beautiful pattern or just have one centre or focal point, the spider's web clearly brings out the notion of multiple interconnecting ties, criss-crossing and interdependent. The spider's web analogy has been applied to many organisations including by Harari (1998) who described Sun Microsystems dependence on other collaborators and competitors to develop its Java (Internet programming language) technology. These network ties included those to Netscape, IBM and Oracle. To accept the validity of a network view, an acceptance of the fact that companies are tied to each other to create a stability of exchange is needed. This understanding is aptly described by Granovetter (1985) in the concept of 'embeddedness' that he brought to the study of business behaviour from sociology. Firms are said to be embedded in network connections to competitors, customers, suppliers, and into the broader business environment. These networks can be resistant to change but can handle change within their structure. As with relationships, some networks are strong and others weak. The embeddedness concept gives the idea of layers of ties or connections, or density of ties, that are central to understanding networks. Jones et al. (1997) argued that networks are defined by relationships between the parties or actors in a system. While all the actors are independent their action is constrained by the network. Networks are durable and long-term solutions for managing inter-organisational/systems interactions. Thorelli (1986) provided a broader definition that compared the entire economic system to a network. It is repeated here:

> The point here is that the entire economy may be viewed as a network of organisations with a vast hierarchy of subordinate criss-cross networks. Our focal network is the one intermediary between the single firm and the market, that is two or more firms which, due to the intensity of their interaction, constitute a subset of one (or several) market(s). Generically, a network may be viewed as constituting 'nodes' or *positions* (occupied by firms, households, strategic business units inside a diversified concern, trade associations and other types of organisations) and *links* manifested by interactions between the positions or members. Note in passing that *positioning* of the firm in the network becomes a matter of as great strategic significance as positioning its products in the marketplace. Networks may be tight or loose, depending on the quantity (number), quality (intensity), and type (closeness to the core activity of the parties involved) of interactions between the positions or members. Thus, custom-tailored products may bind a firm tighter into its output network than if it offers mainly standardised models. (Thorelli, 1986, p. 38)

Thorelli's (1986) definition encompasses some key issues for this chapter including the importance of positioning within a network. The network analysis provided in this chapter is primarily external to a firm. Lincoln (1982) also emphasised the importance of intra-organisational networks (between people and functions). Thorelli's definition recognised the links inherent between strategic business units but Lincoln went further. Indeed, the internal network is instrumental to operating the external one as ties between individuals ultimately get the work done. The role of managers and people is a central theme of this entire text.

Network and relationship perspectives have facilitated new ways of co-ordinating economic activity. Firms can choose between the traditional vertical integration (making it themselves), or going to the market for goods and services, or co-ordinating in relationships and networks. For example, France Telecom[1] developed a co-operative business network specifically to create a more competitive cluster of telecommunication firms that would allow it to become more globally competitive. It now has global links with telecoms firms in Germany, the US as well as with customers and suppliers, (see, D'Cruz and Rugman (1994) for a history of France Telecom's partnership model). Jarillo (1993) described this type of network as a strategic one given the top-level impact of such a co-operative strategy. The nature of these types of co-operation means they are capable of outstanding technological

---

[1] www.francetelecom.fr

breakthroughs as each partner has potential access to a huge diversity of resources through the network and also has the advantage of access to larger scale organisational resources but with the flexibility of the smaller firm. Networks give access to large scale resources without the bureaucracy and organisation systems needed to manage these if owned by one individual company. A comparison between the network form of organising to the market or to an internal hierarchy is provided in Table 5.1, which clearly shows the benefits of gaining from the complementary strength of others in a network and the relative flexibility yet commitment in network ties when compared to other forms of organising.

Table 5.1 Comparison of forms of inter-firm co-ordination (Source: Powell, 1990)

	Forms		
Key feature	*Market*	*Hierarchy*	*Network*
Normative bias	Contract-property rights	Employment relationship	Complementary strengths
Means of communication	Prices	Routines	Relational
Methods of conflict resolution	Haggling-resort to courts for enforcement	Administrative fiat-supervision	Norm of reciprocity-reputational concerns
Degree of flexibility	High	Low	Medium
Amount of commitment among the parties	Low	Medium to high	Medium to high
Tone or climate	Precision and/or suspicion	Formal, bureaucratic	Open-ended, mutual benefits
Actor preferences or choices	Independent	Dependent	Interdependent

Quite often firms do not want to enter relationships for fear of the loss of their autonomy. Oliver (1991) was among the first theorists who found that firms enter networks without fear of the loss of their decision-making autonomy. That is, the boundary between managerial action and a strict rationality is more fluid than was supposed. Perhaps this is due to the fact that you cannot legislate for everything in a contract and you depend on partners to carry out contracts but also act on a range of business norms. Networks temper opportunism (Provan, 1993) and therefore facilitate the smooth economic exchange between organisations. The motivation for network formation may not always be clear. State intervention, the need for industry to economise, or perhaps clever resource management by firms are rationales behind network development. Whatever the reasons, network co-operation is a distinct form of economic organisation and a feature of much of industry, whether explicit or implicit, or even recognised by the participants. The resource sharing potential of networks seems to be a key feature in their sustainability. The fact that no firm owns the network makes it responsive and flexible, and, as it is not relying on market forces solely, facilitates co-operation and the development of network specific knowledge and innovation. Obviously, networks, due to their flexibility, are good at responding to uncertainty, and are necessary when resources needed to succeed are not clearly defined or owned by any one firm. The complementarity of network participants is a great strength.

Grabher (1993) presented four basic elements of networks. These are:

- reciprocity – indefinite patterns of rewarding reactions from others;
- interdependence – long-term interactions leading to stability and a mutual orientation implying a set of interaction rules;
- loose coupling – preserves some autonomy when compared to vertical integration allowing the network to benefit from a broader learning;
- power – facilitates the exploitation of interdependencies, may prevent outsiders from getting into the net, and its use is closely related to the atmosphere in the network, and in particular the trust among the actors.

Many elements within a network are invisible but can eventually gain a momentum that influences the shape of all decisions taken in particular industrial sectors. The 80-mile stretch running north-east from Philadelphia, through the Ivy League university town of Princeton to New Brunswick, and Madison in neighbouring New Jersey, is being referred to as Drugs Valley – the drug business' equivalent of Silicon Valley. It is home to many of the biggest US drugs companies including Merck, American Home Products, Bristol Myers Squibb, Schering Plough, Warner Lambert and Johnson and Johnson and the operational headquarters of GlaxoSmithKline. It is a magnet for skills and expertise, and with the increasing globalisation it poses a growing challenge to the other traditional centres of drugs excellence: the UK, Switzerland and Sweden. To compete successfully in design and related businesses it is becoming necessary to locate in this district. SmithKline's two big US research and development facilities, Upper Merrion and Upper Providence, are in the quaintly named King of Prussia, a pleasant 45-minute drive through the countryside from Philadelphia. The huge development zone also houses the blood and plasma operations of Franco-German drugs giant Aventis. Many British and other European firms serving the industry are also located here including software and financial services.

The chapter will review network analysis and application but will not attempt to present all the theoretical contributions to network analysis as many of the schools of thought are covered in our chapter on relationship theories. However, many good guides to these theories are provided in selected further reading at the end of the chapter including Grandori and Soda (1995), Araujo and Easton (1996), Oliver and Ebers (1998) and Grandori (1999).

Analysis of networks

Micro analysis of networks

Micro analysis of networks begins with the firm and a focal relationship or dyad. A model has been developed by the IMP group (International Marketing and

Purchasing) to help understand and analyse networks. The appeal of micro analysis lies in its focus on the firm – therefore from a practitioner point of view it is appealing to begin at the level of one's own organisation and use it as a reference point for evaluating the connections between the main players in the network. The IMP model has been described by Hakansson and Johnson (1992) and constitutes actors, activities and resources as presented in Figure 5.1.

The focal point in Figure 5.1 is on actors as they control activities and the

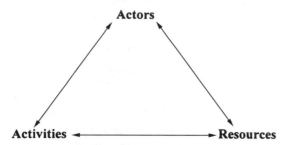

Figure 5.1   Micro network analysis model (Source: Hakansson et al., 1992).

resources in any particular network. Therefore the analysis begins with the identification of actors and the connections between each actor. These connections are both of a social and economic variety and will be at different levels of embeddedness or density depending on the actors involved. A firm may identify itself as very loosely connected to a network of which it would like to be a central part. Its goal over time would therefore be to move to a more central part of the network. The actor focus can begin with your firm or with the critical player in the network. Thus, the analysis commences with a focal firm – it is a micro analysis. The actors are the firms and individuals involved in a network. Exerting control and influence in a network is a key goal of the participants. This can cause tension but is balanced by the stability of network co-operation. Understanding a network may show how difficult it can be for firms to change their market position, for example, a firm on the outside may have great difficulty in becoming more central in the network. Relationships among actors is the basic mechanisms for changing position and exerting control over the network. Thus, the rest of this text provides a link as to how to influence the network. When starting with an individual firm, it is relatively easy to identify its key demand, supply and support networks but then begins the task of analysing these associations to identify critical paths and outcomes.

Activities are that which is done in the network. An activity cycle might be complete when a product is delivered, a research and development process ended. However, activities are usually ongoing and overlapping. Activities are performed by actors but a total activity never completed by one. Actors who perform activities are probably dispensable in that an alternative provider can be found. However, activities can be tightly coupled to another, making the actors performing such activities less dispensable. Performing activities requires resources. Each actor brings resources to a network. These resources can be unique to an actor, or complemented by another actor's resources. Combining resources from a variety of actors is a real strength of a network perspective. Accessing resources of a network permits an individual firm to be greater than the sum of its parts. That is why networks can be very successful at driving innovation. In addition, resource sharing leads to new knowledge in the system that further reinforces the network. Sharing of resources builds learning and adaptation skills in the network. In a way, a network can be viewed as a knowledge resource. Obviously, the combination of resources is endless, and network productivity and performance can be enhanced by making better use of the resources available to the actors in any net.

An analysis of the three basic elements of the network will reveal its structure and identity. Limiting our analysis to two party relationships may be too simple. However, by building out from this we enrich our study of the focal partnership. Anderson et al. (1994) provide an illustration of a dyadic relationship and its connected relationships. This is re-produced in Figure 5.2 to show micro analysis beginning at a focal relationship and then building out into other actors. The activity and resource connection of each actor can be investigated in this way.

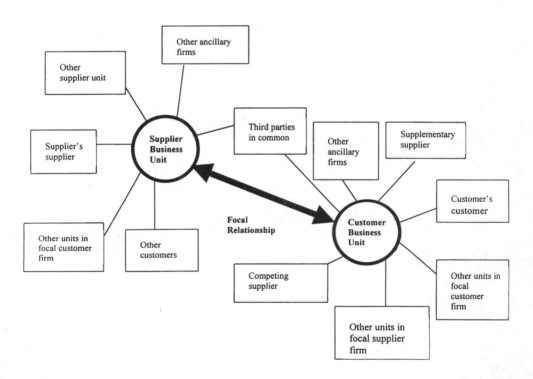

Figure 5.2   Connected relations for firms in a dyadic relationship (Source: Anderson et al., 1994).

Macro analysis of networks

A macro analysis of networks starts from the economic and social system level and eventually finds its way to an individual firm. The influence of how an economy is organised, the impact of industrial policy, cultural and social organisation patterns are some of the key contextual parameters in which industry and firms operates (Nohria and Eccles, 1992; Powell, 1990, 1998). A macro position attempts to unbundle context in its approach to network understanding. Taking a business environment or an industry as an initial analysis position in examining networks is the characteristic of a macro approach. A simple example might be starting with an industry rather than a firm. Regardless of the approach one takes the context is always an important determinant on what happens further down in the network. Many studies have been conducted using macro analysis to explain issues such as location of industrial clusters, family and ethnic networks, business groupings, how industries and firms evolve, analysing the affects of policy makers' interventions in economic systems. For example, Uzzi (1997) investigated 23 entrepreneurial firms in the women's clothing (apparel) industry to examine how decisions were affected by social and structural ties and how these ties influenced the structure of relations between network members and economic outcomes. The author's finding that strong ties and economic co-ordination existed might be unexpected in this case as the industry faces intense international competition, huge numbers of local shops, and low entry barriers. An industry where one would expect market forces to dominate did not have such a structure. The author's approach to the study was to examine the economic organisation of such a network rather than take a focal dyad and build on this core relationship. This macro approach offers further insights into how networks work. In policy debates this is critical but may be complex for the individual firm to use as a core methodology in analysing its network.

The business environment or competitive approach to the study of networks is important. The opening case study provided an illustration of macro network analysis. The location of Silicon Valley as a high-technology network or the entrepreneurial network of small firms characteristic of much of Italy's economic success has lead to the use of network approaches to examine particular economic and social systems. Initially, differences in cultural organisation was put forward as a rationale for these types of networks. In particular, culture was used to explain Asian economic success. For example, Japan is dominated by what were once family-controlled conglomerates. These conglomerates ('Kigyo Shudan') are networks of firms in unrelated business that are joined together by central banks or trading companies. Many Japanese firms are members of trading houses (large conglomerates) such as Mitsubishi, Sumitomo, Fuji. In parallel with these, other forms of strong subcontracting networks linked to a major manufacturer and in turn to retailers are also a common feature. These networks form an internal market in which business is done and ties are strong. Initially, business networks were seen as 'blips' running contrary to the traditional modes of economic and firm organisation that is seen as peculiar to specific cultures and certainly not widespread. Today business networks feature in all economies as our understanding of business ties increase. From Chambers of Commerce to strategic alliances, network forms of organisation have reached new prominence as sharing and pooling of resources has become a mechanism to respond to constant environmental uncertainty and to the complexity of providing services and products in knowledge economies. Therefore, peculiarities of culture is only a part explanation – variety in organisational systems may arise out of culture, but a host of additional supporting institutional and other influences such as financial structures, history, management-labour relations, how inter-firm relationships have developed, may also provide part of the picture.

Economic and competitive analysis of networks adds a further layer in our understanding of the multiple pattern of co-operation among firms and supporting economic and organisational infrastructures. The macro approach sees networks as an outcome of various environmental and particular competitive processes and objectives. Analysing industrial systems in the context of society, policy and culture adds a richness to our understanding of how firms operate in particular societies. Fundamental social processes such as trust have a history impacted by a particular social context. Macro analysis gives us the insight into this context. Whilst macro analysis may not be the first level of network analysis for a particular firm, indeed it may be beyond the training and resources of many firms to do it, it is insightful to analyse relationships from the outside in. Macro analysis of networks is often seen as the preserve of the economist, policy maker, organisational sociologist, and anthropologist. Although once a network position is adopted in planning then the knowledge and resource needed to do network analysis will become part of a manager's job.

Networks and strategy

Traditional approaches to business strategy do not view the firm as embedded in a social structure. This interdependence is fundamental to a network approach. Network strategy is about devising a position in a network and then moving towards it. The traditional approach to strategy is based on the assumption of a firm acting alone as a atomistic actor (independent actor). Chapter 2 contrasts the traditional versus relational view of strategy which is applied to networks by Axelsson (1992). Network views of business obviously see the network as a key strategic component. All the reasons as to why relationships are important also apply to networks by extension. Networks are important in the strategic context as they place boundaries and opportunities on the activities of a firm. Networks can be knowledge and learning resources that add to an individual firm's competencies. Networks can also add limits as unfavourable positions can inhibit movement and lower overall firm profitability. Therefore, two critical strategic network issues are network position and change.

Easton (1992) defined position in terms of role: role vis-à-vis other relationships or the nature of your network connection. If you are a focal firm in a network then this central position and power will bring rewards if used to advantage. Centrality

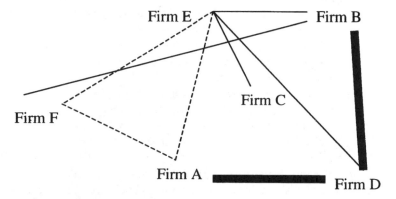

Figure 5.3   Illustration of network ties.

and peripherality are important clues to position. Strength of ties is also indicative of the nature of a firm's connection and the strength of a network.

Figure 5.3 illustrates the strength of position ties. Firm E is connected to all firms in the hypothetical network. This could give firm E an information and resource gatekeeper role or make it the focal (central) firm depending on the network. The thick lines indicate very strong ties while the broken lines indicate weaker ties. Firms D and C are only connected to one other firm in this network. Getting a perspective on the nature of the resources that are exchanged and the power position of each partner will also impact the strategic position of any one firm. High trust networks are likely to have greater transfers of unique information and resources, for example, this might be characteristic of a network that is strong on innovation.

Changing network position could be a key objective for a network strategist. Even though one of the benefits of networks is stability, there is continual movement and change. Actors drift closer and further away. This drift needs to be managed. Positions are changed for internal network reasons or for external ones. The type of change will have a significant bearing on any response (Halinen et al., 1999). Network level change can be radical or incremental. Radical change can have dramatic effects on network structure. The alternative, incremental change, can be affected by an individual network participant. Other firms in a network will be aware of any changes and may react negatively. Incremental change can be planned and long-term and can require resource commitments. For example, getting listed by a focal firm in a network can open many doors in international subcontracting. In fact, the listing by a large multinational can be a 'calling card' to other firms in the network. External environment change, if not radical, can be incorporated in any individual firm's network change strategy (Madhavan et al., 1998). A number of strategies can be used to evolve a focal firm's position in a network. Increasing the number of relationships that a firm is part of or trying to connect to central players can be used to affect a positional change, for example, deregulation of financial services in Europe is forging alliance networks in the banking and insurance sectors. Such elements are foreseeable and therefore can be used strategically. One huge complexity for a network strategist is that to change your position in the network you may need to change others. It goes beyond a single relationship. Making resource investments and adaptations across the network must be considered. Managerial action has to be extended over the network that will add pressure on any individual's influencing and networking skills.

Many firms perceive networks as strategic mechanisms in which to improve competitive advantage through cost minimisation while simultaneously maintaining flexibility. However, sustainable advantage is reached through mutual value adding that requires substantial trust and commitment. Holm et al. (1999) found in a study of 159 European supplier firms, that network value creation is linked to the strength of the relationship between the participants and across organisation value is likely to be high the more committed and mutually orientated the participants. Assessing costs and benefits of network participation is far from an exact science (Ring, 1999). Direct costs might be assessable such as investments, travel, entertainment and even people costs when participating in projects. It is more difficult to uncover the costs of network learning or the opportunity costs of doing other things. Often network performance is intuitively assessed by managers who know the business and who have a sense of what it should be doing. Even though competitive advantage may be found in networks they also contain risks. For example, over reliance on a focal network firm may make a particular firm more susceptible to an industry shock if it were to happen. This is especially problematic when there is a capital dependency in a network. A financial squeeze by a focal firm can lead to closure of other firms in that network. Risk of an abuse of one firm in a network by another, particularly of resources and information is always a possibility. For example, sharing of knowledge in a research and development alliance might leave an organisation vulnerable to abuse by its partners. Obviously, thinking through how to manage such possibilities is one response to this type of threat. Enacting procedures that govern such alliances including, for example, the use of third party guarantees might be another response. Although, it appears that active engagement by managers is the most effective monitoring and safeguarding position.

Network forms and application

Most networks cannot be labelled but were likened earlier to a web and are invisible. These networks have varying levels of co-operation and competition within them. For example, networks set-up to innovate may be very co-operative. Grandori and Soda (1995) classified networks into three types – social, bureaucratic, and proprietary. They did this on the basis of the extent of formalisation (rules governing the network), extent of centralisation (central co-ordinating firm or all parties equal), and mix of co-ordinating mechanisms (decision making, communication etc.).

Social networks are networks that rely on human interaction as the main mode of formalisation and co-ordination. Personal networks, interlocking directorates (a common decision making forum across independent organisations), and industrial districts are three examples of social networks where participants are of equal power. Subcontracting is another form of social network that would have a central firm playing a major co-ordination role as in the case of a main contractor in a building project. Bryson et al. (1993) described the personal networks needed for small business service firms to compete successfully. Their success depended on informal person-to-person networks, word of mouth recommendations and repeat business (including business done while working for a bigger company before setting-up one's own). *Bureaucratic networks* are more formalised and vary depending on the power of the parties in the network. Trade associations and consortia are two common forms of bureaucratic networks in which parties have common power but very explicit roles as in the case of consortia. More unequal bureaucratic networks include agency, licensing and franchising networks where the focal firm has significant market power; for example, McDonalds in the fast food industry. Finally, *proprietary networks* in which ownership of specific assets are pre-specified include joint ventures and capital ventures. The proprietary rights of the parties are spelt out in agreements. Joint ventures are widely researched and used for developing new markets and products. Capital ventures for new business start-ups and larger projects are also a common form of network between venture capital firms and organisations involved in the business start-up/expansion. Joint and capital ventures are often found in innovative networks – an application of networks detailed in this section.

Alliances among independent organisations (strategic alliance is a much used term) are common. Industries such as airlines and telecommunications are replete with alliances. These alliances often evolve as a response to uncertainty and instability in the global business environment. Sharing resources across companies rather than through independent expansion is viewed as the optimum method for coping with these environments. The European aircraft industry has forged many alliances. Airbus Industrie[2] is a combination of German (DaimlerChrysler Aerospace (Dasa)), French (Aerospatiale Matra), Spanish (Casa) and British (BAE Systems) companies who co-operate to compete against US rivals, in particular, Boeing. Their co-operation began in 1967. In 2000, these companies re-formed to produce a super jumbo to compete against the Boeing 747 with Dasa, Casa and Aerospatiale Matra merging. The project is estimated to cost EU 12.8 billion. The aircraft will be assembled in Toulouse, the wings made in the UK, the tailplanes in Spain, and the furnishing and interiors in Hamburg. These focal firms co-operate with a host of other firms tied in a European aircraft network.

We invite readers to study alliances from a network perspective. The density of ties and positions of firms within the network would be a feature of this study in conjunction with an analysis of actor, activity and resource patterns. This analysis would clarify the nature of the alliance, whether loose or tight, and the motivation of the parties. The latter is particularly important that is whether motives are purely defensive or are underwritten by active collaboration. Alliances can be loose in terms of structure and organisation thus in themselves be unstable. They also

---

[2] *www.airbus.com*

carry risks with firms coming together with different priorities, objectives and styles. Selection of an alliance partner(s) is a critical variable in its subsequent success. Child and Faulkner (1998) provide a comprehensive review of managing and developing alliances and joint ventures. A critical theme in their book is the importance of managerial acts and of people and culture in the alliance. Active participation and bringing people together or, at least, creating understanding across the alliance provides a basis for mutual learning and potential solidification of the alliance. A successful alliance evolves from something more than perhaps was foreseen at the beginning.

Managing *innovation* within a network context is within the realm of most firms given the pressure to bring innovations to the market more quickly and to design products to user requirements. The biotechnology industry is part of our end of chapter case. Innovation is a major force pushing collaboration in networks in that industry. Chapter 10 develops the themes of relationship innovation. They are similar to the network themes except with less actors. The idea that competitors, customers, channels, research institutes, suppliers can be active participants in innovation and diffusion is the assumption of the network approach. Instead of independently developing a product/service within one company, a firm can make use of network resources and participants. Bolton et al. (1994) described the organisation of innovation in the semiconductor industry in Japan as an interconnected web of co-operation. Their superior innovation performance over US competitors in this field was attributed to networks of co-operation between banks, suppliers, competitors, and customers which has facilitated effective technology transfer and quick response to market demands. Bringing together of complementary resources is a feature of networks formed for technology innovation. Parties who bring marketing and distribution expertise can be complemented with capital-rich companies, or banks, and with smaller research companies. Each of these is in turn connected to a web of other actors and resources. Benefits gained from this type of co-operation rely on managing the network. Many firms focus on developing this managerial competency. ARM Holdings[3], based in Cambridge, is a leading innovator in microchip technology. The company designs for the core of high performance chips (small portion of a chip but a critical one). It also provides software and consultancy services to the industry. ARM develops new patents that it licenses to other firms. It has technology partnerships with firms such as Intel, Lucent technologies, Panasonic, and Toshiba, and is thus connected to many networks. Its business model is based on networks of partners to which it contributes its innovatory designs. Without a network, ARM would not be able to exploit its technology or grow as fast as it has.

Chapter summary

An introductory case illustration on industrial districts showed how economies can be viewed from a network perspective. Networks were defined as webs of inter-

---

[3] *www.arm.com*

connecting ties between independent parties. Network analysis was presented at both a micro and macro level. The micro approach begins with two firms, or actors, and analyses their ties to other actors through an assessment of activities and resources in the network. This method of analysis is particularly applicable to firms as they usually begin their strategy analysis at this level. Macro analysis by contrast begins at an industry or economic level as is the case of industrial districts and would be difficult for an individual firm to use. Networks were characterised as strategic resources and therefore, changing and analysing network position described as a strategic issue. Indeed, the competitive advantage of certain network compositions was also presented as a strategic issue. Networks based on mutual collaboration tend to offer value adding potential when compared to other types. Different forms of network were outlined based on the degree of formalisation, contralisation, and co-ordination and ranged from personal networks to alliances and joint ventures. Network ideas were applied to the alliance and innovation setting that demonstrated network forms in practice. The end of chapter case analyses networks in the biotechnology and pharmaceutical industries.

CASE FOR DISCUSSION   **BIOTECHNOLOGY AND PHARMACEUTICAL NETWORKS**

The biotechnology and pharmaceutical industries are full of cross-company collaborative relationships that are used to access knowledge, skills and resources of partner companies and organisations. Survival of many biotechnology companies has been due to their co-operation with larger, sometimes multinational, pharmaceutical companies. These larger companies see many bio-technologies as critical to new product development in the pharmaceutical industry. The ability to transfer and process information across partnerships and to manage this transfer process is becoming a critical success factor in ongoing networks in these industries. Obviously firms vary in their ability to access knowledge and skills beyond their boundaries. This variability may represent a competitive advantage for those organisations best able to work within a network.

Biotechnology is an area ripe for study by the network analyst. Its core technologies such as molecular biology and genetic engineering are changing and developing so rapidly that this very uncertainty forges alliances among competitors and agencies involved in the industry such as governments, universities and venture capital firms. Relatively small biotechnology firms have been a key conduit for larger pharmaceutical firms to gain access to technologies that are providing new ways of treating disease and new products such as genetically modified foods. The smaller biotechnology firms often require help from larger firms to overcome barriers to entry. In addition, some small biotechnology firms have had to contract out their clinical trials to combat the high cost and long time frames of gaining government approval through the drugs administration bodies, for example, the Food and Drugs Administration (FDA) in the US and the European Commission for the EU (European Agency for the Evaluation of Medicinal Products). Similarly, many dedicated biotechnology firms have established marketing agreements with larger firms to gain access to established distribution channels and foreign markets. Manufacturing agreements have been attractive to small firms without production facilities, and some biotechs have been willing to license the technology in order to ease cash flow problems. Thus, in commercial biotechnology it has become commonplace for smaller firms to sell scientific and technical expertise in exchange for access to the larger firms' financial resources, manufacturing capabilities, and marketing expertise. The large diversified companies are among the most powerful actors in the pharmaceutical, chemical, food, energy and agricultural industries. Nevertheless, there is a general perception that the market share of these diversified corporations is vulnerable, in the long-term, to innovations based on biotechnology. Even though they may have their own research laboratories in this area, the rate of change and combination of approaches makes collaboration important.

Chiron[4], headquartered in Emeryville, California, is a leading biotechnology firm applying its technology to the cancer, heart, and infectious disease fields. The company pursues its problem solving in these areas through collaboration in its research and development as a core strategy. Chiron has numerous research and development ties with universities, licensing agreements with large pharmaceutical and other health care companies, and manufacturing and marketing ties with other large firms as well. The company reports more than 1000 informal agreements with universities and research institutes and over 60 formal collaborations with other companies. Chiron's partial parent owner, Novartis of Switzerland (49.9%), uses it as a major research alliance. Novartis[5] in turn is linked to a host of other partners for research and development. It sees itself positioned at the centre of a global network of research scientists and facilities that cross over and connect worldwide expertise. Details of its research alliances can be found on its web site. Novartis is a multinational pharmaceutical company that relies on its network of connections to fuel its product development and widen its scientific and technological capabilities. Many drugs research projects require cross-disciplinary input. This is one reason why co-operation with smaller biotechnology companies is so attractive. Biotechnology research is not industry specific per se as it provides a platform for multiple applications in many industries such as in prescription drugs and agriculture and food. Novartis has established procedures for collaboration. Key to these is its insistence that the partnership engage in technology transfer, that is, Novartis must learn from the process. Otherwise it would be simply an outsourcing deal. Some of the biotechnology firms that Novartis has contact with are entrepreneurial whose personnel would not work with Novartis because of its size and their need for the independence provided by a small firm structure. Partnership is sensible strategy in this case. Many of Novartis' close partnerships are formal – rules and procedures govern the relationship and expectations are stated up-front. However, Norvartis has other looser ties to companies and institutions in its network. These ties may provide more formal partners in the future or act as key information resources in a dynamic industry. Novartis continues to do research and development themselves to complement their network activity. About 70% of its new discoveries come from within the company.

Learning from networks is a core strength of the biotechnology and pharmaceutical network described. This learning can be facilitated as cross-company science teams, through joint projects, in seminars, or in licensing or development contracts. Electronic communication and databases of information are also important. However, informal, ad hoc sessions can often deliver insights that can not be planned. Encouraging cross-

---

[4] *www.chiron.com*
[5] *www.novartis.com*

organisational social relationships and unplanned meetings needs to be part of a learning strategy. Ensuring staff are part of their professional community and interact within this in external conferences can also be a major help in information transfer. Roche[6] is a multinational company employing over 67 000 people in 1999. The company's pharmaceutical division is based in Basel, Switzerland and it actively pursues a collaborative strategy not unlike Novartis. Often its partnerships end in acquisition as was the case with the Californian-based firm Genetech[7]. Roche has six research centres across Europe (3), Japan (1), and USA (2). Genetech employs about 4000 people. Their relationship with Roche allows them to concentrate on biotechnology research and to use Roche's marketing and distribution for commercialisation. Genetech is a leading biotechnology firm with its own extensive set of collaborations.

Questions

1. Claims are made about the network position of the companies mentioned in the case. How would you evaluate these types of claims made by companies as an independent analyst?Characteristics of network forms were described earlier in the chapter. What forms best represent the networks described in the case?
2. The case described the network position of a few companies in the biotechnology and pharmaceutical industries. Take a specific firm and analyse its network position using the micro analysis model provided in the chapter.
3. The biotechnology industry is characteristic of a network structure. This may be explained by the nature of the industry rather than the way in which the firms in the industry have decided to organise. Discuss.The case presents information and knowledge transfer as a critical resource in the network, examine ways in which its transfer across organisation can be managed in both a formal and informal way.

[6] *www.roche.com*
[7] *www.gene.com*

Further reading

Axelsson, B. and Easton, G. (1992), *Industrial Networks: A New View of Reality*, Routledge, London.

Biemans, W.G. (1992), *Managing Innovation within Networks*, Routledge, London.

Gadde, L.-E. and Mattson, L.-G., (1987), Stability and change in network relationships, *International Journal of Research in Marketing*, 4, pp. 29–41.

Granovetter, M. (1992), Problems of explanation in economic sociology, in Nohria, N. and Eccles, R.G., editors, *Networks and Organisations: Structure, Form and Action*, Harvard University Press, Boston, MA, pp. 25–56.

Hakansson, H. (1987), *Industrial Technological Development: A network Approach*, Croom Helm, London.

Hakansson, H. and Johanson, J. (1993), Industrial functions of business relationships, in Sharma, D., editor, *Advances in International Marketing*, Vol. 5, JAI Press, Greenwich, CT, pp. 13–29.

Hakansson, H. and Snehota, I. (1989), No business is an island: the network concept of business strategy, *Scandinavian Journal of Management*, 5 (3), pp. 187–200.

Hutt, M.D., Stafford, E.R., Walker, B.A. and Reingen, P.H. (2000), Case study – defining the social network of a strategic alliance, *Sloan Management Review*, 41 (2), pp. 51–62.

Iacobucci, D. (1996), *Networks in Marketing*, Sage, Thousand Oaks, CA.

Perry, M. (1999), *Small Firms and Network Economies*, Routledge, London.

Chapter questions

1. Examine an industrial district of your choice. Does a network approach sufficiently explain the existence of the firm cluster in question or is there an alternative explanation?

2. Define what you consider networks to be and outline their main characteristics.

3. Evaluate the strengths and weaknesses of a network form of organisation when compared to other types of organising economic activity.

4. Compare and contrast the micro and macro methods of analysing networks. Which method do you prefer? In what situation would each be of most value? How would you go about researching each one?

5. Apply micro analysis to a network of your choice. After conducting this analysis what insights did you gain in comparison with an analysis based on the firm acting alone?

6. Develop a plan to change a hypothetical firm's network position from being peripheral to being core.

7. Many network forms are not unique to network theory. In what ways does a network/relationship approach differ from others in examining these forms of organisation?

8. A network application to strategic alliances and innovation was presented in the text. Examine the managerial and organisational challenges of such an application.

CHAPTER 6

Relationship classification and development

Introduction and objectives

In any company's relationships with its customers, it is closer to some of them when compared to others. This may be because certain customers buy more from them or could be due to a closer working partnership that has developed over time. Similar to classifying products using the product portfolio, it is useful to be able to classify customer or supplier relationships to help analyse current and potential opportunities. This chapter addresses relationship classification issues through an examination of a relationship classification matrix, relationship portfolios, and a presentation of approaches to relationship development. After reading this chapter you should know:

- the main literature approaches to classifying relationships;
- the importance of looking beyond labels to the underlying substance of a relationship;
- be aware of a range of relationship when developing specific relationship strategies;
- the potential of managing strategic market relationship portfolios;
- the relationship development process.

The case illustration shows how decisions made about relationships today can affect the future of your business. In the past, many auto manufacturers squeezed their suppliers for price concessions to maintain their profit levels. They were able to do this because of their power as buyers. However, today these same suppliers, through mergers and alliances, represent a countervailing force. The tables have been turned. The auto makers now have to work with some of their suppliers in a different way. Would the same scenario have developed if the car manufacturers had used a different method of managing their component supply relationships? The answer to this question is speculative but shows that no matter how powerful a company is at a point in time, its power advantage may not last. Companies should be careful about using their marketplace power. The case also illustrates one type of relationship – a dominant partner using its power to exploit a relationship.

CAR-MAKERS FEELING THE HEAT

In the past, auto manufacturers have sought to cut costs through aggressive managing of their supply relationships. Initially, as part of this programme, they would play one supplier off against another to bid supply costs down. When this led to fluctuating quality and lack of co-operation they decided to operate a preferred supplier system. Still this supplier was 'asked' to reduce cost by certain percentages each year and pass much of the savings onto to the car manufacturer. Even though these suppliers did reduce costs the preferred supply arrangements allowed them to grow their business on an international basis as they supplied components previously provided by competitors and were expected to supply globally. In general, the turnover of car manufacturers dwarfed that of suppliers. This combined with a small pool of car manufacturers made component suppliers very dependent on the manufacturers who could use their power for price concessions. However, the 1980s and 1990s provided a changed scenario for suppliers. Car manufactures were convinced of the wisdom of out-sourcing a lot of the design and manufacturing of entire systems to suppliers, including such items as dashboards models or axle assemblies which the manufacturers then installed quickly into their production lines. In some areas the manufacturers just co-ordinated parts from several suppliers together. However, this trend gave a short-term cost benefit to manufacturers who no longer had the in-house costs of doing these jobs, but it also paved they way for developing a counter power to the manufacturers. Today, less and less of the revenue of a finished car goes to the manufacturer. For example, the cost of the out-sourced electronics systems is estimated to be growing by 20% per annum. This growth is provided for by supplier of these systems, not the manufacturers. As installation of high technology systems such as satellite systems, collision avoidance radar, and automatic crash location grows, more and more of this value added is provided by specialised outside firms who can now turn the tables on the car manufacturers and leverage their growing power.

Bosch[1] of Germany is the world's second largest independent auto parts group with automotive sales alone of DM28.7 billion. They have always been leaders in innovation and technology to remain cost competitive operating from a German, relatively high cost base. The company supplies a huge range of parts including braking systems, spark plugs and in car entertainment systems. One of the major growth areas identified for the company's future is in electronic control system in which the company is the leader. Its electronic stability programme uses sensors to detect downward movements in a car's progress and applies the breaks selectively to restore balance. Bosch, through technology and innovation, has managed to have a balanced relationship with its buyers. In some cases this relationship is very close including working on joint product development projects.

Source: adapted from Financial Times 23/02/'98 and Dyer (1996).

[1] *www.bosch.de*

Classifying relationships

This section assesses approaches to classifying relationships and develops a classification system based on the relationship strength tool presented in chapter 4. Relationship strength measures the underlying motivation guiding the relationship and the intensity of interaction between the parties. It is measured through an assessment of the belief in and actions taken in the relationship. For example, close relationships have bonds that are dense and binding (belief) and significant unique economic action.

Bi-polar classifications

Jackson (1985) and Sako (1992) have classified relationships in two types: one close and interactive and the other discrete, or price based. These relationships are presented as opposite end of a spectrum or continuum. Figure 6.1 illustrates these two continuums. The 'always a share' and 'arm's length' relationships represent discrete or marked-based exchanges which are primarily based on price and no amount of relationship building is going to lead to customer loyalty or repeat business. The exchange is based on opportunism and may correspond to purchasing situations where risk is low, the product/service well known, and where little differentiation exists among brands. Adding extra services to this type of customer will not induce reciprocal behaviour.

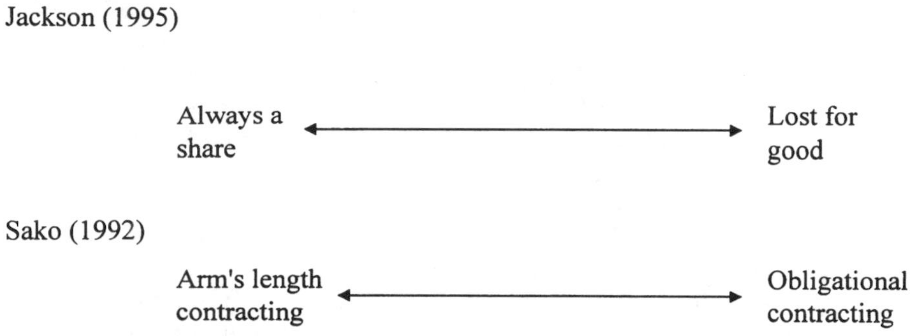

Jackson (1995)

Always a   Lost for
share   ←——————————————→   good

Sako (1992)

Arm's length   Obligational
contracting   ←——————————————→   contracting

Figure 6.1   Bi-polar classification (Source: Jackson, 1985).

On the other side, 'lost for good' or 'obligational contracting' represents relationships that are close. If a customer is lost she or he is unlikely to come back and for this reason they must be managed carefully. These types of relationships are highly interactive and may occur where market uncertainty is high, a lot has been invested in the transaction and the product is complex. These types of relationship are open to a relationship approach to marketing, whereas discrete based relationships are best dealt with on a transaction by transaction basis. If you knew which type of relationships were most appropriate then you could design your products/services accordingly. Many firms try to do this by introducing loyalty schemes and through price discounts. It is easier to practice customer differentiation like this in business-to-business markets where smaller customer bases and higher levels of interaction characterise the relationship. In mass markets it is difficult to restrict services to certain customers. However, information technology is making it easier but it still remains a considerable challenge.

Now that the idea of different types of relationships has been introduced we will describe these types in more detail. The theories in chapter 3 provide a justification and rationale for examining different relationship types. The theories also underline the conditions under which different relationship types represent the optimum way of managing a relationship. Some authors have presented typologies of relationship types that describe in great detail the characteristics of specific relationship types, including the two presented in Figure 6.1.

Descriptive typologies

In chapter 2 we presented a variety of relational exchange domains, for example, supplier, customer, internal, and lateral partnerships. Throughout the text we have added others, such as joint ventures and strategic alliances. However, all these categories, while useful to indicate the nature of a relationship, do not tell us anything about how close or distant that relationship might be. In other words, is the relationship determined or governed by the market or by some form of close co-operation? We examine a variety of governance modes in this section as presented in the literature. We believe the differences among governance forms are fundamental and imply radically different approaches to relationship management. From a theoretical perspective, Heide (1994) presented three relationship types – market, hierarchy (buyer or seller dominant), and bilateral. A typology, from his work, is presented in Table 6.1.

In Table 6.1 market governance corresponds to the discrete or arm's length relationship type. Table 6.1 describes how these relationships are initiated, maintained, and terminated. They are presented as alternatives, not as positions along a continuum as their structures and management is fundamentally different. Market governance is related to the costs and prices of individual transactions. Hierarchical governance modes are supported when one party has sufficient power to dictate the terms and conditions of the relationship. Our introductory case illustration provides an example of this type of relationship. The third relationship type is bilateral. This is where parties co-operate for their mutual benefit and actions are taken on the basis of the consideration of joint goals and outcomes. These three relationship types will be described in practical detail in the next section. While, at this stage, we know that there are different types of relationships and these can be described, we still need to consider how to choose or distinguish between them.

Discrimination between types

In chapter 4 we presented the relationship strength tool to aid in the choice of relationship with which to do business. We build on that technique to classify relationship types. Whether these relationships are with final customers or alliance

Table 6.1 Governance typology – dimensions and forms of inter-firm (Source: Heide, 1994)

Governance / Dimensions	Market governance	Non-market governance	
		Unilateral/hierarchical	*Bilateral*
1 Relationship initiation	No particular initiation process	Selective entry; skill training	Selective entry; value training
2 Relationship maintenance			
2.1 Role specification	Individual roles applied to individual transactions	Individual roles applied to entire relationship	Overlapping roles; joint activities and term responsibilities
2.2 Nature of planning	Non-existent; or limited to individual transactions	Proactive/unilateral; binding contingency plans	Proactive/joint; plans subject to change
2.3 Nature of adjustments	Non-existent; or giving rise to exit or immediate compensation	*Ex ante*/explicit mechanism for change	Bilateral/predominantly negotiated changes through mutual adjustment
2.4 Monitoring procedures	External/reactive; measurement of output	External/reactive; measurement of output and behavior	Internal/proactive; based on self control
2.5 Incentive system	Short-term; tied to output	Short- and long-term; tied to output and behavior	Long-term; tied to display of system-relevant attitudes
2.6 Means of enforcement	External to the relationship; legal system/competition/offsetting investments	Internal to the relationship; legitimate authority	Internal to the relationship; mutuality of interest
3 Relationship termination	Completion of discrete transaction	Fixed relationship length, or explicit mechanisms for termination	Open-ended relationship

partners, an assessment can be made of the strength of the relationship, and on this basis, it can be classified into a range of relationship types.

Figure 6.2 contains our matrix of four relationship types classified using the relationship strength tool (Donaldson and O'Toole, 2000). The relationship strength tool (see chapter 4) makes an overall assessment of a relationship possible, based on its social and economic elements. These are measured through an assessment of belief in (social) and action taken in (economic) a relationship. After making an assessment of a firm's belief and action about a relationship (for example, the level of trust between the partners), and actions taken (for example, what investments have or will be made in the relationship), we can classify the relationship into one of the four types. In the last section three relationship types were presented – bilateral, dominant partner (hierarchical), and discrete. We have added an extra one in our matrix – recurrent partnerships. These are ongoing relationships with high levels of commitment and trust held by the partners, a long-term orientation, but do not have the potential or partner willingness to add increasing components of value to the economic structure of the relationship.

ACTION COMPONENT

		High	Low
BELIEF	High	BILATERAL	RECURRENT
COMPONENT	Low	HIERARCHICAL (Dominant partner)	DISCRETE or OPPORTUNISTIC

Figure 6.2   The relationships matrix.

Where both the belief and action components are high, bilateral relations are said to exist. This does not mean each party is of similar size or importance, but that their involvement and participation in the relationship is at a relatively high level. Where there is a high action component and low belief in the benefits of a relational approach then the relationship form is more likely to be hierarchical, with either the supplier or the buyer dominant. In other cases, where the belief in relationships is high but the need for committed action is low (frequent repeat purchase), the relational form is said to be recurrent. This may happen where one firm re-orders on a regular basis with another and does not expect to be over charged and for the conditions of the commercial relationship to exist as expected by both parties. Finally, where there is low belief in the value of a relationship and a low action component then the relationship form will be at its weakest and we could expect discrete transactions or opportunistic behaviour to take place.

Bilateral relations, where both the belief and action elements are high, are the high relationship strength form. In bilateral relations, partners co-operate for mutual advantage characterised by openness in communication and strategic collaboration. This is a unique and complex relationship not easily copied and which potentially would offer the greatest benefits in the context of relationship performance. This does not mean that they are symmetrical, but merely that they are dominated by a bilateral content and process. The strategic nature of the relationship would involve high levels of interdependence. Harari (1998) describes EDSs[2] relationship with the Rolls-Royce aerospace group. EDS manages that group's software and hardware functions, designing engineering processes that substantially reduce its development cycle times. It would appear that the two have a bilateral partnership aimed at achieving common goals. They co-operate and jointly plan. EDS has built a major research centre near the Rolls-Royce site and many people in EDS report to Rolls-Royce and vice versa. Typically, bilateral relationships would have more planning and resource reviews, would utilise all forms of communication intensely, products exchanged are often customised, more value is added at each stage of the exchange, and price tends not to be a determining factor. An interesting metaphor for describing bilateral relationships is used by Silicon Graphics in its classification of partners with whom it does its product development work as 'lighthouse customers' (Prokesch, 1993). These lighthouse customers are willing to be actively involved and present high level problems to Silicon Graphics to solve using its high performance computer graphics. The metaphor gives the idea that these types of relationships are limited in number and not available to everyone. The case at the end of this chapter requires the reader to analyse this type of relationship.

Recurrent relationships are a hybrid form between discrete and bilateral. Elements of reciprocity and temporal duration creep into the exchange as trust is built between the parties but committed actions are low. For example, investments are medium to low in the relationship but it may equate to certain just-in-time types of supply where preferred status, information on product demand, special payment terms, and long-term contracts are typical features of a buyer's co-operation with its supplier. Recurrent relationships are special partnerships with well developed social structures. The focus is more on operational issues than strategic ones and purchases are likely to be transaction-based rather than relational-based. This form is characterised by matching sentiments in both parties. Often repeated purchases are characterised by this relationship form. Many services are bought on a recurrent basis. Parties are satisfied with the relationship but there is no need to bring it further.

Dominant or hierarchical relationships are a common form of governance and occur where a dominant partner specifies the nature of the interaction between the partners. The weaker partner faces a combination of low belief in the efficacy of a relationship approach but demands a lot in terms of action such as specific investments by a supplier on behalf of their customer, a situation experienced by many original equipment manufacturer (OEM) suppliers. Hierarchical relationships

---

[2] *www.eds.com*

revolve around the decision about who controls the transaction and may be common in own label supply which is reflected in the authority and power-dependency balance in these relationships. In certain situations, the size and power of the buyer/supplier may be better served in a bilateral rather than a dominant one but the influence of environmental conditions, especially competitive forces, may strongly influence this position. The problem in this form is the asymmetrical views held by each party. A good example of an industry characterised by some dominant buyers using their power was provided in the introductory case illustration. The auto manufacturers have been known to ask for as much as a 6% reduction in price from their suppliers on an annual basis. In a mass market consumers often feel that their power is limited. However, with the growth in consumer movements and trends, especially coming from EU level, for increased consumer regulation, the final users' power may be about to change.

Discrete relationships are lowest in the relationship strength concept with minimal levels of belief and action components. Opportunism can be expected to dominate this approach with few, if any, ties between the partners. Firms in this mode are assumed to make rational economic decisions as independent actors in the marketplace. It may be possible to build on the relationship but it is not central to the transaction and it would not be prudent to invest in the relationship. Many purchases offer limited need or ability to build relationships. It may be best here to concentrate on overall brand image rather than invest in what might prove to be costly relationship schemes that yield little in extra revenue for the firm. The nature of investment made in bilateral relationships is that it is unique to it. Many so called relationship tools have been copied, for example, airline frequent flier, retailer loyalty cards, and do not deliver loyalty. Sometimes the very basis for a close relationship, high levels of trust, is just not there. We argue that certain relationship types are not easily developed or managed and that these, particularly, bilateral but also recurrent offer possible competitive advantage. Discrete relationship are only 'relationships' to the extent that parties can come together to do business. Many relationships are discrete or market-based. Applying the relationship label to them, makes it difficult to separate out varying types of buyer-seller relationships. However, by concentrating on the underlying forces that govern a particular relationship, a clearer picture emerges of what is possible in any particular relationship and how to manage it (see other chapters for managerial implications and O'Toole and Donaldson, 2000).

Managing relationship portfolios

Every company must manage a portfolio of relationships. Many of us are familiar with a portfolio of products, business units, or customers but, in relationships, it is the customer relationship, the supplier relationship, or other relationship that is represented in the portfolio. The aim of traditional portfolio management is to achieve balance. Balance can also apply to relationships – we want the worthwhile relationships of today but also to be developing new ones for the future. We also want to know the percentage of difficult relationships and the percentage of ones that do not offer huge potential. Relationship portfolios help managers to decide on resource allocation decisions to relationships and are therefore a strategic tool. In addition, it is possible to develop a range of prescriptive management tactics for each section of a portfolio. The prescriptions will vary slightly depending on the variables used to classify the relationship into the portfolio. We will present two different types of portfolio. The first will be to use the matrix in Fig.2 as a portfolio of relationships – this type of portfolio is based on the level of integration in the relationship. The second portfolio technique presented will use an assessment of the contribution of the relationship to the company in its classification. The aim of presenting two approaches is to develop an understanding of the issues involved in portfolio assessment.

Portfolio approaches have received wide application in the literature, including between a focal firm and supplier (for example, Sinclair et al., 1996; Olsen and Ellram, 1997) and between a focal firm and customer (Shipiro et al., 1987; Krapfel et al., 1991). Relationships are not as easily defined and require an understanding of the combination of resources they represent before we can commit them to a category. We provide a relationship strength assessment tool to aid in this task. In addition, relationships are two-way which means that an assessment of matches on both sides may be necessary for classification into a portfolio. When assessing portfolios, managers need to be aware of both the structure and the costs and benefits of relationships. Each relationship type requires different degrees of investment and produces different outcomes. Some relationships might appear to be successful but when account is taken of the resources put into them, they may not be as profitable as first thought. However, they may be worth investing in for other reasons such as network position, contribution to the profile of the firm or to key activities such as new product development. The price paid for acquiring some customer relationships seem high as reflected in bid prices for acquisitions, for example, the valuations of individual cable television households. We cannot envisage all these households remaining loyal!

The relationship classification matrix presented in Figure 6.2 could be viewed as a portfolio. This classification is based on the level of relational integration. The classification process is aided by the use of the relationship strength tool. The core strategic issue in this type of relationship classification is the developmental potential of existing and future relationships. The classification matrix, when used as a portfolio, should be thought of as a portfolio of evolving or developing relationships.

The classification matrix presents another level of difficulty when managed as a portfolio as we believe relationships are embedded in the culture of the participating firms. The type of managerial philosophy and values required to run a bilateral relationship is different to those needed to run one that is discrete. These managerial attitudes are likely to be pervasive in the organisation making it difficult to manage a portfolio of types. Having stated this, all of a firm's relationships will not be of one type but managing a range of absolute types is difficult in practice. For example, a firm that has some bilateral relationships is likely to use this culture in other relationships while not managing these other relationships in this way. We envisage obstacles to managing a portfolio of types in their absolute sense as it is impossible to simultaneously have the range of organisational and managerial values needed to accomplish them. One approach is to use separate units for managing close and adversarial relationships. On the other hand, it may not be possible to manage a full portfolio of all the four types but it may be necessary. Certain partners may have to be maintained even if not the first choice. One of the difficulties of managing a portfolio is that a company does not have a free hand. You may want a certain type of relationship but a partner may not. Viewing the portfolio as a relationship development tool can help plan for strategies that develop relationship over time.

Turnbull and Zolkiewski (1997) outlined a three-dimensional customer classification portfolio. This portfolio technique is based on the assessment of the contribution of the relationship. Figure 6.3 presents the model, based on three factors: relationship value, net price, and cost to serve. A customer relationship can be placed in any segment of the portfolio based on an assessment of these factors. The dimensions are as follows: the relationship value is the value of the relationship to the firm, the costs of serving a particular account/customer, and the net price of the product/service sold to a customer. Relationship value represents an assessment of the importance of the relationship – placing a financial value on the criticality of a relationship, the quantity bought/sold, ease of replacing the relationship, and the cost savings from repeated dealings. What represents a low or high rating on the portfolio's axes depends on the business and industry in which the company operates. Some of the calculations in making the assessment may be difficult but it could be well worth it. Turnbull and Zolkiewski suggest that managers review the

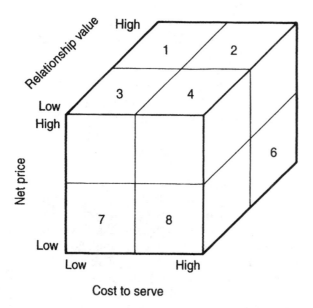

Figure 6.3   Customer portfolio (Source: Turnbull and Zolkiewski, 1997).

calculations of each factor as they can vary with the use of different accounting techniques, relationship costs can be difficult to allocate. Often companies do not consider the value of a relationship, for example, when pricing to include the differential costs in providing after sales service to particular customers. This portfolio management technique can provide a critical assessment of the structure and profit potential of a firm's relationships. Any changes in the position of a relationship in the matrix over time can be reviewed and acted upon. The calculation of portfolio position in itself would be extremely useful in strategic relationship planning.

Developing relationships

Two of the classic models of relationship development are presented in Figure 6.4A,B. Figure 6.4A represents Dwyer et al.'s (1987) model of relationship development and Figure 6.4B, Ford et al.'s (1998) model of relationship development. The models assume a company wants to develop a close relationship. If a company is dealing with a mass market with little potential for an involved relationship, then an appropriate focus may be to develop customers to an advocate stage using the idea of a loyalty ladder (Christopher et al., 1991). The loyalty ladder is presented in another chapter of this text. The loyalty ladder envisages customer relationships being developed through a series of stages, from prospect to being an advocate encouraging other people to buy from the company. Here, we will concentrate on the development of close relationships as these are the focus of the text. This can then be applied to other relationship types. The models presented in Figure 6.4 can be applied to the case at the end of the chapter.

The models examine relationships as developing through a number of stages from initiation to full integration. The model's implications are that firms can manage relationships with customers through these stages and as such, represent a framework for doing this.

Both models use similar stages, beginning with initial contact and developing to a level of institutionalisation where expectations and roles of both parties are set. During the process the parties explore and expand their relationship and establish sequentially more structured and formal relations. This may include the signing of formal agreements during the process in some cases, for example, where a joint product is being developed. Within each stage of relationship development there are many mini stages. Progress from one stage to another is achieved through mutual commitments that happen on a gradual basis as trust and relational norms are established. In the initial stage of a relationship, partner choice and information search is critical. In some instances it may be very difficult to induce buyer switching but in the early stages it is through information gathering and knowledge building that this exchange risk is reduced. Many companies use a problem solving approach to demonstrate the need to change. The first exchanges are likely to be of a limited nature to keep risks low. Usually the transaction can be reversed, for example, in the case of a trial order or interaction with a company's or showroom personnel. The next phase is the development of a 'lock-in' relationship

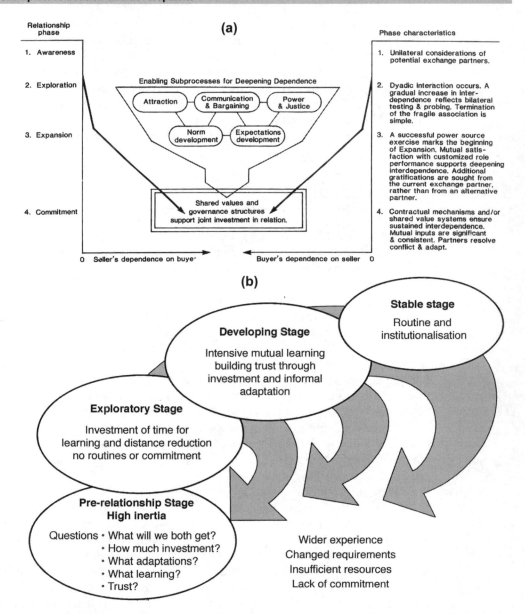

Figure 6.4   Models of relationship development (Source: Dwyer et al., 1987; Ford et al., 1998).

where commitment by both parties to the exchange is reflected through a deepening involvement. Dissolution is more difficult in this stage. In business-to-business markets, this commitment may be reflected in adaptations of processes to suit the partner or investments, such as in training people to manage a specific customer account. In consumer markets, loyalty can be expressed in different ways, for example, through loyalty bonuses or extra back-up service. Relationship development can have risks and each partner must insure that they share in the benefits and do not feel the dependence on the other partner is just one way. Holm et al. (1999) describe the relationship development process between Ericsson and Tokyo Digital Phone (TDP) in their partnership in the Japanese mobile phone market. What is interesting about their analysis is that they link relationship development to strategy and particularly to value creation. We see relationship development as an issue of strategic choice, especially, with relationships that are developed to be close.

Eventually a relationship is likely to become institutionalised to the extent where its norms and modes of working are unique. The challenge at this stage is to keep changing, as inertia could open the relationship to competitive challenge. Dissolution of a relationship is always possible and may be natural. However, if the later is the case then no party should be aggrieved on exit from the relationship. As is so often the case, parties may leave and not voice their complaints to the company but voice them to others and, thus, disturb the pattern of other and future relationships. Dissolution needs to be managed as carefully as the other stages. Many companies fail to treat customer exit as seriously as they should or respond to it (Steward, 1998; Hirschman, 1970).

Chapter summary

The chapter analysed relationship classification approaches and presented relationship development models. It began with an examination of approaches to classifying relationships – bi-polar continuums and descriptive typologies, and developed this, through the authors' research, by building on the relationship strength concept presented in chapter 4, to develop a classification matrix of four relationship types. These are bilateral, recurrent, dominant partner and discrete. The behaviour of firms in these types of relationships was described. These behaviours have many implications for relationship management. The chapter continued with an analysis of relationship portfolios that are a strategic relationship issue given the resource allocation implications of portfolio management. Two examples of portfolio analysis were presented – one was based on relationship integration and the other on an analysis of relationship contribution. Finally, the chapter examined a few key contributors to the relationship development literature and presented their models with an explanation of how they work. The models showed how close relationship can be developed and provided a framework for doing this. The company case allows the reader to put into practice some of the techniques learned in the chapter.

CASE FOR DISCUSSION   **METAL FORMING LTD**

Metal Forming Ltd (names disguised) is a small engineering firm with 80 plus employees. Its core technology is sheet metal. This technology is standard and on the low end of the technology spectrum. Essentially, engineering companies that just, for example, punch holes in metal are competing on the price at which they carry out this process. Metal Forming Ltd has managed to differentiate its product by developing certain relationships. This case describes the company's relationship with two of its partners: AirCon of Holland and Super Chef Inc. of Dallas.

AirCon are designers and installers of clean rooms and clean room equipment. Clean rooms are used in a variety of industries such as electronics and aircraft. They can be used for storage of light or heat sensitive material, or to conduct a specialised manufacturing process. Today AirCon specialise in air filtration and conditioning and provide the electronics and controls for the plant that they and Metal Forming Ltd jointly supply. The relationship started in 1985 when Metal Forming Ltd contacted AirCon after a long search for some European business. It was looking for a company with which it could develop a relationship and where, initially, being small would not be a problem. Metal Forming Ltd narrowed a buyer list down to five and chose Aircon on the basis of its long-term potential to develop business.

Metal Forming Ltd began doing metal work from drawings supplied by AirCon. In 1993 it started to design and manufacture the whole system and ship it to where AirCon was building the plant. All AirCon now has to do is add the electronics and controls. Metal Forming Ltd's computer aided design develops the whole system. In this period both companies have developed their turnover substantially and have been able to concentrate on their core competencies: AirCon in final customer relationships and air filtration and control and Metal Forming Ltd in manufacture. The relationship is very interdependent. Metal Forming Ltd has two project engineers working exclusively with this customer who work with autonomy to manage the relationship. The managing directors of both companies have developed strong working and personal relationships.

Super Chef Inc. is a spin-off company from the US space industry and is basically a research and development outfit. The product they developed is a high speed oven that can cook meals to pre-programmed specifications. Meals are multi-cooked which means that a whole meal is prepared in a matter of minutes or less. These meals can be prepared from fresh or frozen. The oven does all the preparation and retains the flavour of a conventional oven. The ovens are sold to commercial customers and are beginning to reach consumer markets through petrol forecourts where you can pick you meal out of a refrigerator, place it in the oven, and in a few minutes have a fully prepared self-service meal. Super Chef Inc had two subcontractors in the US who manufactured the product. Today the sole manufacturer is Metal Forming Ltd.

The relationship developed through the following stages and took 3–4 years to get to where it is currently. Initially, Metal Forming Ltd produced the metal box within which the oven is contained. Then it moved to the electrical and assembly work. After this they started to do the complete building and testing of the oven. This meant a major development for the company as testing these types of products requires meeting tough microwave standards. To do this the company had to take in new equity, but by doing this, has protected their basic business and developed new integrated computer manufacturing and testing capabilities. Obviously, these competencies cannot be built overnight. Metal Forming Ltd had a previous involvement in testing the specification of basic metal car parts to meet, for example, rust proof guarantees of manufacturers. The company now supplies directly to the final customer rather than to Super Chef Inc. They also upgrade the product in conjunction with Super Chef Inc because they know so much about it. The relationship has developed to a stage where the companies, together with an outside investor, have developed a European joint venture to develop sales.

Questions

1. How would you classify the relationship Metal Forming Ltd has with its two customers? Detail the reasons for your classification.
2. Examine the stages of development the relationships described in the case have gone through.
3. What conditions had to be in place for these relationships to develop?
4. Describe the interdependencies between the companies in the case.
5. Analyse the potential benefits to both partners in the relationships presented.

Further reading

Bensaou, M. (1999), Portfolios of buyer-supplier relationships, *Sloan Management Review*, 40 (4), pp. 35–44.

Cannon, J.P., Achrol Ravi, S. and Gundlach, G.T. (2000), Contracts, norms, and plural form governance, *Journal of the Academy of Marketing Science*, 28 (2), pp. 180–194.

Frazier, G.L., Spekman, R.E. and O'Neal, C.R. (1988), Just-in-time relationships in industrial markets, *Journal of Marketing*, 52 (4), pp. 52–67.

Lambe, C. Jay, S., Robert E. and Hunt, S.D. (2000), Interimistic relational exchange: conceptualisation and propositional development, *Journal of the Academy of Marketing Sciences*, 28 (2), pp. 212–225.

Lewin, J.E. and Johnston, W.J. (1997), Relationship marketing theory in practice: a case study, *Journal of Business Research*, 39 (1), pp. 23–31.

Ring, P.S. and Van De Ven, A.H. (1994), Developmental processes of co-operative interorganisational relationships, *Academy of Management Review*, 19 (1), pp. 90–118.

Singh, J. and Pandya, S. (1991), Exploring the effects of customers' dissatisfactions level on complaint behaviours, *European Journal of Marketing*, 25 (9), pp. 7–21.

Wood, C.H., Kaufman, A. and Meranda, M. (1996), How Hadco became a problem solving supplier, *Sloan Management Review*, 37 (2), Winter, pp. 77–88.

Young, L.C. and Wilkinson, I.F. (1997), The space between: towards a typology of interfirm relations, *Journal of Business-To-Business Marketing*, 4 (2), pp. 53–97.

Chapter questions

1. Discuss the appropriateness of classifying relationships concentrating on what actually happens in a relationship when compared to a description of the category of relationship – supplier, buyer, alliance, competitor.
2. Outline the advantages and disadvantages to using matrices of relationship types to classify relationship.
3. Prepare a plan for moving a relationship for being discrete to bilateral. How possible is this?
4. How can a firm handle the problem of being dominated by the power of its

supplier or buyer who are using the power to manage the relationship for their benefit?

5. Assess the potential of using a portfolio approach to managing relationships. Can one company manage a range of relationship types? Under what conditions might it have to?

6. Using the relationship development models presented in the case, select a company and examine its relationship development with its main supplier.

7. Present a plan for developing a relationship to a bilateral level. Start your plan with choice of partner.

8. Examine the challenges in developing individual relationships in mass markets.

CHAPTER 7

The 5-S framework of relationship management implementation

Introduction and objectives

The bottom line for any business is that improved performance comes in one of three ways – increased sales, reduced costs or a change in the product/customer mix. Nevertheless, the strategic direction of the business is a precursor to effective action at the implementation stage. The task, from a supplier perspective, is to increase the number of customers as well as to retain and increase business with existing customers at a profitable level. Yet, the dynamics of the market place are making new forms of competitive advantage more difficult and ephemeral with instant imitation and rising costs. Given this scenario, it is not surprising that strategic market relationships have come to the forefront of managerial thinking, with its focus on retaining and increasing profitable business with existing customers and the initiation, development and retention of business with new ones. Relationships also mean a focus on employees working as partners and managing internal relationships will be key to effective management of external relationships. Relationships also emphasise the need to initiate, develop and maintain relationships with a number of stakeholders in the firm and related to the firm. This change in emphasis moves management from a craft and set of techniques to a more complex process of intra and inter-organisational interaction based on new relationships. As is often the case, this is easier said than done. This chapter is about how firms initiate, develop and retain profitable relationships, primarily with customers. It is also concerned with how strategic market relationships can be implemented and what guidelines can be given for the management of these relationships.

In this chapter the objectives are to:

- stress the importance of managerial commitment and a new corporate vision incorporating a relationship orientation;
- offer appropriate organisational response to the demands of strategic market relationships based on the 5-S framework;
- highlight examples of macro network responses that a relationship marketing approach might create;

- specify internal responses and give examples of new relationship forms;
- confirm the importance of managerial commitment and relationship-oriented people;
- consider alternative managerial systems and change processes.

CASE ILLUSTRATION   **THE UK ENERGY MARKET**

The UK energy market is now a de-regulated market for the supply of gas and electricity to domestic and business customers. This has provided opportunities for companies to increase their customer base for gas and electricity throughout the UK and more recently to enhance this customer base further with water services and, in some cases, telecommunication services. Major players such as Scottish Power, British Gas, Eastern and Northern Electricity, Southern and Scottish Hydro have been very aggressive in acquiring customers from the competition and delivering value through lower cost operations.

At the same time, these companies now risk losing customers that were previously tied in to their specific area. For example, since de-regulation of the gas market, British Gas has lost 25% of its customers. Although many people are reluctant to change, more consumers, influenced by the promotional effort of the utility companies themselves, are now open to the idea based on price discounts. The result is that prices tend to be forced down to the commodity level with some suppliers 'swimming against the tide' by attempting to compete on enhanced service as a basis for differentiation.

To gain competitive advantage on a long-term basis, energy suppliers are looking at extending their product portfolios that compliment their core energy services in order to find new ways of enhancing service delivery. Innovations include the launch of credit cards, insurance, security products and deals with supermarkets such as joint loyalty cards. A report by Price Waterhouse Coopers (PWC) has forecast that, in future, gas and electricity will no longer be purchased from traditional power companies but from big brand home service retailers for whom utilities will only be a small part of the product and services they offer. They predict that the industry will be split into two. Part A will be an elite few that remain focused on consumer retailing with a strong brand identity. Part B will be those unable to compete in the brand loyalty stakes and will become out-sourced backroom services for billing, customer contact and debt collection. To quote from the PWC report

the time has come for current players to make decisions. If they want to remain in retail, large-scale change is not optional. Companies need to be hard-nosed when assessing their capabilities and initiating major change. Already mergers and acquisitions are moving towards creating mega-utilities with the market size and clout to secure their place in the new world order. For the rest, unless they take positive action to establish themselves either in the home services retail market or as a back-office service provider, the future will be bleak.

Source: Price Waterhouse Coopers, Open Sky Retailing May 1999.

The case illustration suggests that new approaches will be required in the future if relationship implementation is to be executed successfully. Since we are concerned here with implementation, we use the 5-S framework for relationship implementation introduced in chapter 4 – structure, staff, style, systems and schemes.

Structure

Businesses today find themselves being forced to make unprecedented changes in their business models, supply chain, organisational structures and in the way they interface with customers and consumers. In particular, the impact of IT and e-commerce are major drivers of change. SMR are multi-faceted. Companies realise they have to integrate upstream and downstream in their supply chain but, as yet, there are a number of areas where there is apparently no prescription for relationship building.

We consider some examples of organisational development in the pursuit of successful relationship implementation on two levels. First, those changes at the macro level with suppliers, sometimes competitors and other role partners. These include mergers and acquisitions, joint ventures and alliances and out-sourcing. Secondly, from an internal perspective, mainly changes in relationships with customers including franchising, key account management and category management:

Macro network responses

Companies need to realign themselves and alter their structures to build effective relationships. In some cases these new relationships may fail on a voluntary basis because of incompatibility between players. The firms, or more correctly the management of these firms, do not develop the transparency, do not have similar objectives, do not trust each other explicitly and therefore are neither committed to nor believe in their relationship-based approach. However, there are ways in which industry structures change and we consider three – mergers and acquisitions; joint ventures and alliances; out-sourcing.

Mergers and acquisitions (M&A)

Mergers and acquisitions (M&A) are two possible strategies companies could adopt in order to survive and prosper in highly competitive markets. News about mergers and acquisitions are broadcasted on a daily basis – the US and Europe being the most active geographical areas. There are a number of benefits to be gained by this strategy, securing growth and achieving size to mention just two of them. M&A also lead to a reduction in the number of key global players in the market. However, there are also a number of critical success factors and drawbacks that have to be taken into consideration to ensure a successful consolidation of two businesses and the fulfilment of the objectives set for this strategy. While financial benefits are often paramount, we consider the strategic market effects arising from M&A activity.

The drivers for national and international mergers and acquisitions stem from the need to get a leading edge in the battle for market share and sources of funds for expansion. The combined effect of competition, technology and deregulation will further diminish profit margins of traditional businesses, forcing them to acquire stakes in new high-growth markets. They will then be able to offer new and innovative services and pursue national and international expansion via mergers and acquisitions in an effort to extend their geographic reach and have the ability to fully service international customers. Suggested benefits of increased size include:

- it allows the exploitation of economies of scale which in turn can lead to efficiencies in areas such as IT, purchasing, overheads, R&D. It permits more efficient use of the companies' resources and networks thus reducing transaction costs;
- size is also necessary if a company wants to grow because a large number of customers allows a broader product range offering and international networks secure international business customers;
- large companies have, in addition, the necessary bargaining power to set industry standards and influence politics and legislation;
- size can avoid hostile takeovers (although not always if one considers the acquisition of Royal Bank of Scotland and Natwest);
- size attracts business opportunities with the best partners in the market of high growth areas requiring new investment such as telecommunications;
- high volume sales are needed to cover the fixed costs of global operations as margins are squeezed continuously.

Despite the advantages that mergers and acquisitions can provide, there are also constraints and risk factors to be considered, that can impact heavily on the process. Firms involved often under-estimate, or at least have to overcome issues of corporate pride, national politics, government ownership and cultural differences as the main critical success factors for mergers. Further problems include the integration of different business processes and structures and the alignment of management. The size of the merging companies can also be an inhibiting factor as it renders it more difficult to manage and lengthens the decision-making process.

In strategic market relationships, size is only one of many issues about mergers and acquisitions. One feature of new entrants, which makes them very dangerous for integrated companies, is that they are focusing on specific business activities and try to do this by being the best in their class. Thus, both large and small integrated companies should follow the focused approach by 'disaggregating' their activities, thus winning back the advantages of small players, namely faster decision-making process, attracting best business partners and high-skilled staff. Once 'disaggregated', these companies should seek further opportunities to grow within their specialised focus and this is best achieved via strategic relationships.

The benefits of 'demerging' embrace other reasons, including pressure on incumbents to add value to the whole group. Stock markets value focused businesses operating in high-growth areas higher than they rate an integrated company. Thus, by spinning off these parts of the business, incumbents get a relatively high share price for their spun-off business, which in turn increases the total value of the company. An increase in share price also typically follows a 'demerger'. Floating is also very attractive for companies as it allows them to generate money for further acquisitions.

The struggle for growth and profit, the need for high technological investments and for competition on an international level drives companies to deploy strategies such as mergers and acquisitions. The benefits clearly outweigh the risks, thus a continuation of this process can be expected until a few key players are dominating global markets. It is also expected that the focus of mergers and acquisitions will change: 'disaggregated' business units will merge with other focused areas to reap the maximum benefits of scale and focus.

Joint ventures and alliances (JV&A)

In order to meet demand expectations, developments in new technologies and increased competition, firms are experiencing the need to establish relationships with others through strategic alliances and joint ventures. Different people can attribute different meanings to these two terms but usually they imply a getting together of organisations in some form of inter-firm relationship in order to pursue a strategic purpose. Alliances are created for the same reason as joint ventures, normally to achieve some form of collaborative advantage. This will be achieved when something unusual emerges that no one organisation could have produced on its own. The main difference between the two strategic options is that in alliances there is no formal creation of a discrete offspring organisation by the parent organisation, thus there is a more deliberately open exit door. In a joint venture, a new organisation (known as child) is formed and controlled by two or more collaborating organisations (known as parents).

The objectives in JV&A are created mainly to:

- accelerate entry into new markets;
- financial purposes;
- achieve economies of scale (in the areas of R&D and marketing);
- to share know-how.

In restricted markets, such as Asia and South America, where foreign ownership of companies is limited, some formed JV&A is the easiest way to gain entry. In some of these countries, foreign companies cannot own more than the 49% of an organisation's capital. Thus, JV&A are, for global European and US organisations, the only way to penetrate these markets. The benefits for domestic companies in participating in alliances is that JV&A are powerful vehicles for growth and for defending itself in case the home markets are opened in the future to new entrants, introducing global brands or new technologies. A recent example is the $200 million alliance between Hanaro Telecom, a Korean telecommunication provider, and Cisco System Inc. aimed to accelerate and to finance a roll-out of the Korean company's high-speed Internet services and to increase the opportunities for Cisco's business products in Korea (Newsbyte, 2000).

In open markets, alliances have provided the possibility for entering new markets even when their financial resources required to support a direct investment were limited. It also reduces the risk and costs of going it alone. Strategic alliances have also been formed to enter into other industries. In this case the organisations involved benefit from sharing their knowledge and speed up the time to entry. However, by sharing institutional knowledge, companies risk that one day their partners may become direct competitors in their own industry.

JV&As are an alternative option to mergers and acquisitions. However, these relationships are never easy, especially when giants competing in the same market form the alliance. In the last 10 years we have seen the creation of thousands of alliances in many industries, which demonstrates willingness to collaborate. However, achieving a collaborative advantage is not going to be easily achieved as members of alliances have different cultures, languages, ownership structures, management styles and sometimes objectives. Nevertheless, daily news about new JV&A's proves that industry participants are convinced that these relationships can work and that partners are sufficiently motivated to make them work.

Out-sourcing

This section will briefly look at out-sourcing and attempt to determine why companies out-source, what activities are being out-sourced, who are the providers of out-sourcing services and what are the concerns and risks associated with out-sourcing. Companies from all industry sectors are turning to out-sourcing in an attempt to reposition their organisations and secure long-term survival in the new, competitive environment within which companies now operate. For many, horizontal integration is no longer the key to sustainable competitive advantage. Such companies are realising that they are not expert in all areas of the value chain and are identifying 'partners' with specialised knowledge and skills that will deliver increased service levels by assuming responsibility for specific tasks within the value chain.

As the word 'partner' suggests, successful out-sourcing is very much dependent on relationships. Prior to embarking on out-sourcing it is important that company executives determine the type of relationship they want to create and the degree of integration that should exist between the two parties. The type of relationship a company decides to pursue should be based upon aligned goals and objectives. Out-sourcing relationships vary greatly and there is no right or wrong type.

Out-sourcing relationships cover a wide and diverse spectrum from traditional type vendor style out-sourcing relationships to more collaborative long-term ones. Companies should consider how many partners the out-sourcing arrangement will involve. If the business process to be out-sourced is critical to core operations and requires a deep well of resource, a company may consider working with several partners that can pool their resources and skill base. Alternatively, a company may select a single partner, or work with two, to instil a sense of competition into the out-sourcing agreement by awarding each partner a portion of the service and offering the remainder to either partner. For example, two partners may be awarded 40% of the work, with the other 20% awarded to the partner offering the highest level of service or innovation.

Why do businesses out-source? What are the benefits?   Every generation experiences change, but some argue that not since the turn of the last century and the rise of the industrial revolution have organisations had to respond so quickly to such pervasive and powerful change requirements. The current environment witnesses a plethora of mergers, acquisitions, divestitures, joint ventures, and others. Large traditional companies are facing unprecedented competition from start-up companies that were not even in existence a year or two ago. Entry barriers are falling and global competition is on the increase. For traditional companies, this inherent complexity is made all the more challenging by the advent of e-commerce. To meet these challenges, companies are developing new business models and analysing their underlying operational structure. Out-sourcing is acquiring a significant presence in the development of new corporate strategies.

A survey conducted in 1998 by the Outsourcing Institute (1998) identified the following ten reasons why companies out-source:

- reduce and control operating costs;
- improve company focus;
- gain access to world class capabilities;
- free internal resources for other purposes;
- resources are not available internally;
- accelerate reengineering benefits;
- function difficult to manage/out of control;
- make capital funds available;
- share risk;
- cash infusion.

Other benefits identified by industry leaders, not stated above, include improving operating efficiencies, increasing customer service, reducing time delays between customer order and receipt, streamlining processes, improving distribution, reducing property portfolio and increasing shareholder value.

What activities are companies out-sourcing?   Traditionally, out-sourcing decisions have focused on 'core' activities versus 'non-core' activities, with the latter usually being identified as an out-source candidate. However, the Outsourcing Institute suggest that the above criteria is too simplistic and that companies should take a wider view of which activities might be considered candidates for out-sourcing. They argue that many companies have successfully out-sourced activities vital to the operation of their core functions. For example, a bank out-sourced its credit card processing to a credit service organisation. Credit cards are a high-growth business for the bank but state-of-the-art technology and competitive prices are essential for the bank, which now has access to those capabilities through an out-sourcing alliance. Another example provided by the Outsourcing Institute, which substantiates their argument on out-sourcing core activities looked at a telecom company that out-sourced a major part of its international telemarketing.

The Institute propose, that in addition to more traditional core and non-core distinctions, companies should consider two emerging types of relationships.

Firstly, "sharing core" in which a company conducts activities that are vital to the operation of its core processes in a highly integrated relationship with an outsourcing partner. Secondly, "expanded core" which involves the creation of new competencies and capabilities through a partnership or joint venture. These types of relationships usually require tightly integrated operations, transparency, openness and a truly strategic, long-term partnership between the parties involved. Very often companies become uncomfortable in such close relationships and concern grows about losing control, vulnerability and protection of core competencies. The Institute did identify a number of actions a company can take to mitigate their concerns, such as patents, copyrights, confidentiality and non-compete agreements. However, they also argue that such actions are only part of the solution and that many of the fears are most effectively overcome by developing a sourcing relationship based on trust, mutual benefit and alignment of interests.

The Outsourcing Institute identified three major areas companies are out-sourcing. Firstly, information technology includes activities such as maintenance & repair, training, application development, consulting and reengineering, mainframe data centres, networks, desktop systems, and user support. Secondly, operations out-sourcing includes a wide spectrum of activities that covers the majority of disciplines within administration, customer service, finance, human resource, property & plant management and sales & marketing. Thirdly, logistics out-sourcing covers the disparate range of disciplines within distribution and transportation such as freight audit, freight brokering, training, warehousing, information systems, fleet management and fleet maintenance.

Who are providing out-sourcing services?   With the advent of e-commerce, a new business model currently emerging is that of value chain service provider (Timmers, 2000). These companies specialise in providing a specific function within the value chain, with the intention of making that into their distinct competitive advantage. Such functions include the provision of payment or logistics but new functions such as production/stock management are also emerging. For example, FedEx are currently leveraging their expertise in logistics and distribution by offering customers various value-chain services. In 1999, FedEx announced a strategic alliance with SAP, a leading inter-enterprise software solutions provider, to develop and market a first-ever 'one-stop' portfolio of supply-chain planning, management, and execution services. This total solution will allow companies to out-source all or part of their supply chain to a single provider, thus enabling them to concentrate on their 'core' competencies while benefiting from cost effective, globally synchronised distribution of their products.

Problems with out-sourcing – organisational readiness   Clearly out-sourcing has the potential to deliver significant benefits but as more and more out-sourcing activities are undertaken and the collection of third party providers swell, managers have to monitor a range of activities and measure the performance and success of each. As companies delegate a greater number of activities, the following risks have been identified:

- greater dependence on third party service providers as internal skills and capabilities recede;
- loss of control of certain strategic activities;
- resources (financial & time) expended on overseeing out-sourced projects may negate any perceived benefits;
- risk of internal rejection, alienation of staff and labour union problems.

Prior to implementing out-sourcing it is important that the company initiating the out-sourcing exercise review their own organisation to ensure its suitability as a partner. The Outsourcing Institute identified a number of components that determines an organisation's readiness:

- the ability to build relationships – managers responsible for implementing new out-sourcing relationships should have experience with such initiatives and understand the key factors in successful alliances
- management support – it is imperative that top management provides strategic direction, creates a supportive atmosphere, encourages innovation and allays fears about trying new approaches.
- a plan for overcoming roadblocks – undoubtedly, out-sourcing initiatives will run into sceptics, cynics and protectors of turf, therefore, a stakeholder analysis (or similar exercise) should be conducted to mitigate any potential 'rebellion'.

It is evident that out-sourcing has the potential to deliver significant benefits. To the initiating company, benefits bestowed include operational efficiencies, greater cost, time and resource management. To the service provider, the ability to leverage operational efficiencies, optimise process utilisation and in some instances the opportunity to capitalise on new business opportunities. A number of impediments with the potential to impede successful out-sourcing have been identified, however, with sufficient planning and organisational review prior to implementation, many of the impediments can be mitigated.

The lessons from these three trends in the macro network are that a new network environment is being created by partners, customers and competitors. This results in greater transparency between buyer and suppliers yet removes entry barriers for a range of different companies, some large and diverse, some small and highly specialised. Industry boundaries may become blurred requiring deconstruction and reconstruction of the value chain. Reducing costs, global expansions and public scrutiny demand new business models and unprecedented change.

Micro network responses

Those already operating within an industry will also have to look at their organisational structures if they are to respond to customer, competitor and external changes in their environment. With ever more demanding customers in different markets comes the challenge to fundamentally re-think on how to compete and deliver appropriate customer solutions. These might include:

- bundling products and services;

- the battle for customer loyalty;
- branding;
- value based relationships;
- co-operating to compete.

Within these strategic objectives there are also organisational implications. Many of these are product/industry specific and the following merely represent three approaches brought about by the trend in relationship enhancement in the supply chain:

Franchising

Today, most new franchise ventures conform to a standardised business format. This contemporary system of distribution evolved from older forms of franchising and licensing arrangement known as 'product' or 'trademark' franchising. These earlier franchise forms typically involved manufacturers granting intermediaries and retailers permission to sell goods such as soft drinks, petroleum and motor vehicles with some centralised marketing support. Business format franchising, by contrast, encompasses a more comprehensive set of procedures designed to support the expansion and operation of a whole franchised business concept and is relationship-based.

> The business format franchise is the grant of a license by one person (the franchisers) to another (the franchisee), which entitles the franchisee to trade under the trade mark/trade name of the franchiser and to make use of an entire package, comprising all the elements necessary to establish a previously untrained person in the business developed by the franchiser and to run it with continuing assistance on a predetermined basis.
>
> (Mendelson, 1993, p. 2)

This definition highlights a number of features commonly associated with business format franchising. Firstly, the relationship centres on a branded product which is owned and controlled by the franchiser. In fact, the significance of branding within franchising is so great that the term 'brand franchising' has been used interchangeably with business format franchising. However, because branding is common to most forms of franchising it cannot be used to distinguish types.

Secondly, business format franchising is commonly differentiated by its wider range of franchise system elements including contract design, franchisee recruitment and selection, site selection, product specification, fee methods, support services and quality control procedures. However, Dnes (1992) compared 19 UK franchise systems and established that 'product', type franchises such as car dealerships, also involved a wide range of franchise system elements. In addition, Dnes found interchangeability in the payment methods used across franchise forms. Business format systems, for example, were found on occasion to use transfer price agreements commonly associated with 'product' form systems.

A third defining feature is the methods suitability to previously untrained recruits. In practice this characteristic will hinge on the complexity of and skills required to run the franchise operation and on the franchisers organisation or distribution structure. For example, small independent operators are not allowed access to corporate franchise systems (Kaufmann, 1996).

Such heterogeneity and interchangeability in franchise system characteristics makes precise typographical definitions difficult. In essence, however, business format franchising is more holistic and more franchisee/franchiser interdependent than other forms. It is therefore suited to products that rely on a broader set of procedures to achieve success in the market place. Such products include services based on integrated production and delivery systems and standardised operational formats.

Although most franchise outlets are directly monitored by a franchiser, others are supervised through corporate or master franchise structures. These essentially involve delegating the right to operate the system to an intermediary company. In master franchising, the intermediary is granted the right to sub-franchise. In corporate franchising no such right is granted.

Key account management

Key account management has been around for some time but has been given additional impetus by the trend towards relationship enhancement. The changing structure of major retailers, distributors and others, necessitates that for many companies certain customers are of strategic importance. The Pareto rule which states that 80% of the business comes from 20% of customers is often exceeded and it is far from unusual to find perhaps 95% or more of business coming from a handful of customers. These important accounts need to be given the attention and service they deserve. Further, since these are normally large organisations with buying groups with relatively sophisticated purchasing systems they require a strategic focus. A unique approach is required for such accounts and it is vital to keep these customers loyal by customising the product-service-information mix (Cespedes, 1996). Key account management requires competencies in a number of different areas of strategic formulation and implementation, systems and process design and relationship building (Millman and Wilson, 1996). Stages in key account development have been depicted as shown in Figure 7.1.

Key accounts are customers of strategic importance to the firm and are likely to posses some of the following characteristics:

- they account for a significant proportion of existing or potential business for the firm;
- they form part of a supply chain in which efficiency is enhanced by co-operation rather than conflict;
- working interdependently with these customers rather than independently, has benefits such as lower transaction costs, better quality or joint product development – perhaps even all three;
- supply involves not just product but other service aspects, whether technical support, 'just-in-time' manufacturing or market development potential;

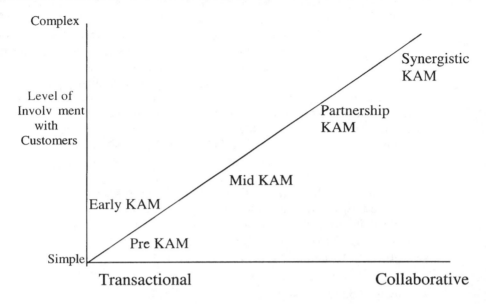

Figure 7.1 The relational development model (Source: McDonald et al., 1997).

- there are advantages to both parties in close, open relationships rather than a focus on transaction efficiency alone.

In some cases, the relationship is, or becomes one-sided, costs rise for the supplier or there is over-dependence on a large, important customer. New and different organisational problems arise because the co-ordination between two organisations becomes difficult and complex to manage. In deciding whether or not to use key account management, an analysis of the type of relationship is crucial. It is clearly incumbent upon the supplier and the salesperson to invest in identifying the type of relationship they enjoy with their customers. This should be coupled with consideration of the stage in the relationship, both now and in the future. We would advocate the use of our matrix, developed in chapter 4, to assist this process.

The various stages in key account management development are:

Stage 1, pre-key account management (pre-KAM) describes the preparation and identification of potential key accounts now and in the future. If exchange is low cost and transactional, KAM is unlikely to be necessary or desirable. A service strategy focused on making it easier to buy and making transactions quicker, simpler and of lower cost using technology (electronic data interchange, telemetry or similar) is more appropriate. At stage 2, early-KAM, the need is to build on the initial order and find ways of keeping the account. It also involves developing and growing so that the customer continues to do business with the firm. This will normally be done by involving more personnel and intangibles such as training and advice, technical support or promotional assistance. The rewards from efforts at this stage might be difficult to assess and it is not about giving the customers everything but about increasing the value of the supplier to the buyer.

The third stage, mid-KAM, is crucial in that, while other suppliers may still be competing, the buyer is favourably disposed to you and your company. Reassurance of responsiveness and flexibility become more important and the objective is to seek and reinforce preferred supplier status. Following this, there is increased contact between salespeople and other staff and the relationship becomes more of a partnership. The buyer will now want and expect preferred status with appropriate cost reduction. Joint product development and promotion are now planned and expected. This results in market growth, reduces transaction costs and promotes continuous improvement in performance on a range of dimensions. Many companies who talk a relationship game do not practise it at this partnership level (Donaldson, 1996).

Stage 4, partnerships can blend into synergistic KAM, which is the ultimate in relationship development, short of vertical integration. They still operate as independent businesses but both companies see it in their interests to acknowledge interdependence and seek economies in operations and market development. In organisational terms, the problem is one of internal co-ordination within the firm and external co-ordination between supplier and customer. In this situation, the division of roles between a salesperson and product or marketing manager becomes blurred and the title of customer account manager perhaps better encapsulates the nature of the job, involving skills and knowledge different from those of working with one buyer or customer contact.

In organisational terms, key accounts operate on a national, European (other economic region) or global basis. No one organisational type can accommodate these complexities. Local buyers and global suppliers can create organisational difficulties and the decision is likely to reflect opportunities for synergy. For example, Honeywell Process Division operates key customer account managers for the major oil companies but use a more conventional approach for some UK food-processing companies. Component suppliers in the UK took a long time to develop adequate relationships with Nissan following their location in north-east England. In organisational terms, identifying the type of relationship and the stage in that relationship are both crucial to the organisational solution.

Category management

In consumer goods marketing, with increasing channel integration, competitive advantage is difficult to achieve with major retailers more interested in categories of products rather than individual items or brands. This itself stimulates relationship orientation but the idea of an agent representing many principles or manufacturers is not new and has been used in a variety of industries for many years, e.g. small tools and publishing. In the food industry, the growth of multiple chains to a dominant position and the importance of larger non-retail users have led to a problem in representation for the smaller company and the large buyer. One type of relationship management to overcome the problem of size is the use of the food broker who acts on an agency basis for several manufacturers selling a variety of products to retailers. Mostly, the tasks relate to merchandising and promotional offers where the cost of individual salespeople for each company is too high and for each store manager too time-consuming. The specialist in, for example, delicatessen items, dairy products or confectionery is preferred to individual representation on individual lines. The retailer gets a 'mix' of product from one broker. The manufacturer get representation they otherwise could neither get nor afford. The skill of such brokers is in balancing the items carried and matching these to customers' requirements. In retailing a new area, category management has emerged to handle the complexities involved in these situations.

In an effort to add value in distribution, suppliers have offered and supermarkets have accepted greater adoption of the concept of category management in the supply chain. An example of this approach is the Glasgow-based McCurrach's which is one of the largest food brokers in the UK. Although founded over 100 years ago, this company has seen its sales grow rapidly in recent years and it now represents over 50 clients such as Guinness, Campbell's and AG Barr. Their role is to maximise customers' sales by getting products into stores, ensuring appropriate shelf space and in-store promotions. McCurrach's employ 100 people at present and have invested £500 000 in new technology to provide the best service possible for client and customer. Such an operation involves specialists in delivering relationship-enhancing benefits in merchandising, logistics and account management. This requires a product, information and service mix, which meets the demanding needs of retail customers. In other categories major suppliers have become the category leaders. Proctor and Gamble have 26 staff exclusively working for Safeway and are permanently based in Safeway's premises. These examples highlight that information sharing between suppliers, intermediaries and customer is immense and to share such proprietary information requires a high level of trust. This is relationship orientation in action.

Staff

New products, new markets, changing conditions, will require a response over time to maintain an accurate reflection of business goals, but in all businesses, especially service ones, the people element is crucial for relationship implementation and relationship enhancement. The move from sales orientation to marketing orientation to relationship orientation has changed the supplier's approach. The need is to understand buyers' requirements more accurately and provide appropriate solutions in the product, service or information mix to satisfy their customers. For example, this has led to a more consultative role for salespeople advising buyers and decision-makers. In the computer industry and industrial direct applications it is common for three or more persons in a team to advise customers. Such teams have product, technical or financial expertise to assess customer needs and so tailor the product/service package to be most effective. A team in this context consists of members of a group dependent on interaction with each other in order to meet and exceed customer and corporate objectives. Such teams can face problems particu-

larly in location and distance, team identity and culture. This requires organisational politics to be put aside and it is a must that trust and commitment on the part
of team members should be put towards attaining the group's objectives. The role
and tasks to be performed should be explicit, the organisational support required in
place and the incentives and rewards need to be fair and seen to be fair.

To be effective in teams requires different managerial skills. It is important that
team members do meet face-to-face initially. The means of communication with
each other and the group need to be clearly specified and the atmosphere of group
learning must prevail. The advantages of cultural differences, skills and ideas must
be tempered with some focus on outcomes and discipline in achieving objectives.
Part of this is accurate and speedy feedback to the group on their relationship
performance and outcomes. Training is crucial in execution of this organisational
transformation but what does this mean in practice?

Using a leading IT company as an example this means combining selling, service
management and profitable delivery. In charge of the team is the Client Director/
Manager supported by the core team and specialists in customer co-ordination,
services, logistics and technical support. At the front end are the project managers,
the service consultants with specific industry and market knowledge and service
delivery teams including telephone sales and service support. In reality, a number
of objectives can be met. First, the team can set joint goals and objectives with their
customers – this is a consultancy role to assist customers expand their own business. Second, they can resource to meet the customer's and their own objectives in
terms of turnover, profitability and future business. Third, they can manage the
existing day-to-day business in terms of logistics, supply and service. These internal relationships are vital to get rid of the 'them and us' mentality between sales
and production, buyers and sellers, workers and management. Finally, and most
important of all, team leaders must identify future customer's needs and opportunities to grow the business. This combines a customer strategy with client management and contact support, thereby offering a relationship-based solution.

As relationships become a more common managerial approach and organisational interactions more complex, the role of the manager in this process becomes
one of interdependent management between parties and entails co-ordination and
control. A complex trade-off between cost, adaptability and risk may be required in
such relationships. Management should be concerned with all efforts and activities
directed at establishing, developing and maintaining profitable relationships. At
the strategic level, senior management must analyse the business unit situation
both in respect of its internal and external environments and decide upon which
markets have to be served now and in the future. The type of products or services
which satisfies customers in these markets and the areas of the business the
company both wants and does not want to serve, including specifying the types
of customers the business does not want to deal with. In the new relationship, most
firms must select those with which they aim to do business, rather than attempt to
serve all. Formalisation of these objectives into a strategic statement or operational
plan is required to manage relationships in the most appropriate way.

At the tactical level, to manage relationships effectively requires not only an organisational structure but also deployment of human resources, recruitment and selection of appropriate staff, training and a system of evaluation and rewards. At the operational level, management must take into account the competitive situation and the needs of individual customers and match these to the organisational objectives set at the strategic and tactical level. The result is a combination of inside and outside sales people, key account management, customer service, support personnel, tele-marketing and other forms of organisational integration and communication. However, identifying categories and forms of relationships does not mean that they will automatically develop. A first step is building the foundations for sustainable relationships by establishing what is required to make an organisation relationship oriented whether from a supplier, buyer, or other perspective. Relationships, mostly, have to be made to happen. This can be achieved if relationships are viewed as strategic and require a relationship orientation.

Part of this orientation is individual and the organisation must commit to relationship building as a way of doing business. Our experience, and almost all the cases we have studied, suggests that a key ingredient in successful relationship implementation is managerial and staff commitment. The owner or chief executive often inspires this but we have also found many others to be involved in this role. The importance of staff is that they not only facilitate relationship implementation but also embrace the future pattern of a business that incorporates the needs of customers and guidance and direction for the business. Three main groups have to be taken into account in the business:

- internal stakeholders – owners, managers, shareholders, unions and employees;
- external stakeholders – financial community, trade associations, government;
- market-place stakeholders – customers, competitors, creditors, suppliers.

The constructive involvement of all three groups should result in a balanced, composite statement of intent but the evolving nature of business will force change on this statement.

The need for staff training and development is crucial. We use the relationship ladder idea to demonstrate the escalating commitment involved in relationship building between staff (Donaldson, 1990; Christopher et al., 1991; Stone and Woodcock, 1995) (Figure 7.2).

Relationships develop by moving from some form of initial contact, usually at a personal level, at the lowest rung, towards a business partnership and relationship development, at the top of the ladder, where the customer becomes an advocate for the firm. At level one, the first stage in a relationship, the task is to build personal trust and bonding between the parties. This will normally be done through an individual salesperson and a buyer, but may involve other parties such as engineers, designers or operations personnel. Alternatively, it may involve customer service personnel on the telephone. Initially the customer is a suspect or unqualified lead who could conceivably benefit from the product or service. When this need is made explicit and the suspect has confirmed their ability to purchase they become a prospect. As the customer moves up the ladder they become aware of your company, your offer and your personnel. Prospects only become customers

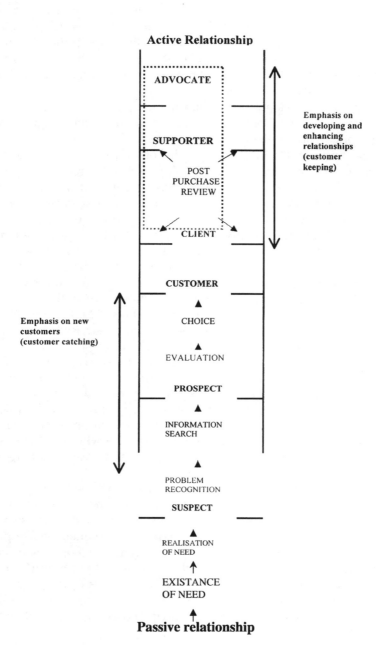

Figure 7.2 A 'multi-dimensional' relationship marketing ladder of customer loyalty (authors original: constructed from ideas from Donaldson, 1990; Christopher et al., 1991; Stone and Woodcock, 1995).

when they buy from you. Some customers may buy only once while others may purchase repeatedly as well as buy from a competitor. Customers who are loyal to your company become clients who not only purchase regularly but also open a dialogue and build a relationship. If this generates positive word-of-mouth then the customer becomes a supporter and will favour you as a supplier on several levels, buying across categories and seeking alternative services from your organisation. At the top of the ladder the customer becomes an advocate, encouraging others to do business with you.

A key ingredient in relationships is acknowledgement that a long-term relationship is desirable to both parties and to match the requirements of the buyer in terms of product, price and service with the capability of the supplier. For successful relationships, individuals must respect the other party, be confident that they will be treated fairly and that further development of the relationship is beneficial to both individuals and their organisations. At lower levels on the relationship ladder, relationships are personal, usually, though not exclusively, between the sales person and the purchasing executive. At higher levels, performance has more influence. If product quality, quantity, delivery time, price and credit terms operate as agreed and both parties perform as promised, then the relationship will continue and develop. The supplier can enhance the relationship by being pro-active in terms of suggesting new benefits. For example, an automatic re-ordering process may be installed which not only links the buyer to the supplier but also reduces the costs to both parties. Further, at this stage, supplier reliability confirms that confidence in the relationship has been well founded. By listening carefully to the buyers needs and being prepared to be flexible and responsive in meeting these needs, the relationship will be enhanced and developed. This level on the relationship ladder is one where performance on a number of agreed dimensions meets expectations. Hence, at this level, the relationship develops as a result of competence and performance by both parties, especially because the supplier keeps to these promises. This extends the relationship from the personal level to a more complex interaction between organisational members who become more familiar with each other, share the same values and aims and can resolve differences in a co-operative rather than an adversarial way.

At higher levels, both parties have experience of each other and are looking for further mutually beneficial outcomes from the relationship. This may be in the form of cost saving as a result of quality systems and processes. It may also be the result of joint negotiations and involvement on product development and improvements. This will be most productive when both parties agree to co-operate on commercial and technological dimensions to further the business to their mutual advantage. At this stage in the relationship the business of both parties grows by co-operation rather than operating as distinct and separate units. No formal linkage, as in a strategic alliance or joint venture is yet anticipated although this may become an outcome in the future.

Style

The analysis of the situation, as well as strategic process, is important but, as noted in chapter 4, there are different approaches to strategic planning. Similarly, there are different approaches as to how managers approach the achievement of their objectives. One approach is that in the world of business, management considers the environment and positions the firm and its strategy within it. Such managers are primarily rationalistic problem-solvers and are either 'doers' or managers of 'doers'. Therefore, from a supplier perspective, such people, in marketing, would favour the traditional approach aimed at manipulating the marketing mix to increase the effectiveness of the firm in winning over market forces. Such managers also favour a task-centred approach to their relationships with employees and generally would attempt to control their relationships with other stakeholders. However, these managers are rarely considered deep thinkers or originators of radical innovation.

A second approach is a more conciliatory style of management with an emphasis on conceptual thinking about management issues in an effort to find pragmatic solutions. The manger in this situation attempts to make things happen by aligning the organisation's efforts and by building good organisational behaviour to achieve their goals. One problem is that there are conflicts inherent in their position, for example, between meeting the needs and wants of customers versus the need to provide returns to shareholders or other paymasters. A second problem might be that no matter the good intentions true innovation in serving customers is sacrificed by 'me-too' competitive reactions. The threat of losing business may force companies to improve their relationships but only in a reactive way.

We are now adding a third dimension represented by a relationship-oriented culture, i.e. where the world of business is seen as achievable through co-operation. Relationships are multi-dimensional and stakeholders have various demands at different times. This may pose a problem and is why managers must build relationship competencies and aim to achieve their objectives in partnership with others.

Strategic action begins with a mission statement, which should not be a vapid platitude but an enduring statement of purpose that distinguishes one organisation from another. The mission statement is but one indicator of the importance of corporate leadership and top management commitment to, and involvement in, relationship-based management. Such a statement should encourage management debate to allow effective articulation of the organisation's purpose. It also serves as a device for ensuring that strategy formulation remains within the objectives of the firm and acts as an integrating philosophy to guide planning, the setting of objectives and performance evaluation. This is true for employee relations, customer relations and indeed, all forms of relationships that an organisation is faced with in its dealings.

The relationship-based organisation will be characterised by top management commitment to working with customers on a long-term basis. Such an organisation, faced with oversupply in end markets and softening demand, may prove more resilient to low-price competition. Firms pursuing new business have to prove superior in some competitive dimension and overcome the inertia between existing partners. Suppliers, defending their existing business and operating in a relationship mode where interaction between buyer and seller is of major importance, can only lose business. The supplier's objective, in this context, is to service and consolidate existing customers by preserving and expanding the volume of business. This means maintaining and reinforcing inertia, increasing co-operation and participation with customers and ensuring a favoured supplier relationship.

In business-to-business markets, to effectively manage relationships, particularly from a buyer or supplier perspective, both parties are required to establish rules which recognise the nature of their relationship. We have suggested that action and belief would be part of this process and that some rules of relationships can be established taking cognisance of environmental conditions. Relationships typically suit both parties but are not mutual admiration societies and often involve extensive negotiation, conflict and individual desire for a favourable outcome. The importance of relationship building is likely to be a function of the action component by both parties over time, based on such diverse areas as technology, risk, strategic positioning, fixed investments and switching costs. Business relationships are not the same as human relationships and the ideas of friendship, caring, support, loyalty, honesty, trust, openness and self sacrifice which have been found to be important in personal relationships (Duck, 1991), do not necessarily transfer to the same degree in business relationships. However, the key ingredient in both is belief that relationships, by representing win-win situations, are the way forward. Studies into organisational relationships appear to centre round co-operation, relationship commitment and trust, based on the anticipated benefits accruing from relationships (Morgan and Hunt, 1994). These benefits include shared values, similarity, open communication, a lack of opportunistic behaviour and lower overall costs. The emergence of relationships as the focus of our attention suggests that new ways should be found for organisations, at the individual and group level, to interact with each other.

Systems

As part of our research we have examined the influence of organisational variables upon exchange relationships (Tzokas and Donaldson, 2000; O'Toole and Donaldson, 2000). Our personal interviews with suppliers and customer firms suggest that management should direct its efforts in a number of directions, as illustrated in Figure 7.3.

We found evidence of mutual effort in the relationship plans that were developed between the supplier and the customer, and in ways that both parties involved themselves and evaluated the relationship over time. This included

Education and change of processes within the supplying firm
This embraces a relationship orientation throughout the organisation with close integration between different functional areas and relationship plans that allocate resources on the basis of the changing nature of the relationship in time.

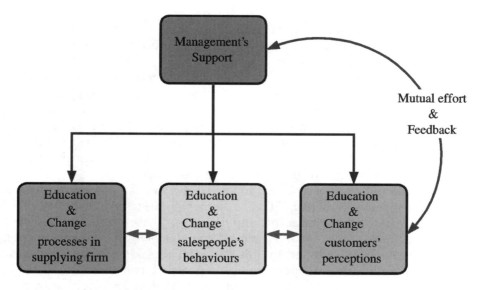

Figure 7.3 Management support for relationships.

Education and change of employee's behaviour

Contact personnel must be empowered and involved in the change process, rewards must be linked to mutually agreed objectives with customer input and training given in process based control, combined with transformational leadership into a relationship mode.

Education and change of customers' perceptions

We found a number of ways by which customers can contribute to the creation of the benefit they can get from the supplier. These are as follows:

- *Openness* – given trust, the more the supplier can understand the specifics of a business problem the better the solution they can offer
- *Setting mutual relationship objectives* – when relationship objectives of both the supplier and the buyer are mutually set and agreed the more the effort by both parties
- *Appreciation of the processes in the supplying firm* – the more the customers appreciate the different operational processes of the supplying firm the more they respect the terms set.

One way, we identified, for this appreciation to occur is through joint effort in the development of the relationship plan and a clear explanation of what the supplying firm is ready to do at the various stages of a business relationship alongside its expectations from customers. In addition, our study of leading edge companies identifies key activities firms should be undertaking to compete effectively in today's markets. These include:

1. Choosing customers. The traditional approach to winning business requires a radical re-think so that there is mutual benefit in the exchange process. Suppliers need to qualify their prospects, plan appropriate strategies for the business they do and manage the relationship.
2. Management must instil in their teams a relationship mentality incorporating best practices in co-operation and teamwork or, as it was put to us, an absence of politics in the organisation.
3. Reward systems must change to reflect the job that management wants done. If relationships are to the fore then individual incentives, especially financial incentives for salespeople, need to be replaced with performance bonuses based on the tasks performed and reflecting teamwork.
4. Global issues are a priority for global companies and a key output is for suppliers to exhibit, on behalf of their customer, knowledge of the industry in which they operate to capitalise on opportunities. These opportunities are increasingly across national and international boundaries. At the individual level, employees may be less affected by this issue but it is key in management support. The identification of opportunities capable of being replicated across customer groups is one of the most significant marketing opportunities in a firm's competitive armoury.
5. The sales plan is being replaced by the customer account plan, which in turn may be as significant, if not more, than the marketing plan. Customer account plans must include objectives for managing the relationship, using IT for competitive advantage and relationship enhancement, and in the continual search for organisational solutions that cement the bond between company and customer and vice versa.
6. Key dimensions of supplier performance include relationship productivity, relationship enhancement and the individual's capacity to act as a relationship manager.
7. Finally, in terms of industry focus, most of the research in relationship marketing has been conducted in an industrial or services setting. Indeed, while the relational view of business has been espoused in the fields of industrial and services marketing, it is not widely accepted in consumer markets mainly because the firm is dealing with many customers who, in many cases, remain anonymous to the firm. However, the assumption that relationship marketing is radically easier between companies or in service contexts than between consumers and their suppliers is open to question. We would argue, therefore, for more research in a consumer context and across industry sectors. The usefulness of our suggestion can be made clearer if one considers some of the recent technological advances in the field of telecommunications that allow an active interaction between firms and vast numbers of individual consumers (e.g. interactive TV, Internet, call centres and so on). Some of these issues will be addressed in chapter 8. Further research, taking account of these developments, would allow an exploration of the challenges and opportunities that new technologies impose onto relationship skills and their management.

Schemes

Relationship implementation requires that new activities and positions in the organisation come into place. The traditional sales department needs to be integrated into a relationship mode by combining marketing, human resources and operations that become more closely aligned with customers and intermediaries. This has generated a new area – customer relationship management (CRM). To be both customer-facing and efficient in back-office support is a major challenge in relationship building. The pressure to deliver better quality products, get them to market faster and keep abreast of technology is a key managerial objective. CRM applications cover pre-transactions, transactions and post-transaction activities. Pre-transaction embraces telemarketing, call campaigns and integrated communications using web-based sources, personal and traditional promotions. Transactions relate to order progress, order status, scheduling, and account and billing processes. Post-transaction activity include service support, customer profiling opportunity identification and relationship management.

The systems and software required, at all stages, must be supported internally within the organisation and externally with customers, regardless of channel or source, and viewed as part of efficient supply and service management. In addition to traditional face-to-face contact, the organisation will need to manage and integrate all telephone interactions, call-centres with computer-telephony integration (CTI), interactive voice recognition (IVR) and web-enabled callbacks as well as traditional mail, e-mail and fax communication. Order processing, account billing and order fulfilment have to be fast and accurate. Depending on the type of application, CRM requirements may vary between different organisations. One example may be where there is a highly automated front-office support for mass-market standardised products. In this case the cost of personal involvement is unlikely to be supportable. What is required is to simplify the product, service and information to deliver what is expected on time, accurately, with a minimum of variation. Customised software such as Siebel e-Business 2000 allows organisations to create a single source of information for tailoring products and service offerings to meet the unique needs of each customer. The result is an enhanced ability to satisfy customers virtually anytime, anywhere, through any sales or service channel.

Another example might be where there are complex products that require extensive distribution and considerable back-office integration, usually in the large, traditional organisations. Processing orders for complex products and services requires much more front-end support and usually a relatively high degree of personal interaction. Here, relationships are central to the operations.

An alternative way to view this challenge is to retain customers and build loyalty through some form of loyalty scheme. There are many ways to achieve this result but, at its heart, is how do you build and sustain a relationship with your customer and reward the customer for continuing to do business? This is one aspect of relationship management implementation in action. Various studies have confirmed the worth of retaining existing customers and the costs of churn on profitability (Reicheld, 1996; Peppers and Rogers, 1997). It follows that ways need to be found to continually re-enforce the relationship with the customer. For consumers, more direct incentives are often required. The most prevalent example of which is the loyalty card. Loyalty cards are really a misnomer in that they are often little more than a retention technique or another form of sales promotion. Nevertheless, their prevalence in many firms and industries demands that as a relationship implementation technique, they should be given some consideration. Tesco in the UK is perhaps the most successful example of this form of loyalty encouragement but its success is part of a wider customer relationship management programme.

The value of such a programme is that it is a new form of two-way communication between customer and company where information enables the organisation to become and act more customer-centric. The first step is to know the customer, then to understand their behaviour, to adapt this to suit communication with them and finally to regard and value them as customers. It has enabled data to be kept, which enables target marketing and a new dialogue between customer and supplier. This means that customers who value quality and service can be separated from those who value cost and simplicity. The information accumulated can be used to segment the market with a level of sophistication previously unheard of. Further, the objectives of knowing, valuing and responding to customers creates a superior value proposition. Tesco have 14 million customers per annum, this represents 650 million shopping baskets, 45 000 product lines at 700 outlets paying in five different ways. This data is of no value unless it can be used to enhance the relationship and increase the propensity to do business. So customers can be split between high spend customers and low spend, on the basis of life stage, on the basis of a typical basket of produce, on their promotional behaviour and on their brand advocacy. This information enables the relationship to be based on price sensitivity, on value, on share of purse, on own label versus brand loyalty and on the propensity to take up new products and new offers. Further, it offers new opportunities in financial products, travel and other services that hitherto were not seen as the domain of the supermarket, thus expanding the business.

Chapter summary

This chapter has reviewed what is required to implement relationships in different situations. Using the 5-S approach, key issues relating to specific aspects of relationship management implementation have been suggested. In terms of structure there are macro level solutions such as M&A, JV&A and out-sourcing. Internally, or at the micro level, from the many organisational suggestions, franchising, key account management and category management have been considered to reflect the need for organisational change to respond to relationship issues. Crucial to a relationship orientation is involvement of staff, at all levels, in implementing a relationship strategy. New structures, such as the relationship ladder, are important in being able to deliver this relational approach. In our view, a key to successful relationship management is to engineer new systems of the way the organisation interacts and builds relationships with a number of role partners. Finally, various schemes such as customer relationship management and loyalty schemes were introduced as examples of relationship management in action and will be considered in more detail in the next chapter.

ABB POWER AUTOMATION

Asea Brown Boveri is a global technology and engineering group mainly serving customers in the field of electric power generation, transmission and distribution. The ABB Group employs more than 200 000 people in approximately 1000 companies covering more that 100 countries. The main 1999 key financial figures are revenues $25 billion; return on equity 28%; R&D investment over $2 billion (8% of revenue).

Further information on ABB group world-wide is available on the website *www.abb.-com*.

The ABB group is divided into business segments, one of which concerns power distribution which focuses on the products, solutions and services to distribute electricity locally to end-users. The service includes business management software to operate electricity-trading systems and the main customers targeted are the utilities that bring electricity from high voltage substations to the end customer. The utilities 'manage the wires' and ABB Power Distribution delivers complete solutions, substations, power-lines, cables and infrastructure. The power distribution business unit aims to play a role in all electrification projects both new and retrofit for urban and rural utilities and industries.

With de-regulated markets in many countries and the search for productivity improvements there are growth opportunities being created world-wide by ongoing deregulation and privatisation. As the utilities focus on down stream end customers they are keen to work with partners such as ABB Power Distribution to improve the efficiency of existing electrical power systems, reduce cost and increase efficiency. The challenge for a utility is to develop their power systems while maintaining network stability at the time as network operation and maintenance cost must be reduced. The need for a distribution automation and management system is therefore addressed by this division.

Specifically, the technical areas the business would be involved in include secondary substation control, remote fault detection, location and switching, load management and quality and facilities management support. At the same time they may assist the utility with their demand side management in terms of load and tariff management, remote meter reading and pre-payment systems administration.

The main customer benefits would include:
– improved performance, reliability and quality of their power distribution network;
– lower outage penalty costs;
– more economic use of customers asses base;
– tariff control;
– reduction in asset expenditure and increased asset life;
– reduction of staff;
– future planning advantages.

Questions

1. You have been asked to develop a customer account team with a brief to prepare a

solution for a major utility company. Identify the personnel you would want on this team and the role each would play in driving a customer solution.

2. What issues need to be addressed for both attracting new customers and servicing existing ones?

3. Explain how you might grow this business by comparing market development options versus expanding the product portfolio.

4. From a sales perspective, how would you balance the emphasis between technical or commercial solutions for your customers?

5. What form of customer contact scheme would you recommend for ABB?

Further reading

Buttle, F. (1996), *Relationship Marketing: Theory and Practice*, Paul Chapman Publishing, London.

Christy, R, Oliver, G. and Penn, J. (1996), Relationships marketing in consumer markets, *Journal of Marketing Management*, 12 (1–3), pp. 175–187.

Corcoran, K.J., Petersen, L.K., Baitch, D.B. and Barrett, M.F. (1995), *High Performance Sales Organisations*, Learning International/McGraw Hill, New York.

Desatnick, R.L. and Detzel, D.H. (1993), *Managing to Keep the Customer*, Jossey-Bass, San Francisco, CA.

Furlong, C. (1993), *Marketing for Keeps*, John Wiley and Sons, New York.

Hartley, B. and Starkey, M.W. (1996), *The Management of Sales and Customer Relations*, Thomson Business Press, London.

McDonald, M., Rogers, B., and Woodburn, D. (2000), *Key customers, how to manage them profitably*, Butterworth Heinemann: Oxford.

Normann, R. (1991), *Service Management: Strategy and Leadership in Service Business*, 2nd edition, John Wiley and Sons, Chichester.

Payne, A., Christopher, M., Clark, M. and Peck, H. (1995), *Relationship Marketing for Competitive Advantage*, Butterworth Heinemann, Oxford.

Chapter questions

1. To what extent do you consider M&A or JV&A to be a failure by at least one of the party's to develop and sustain a business relationship? Give examples to support your argument.

2. Outline some of the benefits of out-sourcing. To what extent does a business run the risk of losing core competencies in search of these benefits?

3. Consider the factors that both buyers and sellers should take into account before accepting KAM relationships.

4. Why has category management developed so successfully in UK retailing? Suggest some controls and safeguards that may be necessary with one supplier such as Unilever controlling a category.

5. You have been asked by your MD to draw up a 2 day training programme for staff to enhance their relationship skills. What would such a programme look like?

6. Consider the mission statement of your organisation or an organisation of your choice. Critically appraise its relationship focus and suggest changes that would enhance relationship orientation throughout the organisation.

7. Using suggestions given in this chapter or devising new ones, specify key activities that management need to consider to transform an organisation into relationship mode.

8. Identify organisations that have loyalty schemes. Which of these do you consider to be most effective and outline the reasons why?

CHAPTER 8

Customer relationship management

Introduction and objectives

In this chapter, we explore the basic marketing relationship, supplier to customer, or what has been referred to as the classic dyad – the parent relationship (Gummesson, 1999). To date, most work on Customer Relationship Management (CRM) has focussed on database management, direct marketing techniques and customer relationship mechanisms. This has been most noticeable in business to consumer markets, especially services and financial services in particular. Many schemes, although not all, are little more than sophisticated selling. More developed programmes explore new ways to view customers and seek a single view of the customer in order to manage relationships more effectively. However, it is users who will define how CRM is applied and its effect on strategic market relationships. We should keep in mind that in our relationship world, sellers do not have full control from design to delivery over the systems in a relationship environment. Advice on customer management systems often implies that customers are passive or only involved through use of the system. It is our intention to demonstrate the impact that strategic market relationships can have on the way a firm operates in this prime relationship.

From the supplier perspective, a fundamental question for any business must concern the basis of their relationship with different role partners, especially buyers. Firms must choose the type of relationship appropriate to the product and market conditions in which they conduct their operations. Some buyer/seller relationships depend on technical performance and one party may be locked into a relationship, voluntarily or otherwise, due to technical dependency. Increasingly, customers can choose between technical options offering similar solutions. However, relationships can also be built on the functional aspects of a product or service. This entails how the service is delivered, the degree of support that is employed to enhance customer value and the effectiveness of the supply chain in meeting end user requirements.

Our purpose, in this chapter, is to reflect on how a product or service is supplied in a relationship context. This is where the customer is seen as an asset and can be highly involved in the company's offering. The way companies manipulate their sales and service system impacts on relationships. Credibility and customer bonding can be lost or enhanced at the point of sale or indeed in how we communicate.

In chapter 7 we built on our 5-S structure to identify managerial issues and in this chapter the focus is on the schemes and systems that can be used to explore the prime relationship between seller and buyer. Bear in mind that this relationship may depend also on the distinction between transactions and relationships as much as between technical versus functional quality. In our research, we found that, in

---

CASE ILLUSTRATION   **UK PRIVATE CLIENT STOCKBROKING**

During 1999, a considerable number of new stockbroking companies were launched. Some were created by existing stockbrokers but the majority were start-up ventures aiming to stake an early claim in what is expected to be a major market shake-up due to the combined effects of the following:

- anticipation that the Internet was fast becoming a viable and crucial trading channel;
- increasing financial sophistication of the public;
- stockbroking market changes, which have reduced the paperwork necessary for transactions.

Whilst the stockbroking market in the UK is expanding, the increase in provider numbers is growing at a faster rate and there are already signs of increased pressure on price and margins (Compeer, 1999). It is essential, for existing traditional stockbroking companies, to devise strategies that can see them through the struggle for business that is starting to occur.

The potential for relationship management has always been present but the opportunities within the private client stockbroking market have never been greater. To realise this opportunity, it is necessary to better understand what different clients are looking for in this business area. Until the early 1980s, the stockbroking market was perceived as a club. Membership of the London Stock Exchange was confined to individuals, not companies, and the individual members worked for stockbroking partnerships in a similar way to how law chambers still operate today. Owning shares was only for wealthy individuals who transacted via a stockbroking partnership.

The Stock Exchange motto was 'My word is my bond' and a trade was a verbal transaction undertaken on the floor of the stock exchange. It was once common practice for companies registered on the Stock Exchange to announce their results in their broker's office, allowing the broker's partners to advise their clients to buy or sell based on what would now be considered 'inside information'.

In 1986 we saw the arrival of the 'Big Bang' allowing companies to become Stock Exchange members for the first time. Stock Exchange partnerships were bought by the banks and became part of wider financial operations targeted mostly at corporate customers, pension funds and wealthy individuals. During the1980s, the market expanded with the privatisation of many government stocks. Beginning with the first sell-off, British Telecom in the mid 1980s, there has been a steady stream of government privatisations, which has been followed by another stream, generated by the demutualisation of building societies. This period changed the perception of stockbroking from that of a gentleman's club to an accepted form of investment and it is now very much a middle class activity.

The UK Private Client stockbroking market is the personal financial part of the UK Stockbroking market. This market comprises stockbrokers, fund managers in banks, private fund management companies and solicitor investment managers. Stockbroking companies conduct trades, with the wholesale side of the market (represented by companies such as Merrill Lynch) on behalf of private individuals who are known to them (known as Private Clients). Individuals who do not have a direct relationship with a stockbroker can still buy and sell shares but this is carried out via a third party (who has a relationship with a stockbroker) such as a bank branch or accountant. By the end of 1998, securities valued at a total of £290 billion were owned by UK Private Clients (Compeer, 1999). The state of the Private Client market is normally indicated by the ratio between share sells and purchases. A high sell ratio is considered bad as it indicates people exiting the market. This was the case during the peak of government privatisation, when the ratio of Sold to Bought was almost 2:1, indicating that the majority of people were disposing of their shares as soon as possible after acquisition. The UK market is currently in the middle of a 'bull' (upward) period with the sell/buy indicator now at 1:1.25. These means clients are adding to their portfolio thereby guaranteeing future trading activity. In 1999 commission/net revenue for the Private Client market hit £1 billion for the first time.

There are three primary relationships that Private Client Stockbrokers engage in. First, discretionary, which is the traditional fund management service, whereby a fund manager proposes and agrees an investment strategy with an individual client. The manager takes into account the individual's personal circumstances such as tax position, other (non-stock exchange related) investments, risk profile, personal ambitions etc. and market position and direction. Once decided, the strategy is implemented without further consultation. Progress is reported upon regularly. Wealthy individuals who do not have the time or inclination to carry out their own investment programme normally use this type of service. Members of Parliament may also use this service as it can be carried out 'blind' so they cannot be accused of Insider Trading on using and abusing government knowledge. This service is often, but not always, fee-based on the portfolio value. This relationship is high on trust and commitment and matures with time and experience.

The second type of relationship is based on the advisory service provided by the Broker. This service is aimed at a less-wealthy market or at those individuals who wish to take an active part in the investment programme. In this instance, the fund manager will advise the customer on the steps he should take and then, if agreed, execute agreed steps on his behalf. Trust is still high but the importance of the relationship can vary. The value of the client's portfolio will influence this relationship and the level of commitment to the relationship will be variable.

Third, is the execution-only service. This is the most recent type of service as the customer decides which shares to purchase or dispose of without personalised advice, and executes the shares through an order-taker on the telephone or, more recently directly via the Internet. With most execution-only services, the customer has access to limited stock-related advice but would have to take into account their own personal circumstances and risk. This service is only offered by stockbrokers and by clearing banks through their subsidiaries. Although there is still a degree of trust, belief in and commitment to the relationship is weak. In these circumstance cost to service will be a significant issue and here the move to on-line is greatest.

A stockbroker that is positioned to provide the top two or all three services is known as a full-service broker, whilst a company providing the lower end service only is generally termed a discount broker. The UK market for private client stockbroking is increasing steadily, in particular in the execution-only and discretionary areas, whilst advisory services stagnated temporarily in 1998 but resumed growth in 1999. In order to not simply survive but prosper, it is essential that stockbrokers take a strategic approach that can raise services offered out of the commodity level. Relationship management has never been more crucial in meeting this objective.

This case illustrates the possibility of using relationship-based management as a strategic defence in an increasingly impersonal, electronic business environment. Different scenarios could be drawn for business opportunities in this market. One view is that there may be a rush of high volume but low value transactions for an increasing number of customers, conducted electronically. This is unlikely to appeal to traditional brokers but if they are complacent then they may find that their business moves elsewhere. Traditional brokers who can improve the efficiency of their existing operations, yet offer real added value services, may be able to increase both volume and value. By offering specialist advice, a range of services and value for money, they will be able to manage a portfolio of relationships from electronic transfers to full service provision. To make relationships work, a supplier must place greater emphasis on service support to establish and enhance the relationship. This support is likely to require the integration of product quality with service quality and to reflect the supplier's competence.

Sources: Compeer, 1999; Deloitte and Touche, 2000; www.innovation.gov.uk

most cases, product quality and service quality should be combined to establish and maintain a strategic market position. In business-to-business exchange processes, strategy can be formulated by considering the behaviour of individual accounts over time rather than customers being members of markets or market segments. This is not always the case in the business to consumer world.

By the end of this chapter, the reader should:

- appreciate the managerial philosophy behind CRM and view this as an opportunity to develop meaningful and profitable relationships for both buyer and seller;
- realise the importance of business development, not just product development, with an emphasis on quality, people and customer dialogue;
- understand the need to support relationships and the importance of customer relationship management;
- be clear what is required to deliver customer satisfaction and sustain relationships;
- understand customer retention and customer loyalty in a relationship context.

The following case study illustrates that relationships have always been important but these do not stand still in a time warp. Today, the personal bond in relationships needs to be reinforced with new ways of working, incorporating streamlined processes and value for clients.

CRM implementation issues

In this chapter we re-visit the elements of relationship management from chapter 7 as they relate to the implementation of CRM practice. Several components that we have identified as important in the implementation of CRM are shown in Figure 8.1.

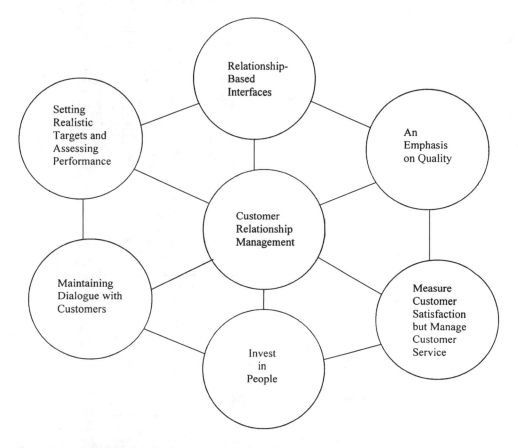

Figure 8.1 The components of customer relationship management.

Relationship-based interfaces

Most large firms, to be effective, need to act like a small firm. This means being in touch with customers, responsive, flexible and adaptable. Most small firms, to be efficient, need to achieve some of the economies enjoyed by large firms. This means lower purchasing costs, economies in scale for advertising and selling and cash resources to fund their plans for development and expansion. This is the modern business paradox. Our advocacy of a new order in management, based on relationships, is in part a response to the inability of large organisations to do what small

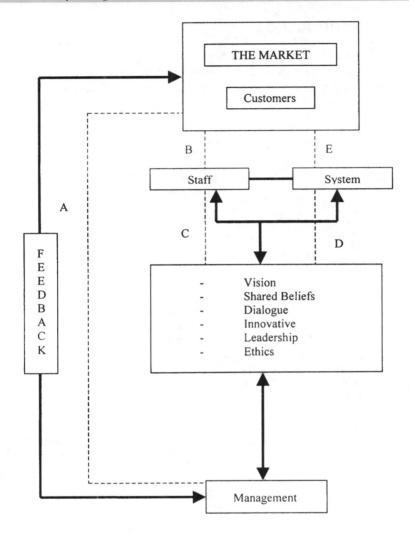

Figure 8.2   Relationship system interfaces.

firms must practice to survive. That is, keep in touch with customers, respond to the trends in the market and, in particular, to the changing demands of customers. Relationships can also provide a way for small firms to mobilise the resources enjoyed by large firms. In practice there is a gap between what firms do, what they should do and what is most desirable for any particular firm to do for any given market or group of customers at any particular point of time in their development.

We will use gap analysis to itemise some of the difficulties in achieving relationship objectives but this is the conflict between strategy and implementation. A firm's strategy can have a clear focus but management may be unable to execute their strategy in the way intended. One approach to this challenge is to adopt the idea of managing gaps in both the delivery and execution of relationship management as shown in Figure 8.2.

Gap A – the management-customer interface

As organisations grow in size, managers become less direct and less frequent in their contact with customers. Those relationships most important to the business deserve greater amounts of management time and attention but senior managers may deal directly with one or two key accounts and lose contact with others. However, as noted already, you cannot have relationships with everyone in the same way and to the same degree. Therefore, there is a danger of a lack of understanding by management of the gaps between an organisation and its customers. Senior managers must be aware of market trends and real customer needs and reflect this in their operations that can drive future business. Relatively low levels of customer contact mean that management must close this feedback loop with formal market research and other customer information-generating mechanisms. We have found that leading-edge companies, in service and relationships, are obsessive about knowing what their customers feel about their performance (Donaldson, 1995). Investing resources in market research, complaints procedures, help lines and management involvement at the front end are all exhibits of this obsession to improve the way they do things which customers value. On a more formal basis, the ideas of competitive bench marking and assessing best practice characterise the desire to be 'best in class'. At the heart of this is the simple philosophy behind a relationship-oriented business that involves the customer in the exchange process. For example, Cisco have a Director of Customer Advocacy Information Systems to ensure the voice of the customer is heard at board level.

Gap B – the staff-customer interface

The front line staff that are in contact with customers are often the lowest paid and least influential in company policy. Yet, staff must be aware of and understand the expectations and needs of their customers. Customers will often rate their supplier's performance based on their dealings with the staff they contact. Staff should be regarded as ambassadors of the company and they will influence the image the company has in the market. These may be retail salespeople, call centre staff, receptionists, delivery people or managers themselves. A professional approach, good interpersonal skills, an ability to communicate, positive attitude, good product knowledge and the 'smile factor' can all play a part in image and in customer satisfaction levels. To achieve this for low paid employees is a real management challenge and an important driver of the relationship organisation. As Tom Peters has suggested, staff who do not come into contact with customers need to realise that it is vital to support those who do (Peters, 1992). Taking as an example, Tetra Pak deliver over 200 million packages every day in over 150 countries. Based on three divisions for cartons, plastics and processing, each of these divisions works in partnership with 70 market companies to produces the best solutions. These market companies account for 70% of their 18 200 plus workforce. We return to this issue of employee involvement in relationships later in the chapter and consider ways to make it happen in organisations. Staff who understand the organisation's culture, are trained in how systems operate and are rewarded for superior customer service will make a positive contribution to performance by retaining profitable customers which far outweighs their training costs.

Gap C – the management-staff interface

The quality of the service offered by a company is only as good as the calibre of its staff. Recruiting the right people, training them in the culture and in the tasks to be performed, evaluating their performance and rewarding them appropriately, is basic good management practice. A participative and involved management style is likely to express this better than a dictatorial one, but a relationship orientation requires acceptance by subordinates that management believe what they say and that they are prepared to invest their time, money and effort to prove it. These basic leadership skills, all too common by their absence in many businesses, are highly noticeable by their presence in leading-edge firms. While the chief executive is often the most important and visible person in this process, we have found that this is also a key marketing role. The marketing manager will often orchestrate, match and manage the interaction of personnel in their own organisation with those of the buying organisation. Training staff to deal with customers also shows management commitment to their customers which, in turn, generates enthusiasm and commitment in subordinates. Often the best examples of people involvement can be found in high tech companies such as AMD. As a global supplier of integrated circuits their growth has been fuelled by its focus on customers and empowering employees. Their mission is to 'empower people everywhere to lead more productive lives'. The company manages its relationships internally and externally to realise this mission.

Gap D – the management-system interface

Systems that a company employ for order entry, order processing, enquiries and complaints, influence the customer's perceptions of the firm. These systems need to be user friendly not merely cost efficient. The design of systems should take into account how a customer will use that system in the exchange relationship. Many systems, particularly the adoption of new technology, have all too often been to suit the company and not the customer. A basic reason for adopting and installing new technology should be the positive effect it will have on inter-organisational relationships. 'Best-in-class' companies use new technology not only for administrative and operational convenience but as a source of strategic competitive advantage to manage better their relationships. IBM's partnership with Siebel reflects the importance of collaboration to effect better downstream solutions in CRM. By involving multi-channel partners they are combining web-based operations, with different distributors and partners across the world. Old and established relationships become reinvigorated by finding new routes to markets, different solutions and greater customer satisfaction and retention. These represent win-win solutions for customers, distributors and suppliers.

Gap E – the service-process interface

Managers must seek continuously to make improvements in their systems to enhance quality and service and to curtail costs. Traditionally, organisations employed work study techniques to make their processes more efficient. Today organisations find that open, flexible and customer friendly systems are required. This process requires management to understand how their systems work, to identify which tasks are to be performed and to enable decisions to be made at the lowest level possible in the organisation. This changes the role of manager from one of 'do-as-your-told' to one of advisor, mentor and coach. It changes the organisation from what its does for customers to what it does with customers and positioning the organisation within its supply chain. Nortel, with its delighting customers programme, has achieved new forms of relationships and ensured that all customer-facing processes are realigned/reengineered or tailored to customer specific requirements.

Efficient systems require the right atmosphere and surroundings. For many organisations this has a profound effect on their customer relationships. For example, banks and building societies spend considerable amounts on up-dating their premises to appear more user friendly and open than their traditional image had suggested. Care must be taken that these trappings are supported by a genuine managerial and organisational commitment to serving the customer better and to relational development. The glue holding CRM together is corporate vision, shared beliefs, internal dialogue, innovative leadership and business ethics.

An emphasis on quality

Fit for purpose and basic levels of customer satisfaction are no longer enough to secure, far less sustain, competitive advantage. To identify how well customers' needs are being met we need to understand quality differently. Many firms have been successful by being first with the right product or technology. Xerox became market leader with superior copier technology but this later became adopted and surpassed by others. As products become standardised, or offered to meet a specification, then cost may become the dominant factor. Cost leadership can be a significant competitive advantage such as Direct Line dominating the UK motor insurance market. However, both cost and product advantage are difficult, if not impossible, to sustain. Suppliers must focus on quality in a wider sense of the augmented product, including supporting services if they are to emerge with a competitive advantage in a specific market. Japanese companies in electronics and motor manufacture demonstrate such an approach but even here there is evidence that this too is difficult to sustain.

To gain a competitive position in a crowded market place, it is important to deliver superior added valued for customers via, for example, branding, style, perceived quality or after sales service that offers greater levels of customer satisfaction. With industrial products, training in effective and efficient use of products, product enhancements and up-grades, technical advice and support can be more important than specification and price (Donaldson, 1995). Service can be a major source of competitive advantage by customisation, adding value and enhancing the quality of the relationship. Poor service is the dominant reason for losing business. In one survey, 44% of customers changed suppliers due to what the customer perceived as poor core service (Keaveney, 1995). This has also been cited as the major reason for poor customer retention rates and low profitability (Reicheld, 1996).

Those who view service as cost incurring or limited to those activities surrounding distribution, concerned only with availability, speed, accuracy and other order processing tasks, are unlikely to be managing effectively their customer relationships. To the old style suppliers, customers were merely numbers to add to the production schedule. Not so now, where customers are not products of a system but individuals, groups and organisations seeking benefits from suppliers that enhance their own operations or consumption process. Success will be achieved by saying what you will deliver and delivering what you say. Buyers choose and retain those suppliers who offer the best value, as they perceive it, whether product tangible or service intangible. The best product, by itself, is no longer enough. As one respondent, an electronics supplier, put it "you might be the best manufacturer in the world but if you can't respond to customers' needs you are not going to survive."

However, suppliers must be cautious of using service as a lever instead of part of a sound relationship strategy. Customers may resent that over dependency if it reduces their freedom and the benefits are not significant to them. Hence, partnership is advocated where the result is a win-win situation but not with the objective of control or dependency. A service strategy must do three things. First, it must impact on the bottom line, second it must impact and count with the customer and third it must stay focused. Caterpillar developed its fast response times and unequalled reputation for after sales service around 1980 and it still provides a competitive advantage today because it meets these three difficult requirements. Recognising customers' servicing needs and finding innovative ways to satisfy these needs will provide greater opportunities to operate in relationship mode.

Historically, the focus on service enhancement appears to have evolved in line with the developments in relationships. First, customer service was seen as the area of physical distribution and logistics and when we ask buyers for their customer service priorities they tend to be narrowly defined in this area. Yet what appears to have been happening is the development of supply chain management and the impetus to deliver downstream superior customer value. A second stream emerged which placed service as part of the marketing mix and gave it wider scope, not least because of the emergence of service industries dominating the economy. Again, the link to the need for relationships in these types of businesses can be made. Following the pursuit of excellence by identifying criteria for business success, service moved to centre stage where it was seen to be a necessary ingredient in the corporate philosophy and mission of the business and drew buyers closer to their suppliers and vice-versa. Leading, well-managed firms perceive service quality as being central to their customer relationship strategy. Thus, service has itself followed a process of evolution which embraces the concept of relationship management in a wider context than traditional exchange processes.

Multinational or global companies are now enjoying scale economies, not in plant or production but in service capability such as marketing skills, financial services and global logistics. Relationships are part of this development because it costs less to serve repeat customers than it does newly acquired ones. Start-up costs are lower with new customers and word of mouth spreads a positive reputation which reduces costs. For these reasons it is tempting to be company-centric in relationship management but this becomes no more that sophisticated selling. What is required is new perspectives in organisational culture, embracing shared values and relationship orientation. Several questions then need to be asked about service operations. First, what services are valued by what customers? Secondly, how often are these services required? Third, how can they be supplied at lowest cost? Finally, what effect do these services have on our relationship with this customer and with others?

Product related factors

Consider first, product related factors. Intel have for some years pursued an advantage based on processor speed but often the perception of superiority in the brand is as important as real advantages. Therefore, a key aspect of the Intel approach is to work with customers such as IBM, Compaq and others to establish market credibility. Their technology is matched with customers relationships to provide downstream success in their supply chain. Firms will not survive with inferior product or price or not for long, and relationships are no substitute for competitive disadvantage. We have found that those firms with superior products are often those committed to serving their customers better. If you are committed to your customers you are also committed to giving them the best products on the market, a philosophy Intel, for example, consider sacrosanct.

Customer related factors

In addition to product issues, customer related factors must be considered. Driven by increasingly well-informed buyers, suppliers realise that customer-led solutions, whether product or service based, are vital as they create customer-led opportunities in the wider market. Vendor rating scales are a good example of customer led service because the buyer becomes involved in the process. Not only do these include reliability of delivery, complaint handling and ease of contact but service enhancements such as information on product usage, sharing proprietary information and giving advice on wider issues including market trends and product applications. This is the difference between a product offering and valued quality services.

Market related factors

Market related factors, especially competition, are often a driving force in customer relationship enhancement but being reactive is not enough. Firms must be proactive and innovative in service, not reactive and passive. When working with customers and intermediaries in growth markets, it is easier to win and retain business than in declining ones but relationships build market inertia. This creates a barrier to entry for competitors and is a sound strategy if a spirit of co-operation exists.

The product, customer and market related factors outlined above show a need to review the meaning of quality. The ideas of total quality management have been significant in improving the tangible product and the service support that add value to the total offering the customer receives. Quality commands higher prices in their served markets and can also reduce costs through less wastage and greater economies. British and International Standards require that organisations give consideration to the verification tasks required to deliver the product or service in accordance with the quality objectives which are either those prescribed by the supplier which are perceived as satisfying a market need or requirements prescribed by the purchaser. These standards also state that an organisation providing a product or service needs to meet the customers' expectations fully but in the most economical way. These requirements give additional and formal recognition to the importance of a relationship-based approach.

Increasingly, firms accept that a co-operative approach to trading is preferred to an adversarial one and performance ought to be defined and measured in expressions of adaptability and flexibility. It follows that one of the right things to do and to do well, is provide relevant quality service. To achieve this without sacrificing price and quality is the managerial challenge of today and the strategic importance of relationships is, in part, the result of the link between quality, marketing and service (Christopher et al., 1991). The outcome is that product quality and service quality should be combined to establish and maintain a strategic position whether pursuing market penetration, development or diversification strategies.

Total quality management (TQM) is also part of this process with its focus on continuous improvement and respect for people, exemplified by the Japanese *Kaizen* (continuous improvement). This embodies concepts such as learning, system and process development and innovation. A feature of TQM is cross-functional co-operation intra firm, with relationship building inter firm between suppliers and customers. This is part of an identified trend from traditional adversarial relationships to one that requires trust and mutual respect. TQM therefore promotes relationship building by bringing vendors closer to the buyer's organisation and its business activities.

Measure customer satisfaction but manage customer service

We have all experienced going to the cinema to watch a film highly recommended by friends, critics or others and being disappointed in what we saw compared with our prior expectations. Conversely, we have gone to see a movie with low expectations and come away entertained, uplifted, even exhilarated. Feelings about satisfaction with products and services are highly dependent on our prior expectations and affect not only the enjoyment of a film but a vast range of goods and services we purchase as consumers. Providers often underestimate the importance of consumers' perceptions about a purchase and it is important, for any enterprise, to understand and define the various benefits, real or perceived, that a prospect expects prior to purchase and how to manage the gap between expectations and performance during and after the purchase process.

After determining the type of relationship and developing an integrated organisation capable of delivering the appropriate level and quality of service, it is necessary to communicate what that level is to customers. An organisation that is confident about its service delivery capability can influence customers' expectations of its performance. It is imperative that only a level of service that can be consistently performed should be communicated. By influencing expectations, organisations can minimise the differences between what customers expect and what they actually get. Communication messages are not always easily controlled since messages to the customer concerning service quality arise from diverse sources such as telephone answering, literature, surroundings and so on, some of which result in signal confusion for the customer. Communications can shape customer expectations but all aspects of an organisation's communication output should collectively deliver a consistent and coherent message.

To repeat, in order to meet customers' needs adequately, we need to think differently about quality. Customers who have low expectations and receive average service have a greater degree of satisfaction than do those customers with high expectations who receive average service. So quality is often perceived as a function of the gap between consumers' expectations and their perceptions of what is actually delivered (Parasuramann et al., 1985). In relationship management, we need to move away from the win-lose mentality to a win-win model by both managing customers' expectations and delivering superior customer value. Product quality related to physical aspects of a product or service is capable of objective measurement by the customer but form only part of the customer's satisfaction. Areas such as advice, support and the quality of personal contact between buyer and seller may be of equal or even of greater importance. This quality is delivered most effectively in relationship mode.

Important in the satisfaction equation are customers' prior expectations of product or service performance and the confirmation or disconfirmation of expectations, resulting in customer satisfaction or dissatisfaction. Prior expectations are pre-purchase anticipation about a product's performance based on previous experience, word-of-mouth communications and marketing efforts. Confirmation of expectations is a result of product performance meeting expectations. Positive disconfirmation is experienced when service performance exceeds expectations, while negative disconfirmation occurs when service performance falls short of expectations. The first two of these possible outcomes will lead to customer satisfaction but the last will lead to dissatisfaction. So, we need to be concerned, not only with product satisfaction but also the customer's satisfaction with the organisation. This may be the core product, the quality of added services and the general level of satisfaction with the organisation and the relationship. This more holistic view of service and relationships as drivers of customer satisfaction can mean that even a well performing core product is not sufficient for a customer to rate quality as satisfactory, it has to be more than this. The product may be the hero but service is the star.

To manage this problem from a supplier perspective we can view relationships as part of a journey which begins with the customer searching for a suitable organisation and ending with follow-up after the transaction has been completed. On this journey there are many different 'moments of truth' which contribute to the customer's experience in dealing with the organisation and the customer may judge by the weakest point of that journey. Customers hold a mental report card of their experiences that the company needs to tap into and evaluate. The advantage of this approach is that it can be profiled for different types of customer and for different organisational communication. This overcomes the problem, identified in the introductory section, of how to manage different relationships for different customers, yet deal with the problem of inconsistency in strategy over both short-term and long-term horizons.

Investing in people

The gap analysis in Figure 8.2 highlighted, at several points, the importance of the people factor. Relationships internally are as important as and a precursor for external relationships. Implementation of a relationship orientation can only come from the people in the organisation understanding the objectives set and meeting the standards required. Many people within an organisation can affect different relationships with external role partners and members of staff must be aware of expected standards and especially customer needs. In service industries, Gummesson suggests that all employees are either full-time or part-time marketers, capable of influencing customer relationships which ultimately determine how successful the organisation is in the long-term (Gummesson, 1999). In other firms, e.g. shipbuilding, relatively few employees are in contact with customers, or need to be. Nevertheless, there is still a need for an integrated organisation which share the common commitment to quality and ultimately customer satisfaction. This has been referred to as internal marketing, focusing on treating fellow employees as internal customers and their jobs as internal products. Internal marketing has four main objectives:

(a) To help employees understand and accept the importance of interactions with customers and their responsibility for the total quality and for the interactive performance of the firm.

(b) To help employees understand and accept the mission, strategies, goods, services, systems, and external campaigns of the firm.

(c) To continuously motivate employees and inform them about new concepts, goods, services and external campaigns as well as economic results.

(d) To attract and keep good employees.

This extends the idea of the value chain backwards to the employee carrying out a task for an internal buyer prior to supplying your customer. Internal marketing, by striving to gain the commitment of employees, is a means of developing a corporate culture which places the customer first and sets out clearly the importance of relationships to the business. The management task, internal marketing, is to identify the service role that different individuals and groups of employees play and by emitting signals that reflect commitment and a service philosophy. Keeping employees informed, trained and rewarded for standards of excellence can achieve management objectives and competitive advantage.

Internal marketing needs to be formalised and managed if a company is to be effective in its relationships with its customers. This can be achieved at three levels. The lowest and simplest level is consistency, or the absence of inconsistency. This would mean, for example, that staff handling low price, no frills, products with minimum service support, operate efficiently and accurately. Level two is integration, where the service is compatible with customer requirements and the relative price and competitive position. At this level, staff must be adaptable and responsive to customers' needs. The third level is where the service exerts leverage on the purchase decision and the buying group. Staff operating here need higher level interactive skills which requires, not only the right people, but investment in training, staff participation and an appropriate reward system. Firms, some of whom may claim to be customer led, who reward staff on traditional output measures such as number of orders or sales value, are unlikely to be operating satisfactorily at this level. What is required is a reward system based, for example, on the number of customers retained and how satisfied these customers are with the service provided. Achievement at level three will place most firms way ahead of the competition. A fourth level, few firms attain, is the 'wow' factor when staff far exceed expectations and delight the customer with exceptional relational performance.

Maintaining dialogue with customers

In the days before mass marketing, the local bank manager knew the names and ages of his (for they were all male) customers' children, the corner shop knew which breakfast cereal to stock for local families and businessmen bought their suits from bespoke tailors. That has all changed with vast increases in the scale of operations, the quest for volume and profit growth with cost-cutting, rationalisation and automation. Many people never see their bank manager or even know their name, the corner shop has been replaced by the impersonal supermarket and most people make do or even prefer off-the-peg suits. Yet another metamorphosis is taking place. Information technology is making it possible for large organisations, with many customers, to personalise not only what they do but how they interact and serve their customers. Mass marketing and mass communication is being replaced with one-to-one communication and new forms of promotion and customer relationship building. Instead of focussing on efficiency alone, many businesses are realising the potential in customer service and relationship management as the basis for business growth and development. CRM has become a hot topic with the ability, if used intelligently, to transform organisations and win new customers and revolutionise markets. Like relationships it is not a panacea for all businesses but many organisations will have to embrace CRM or face loss of customers where others can offer new value-enhancing packages that traditional firms cannot match.

The benefits of CRM include:

- the ability to identify customers and their individual profitability;
- identification of individual customer's specific needs;
- tailored products to individual customer requirements;
- retain customers longer;
- cross-sell other products in their product or service portfolio;
- ability to identify new product opportunities;
- capability to target high value prospects.

These developments enable firms to take a more holistic view based on the lifetime value of a customer as a stream of revenue generation. This relationship is not only the value of current transactions but the opportunity identification based on a long-lasting relationship. Companies providing high levels of customer satisfaction, who delight their customers will retain them and be able to sell them more because they want to buy more from these firms.

The CRM approach, based on a new, individualised, one-to-one approach has been described as follows (Peppers et al., 1999):

1. Identify your customer individually as customer, not just transactions.
2. Differentiate your customers by value, then by needs to identify manageable clusters – most valuable, most growth potential, BZ's (below zero) – those you lose money on.
3. Every time you interact through telephone, letter, internet or face-to-face, capture and record the feedback and never ask the customer to tell you the same thing twice.
4. This information enables you to customise your service and provides a reward to the customer for collaborating.

As noted earlier, service and relationship orientation are linked by employees. Heskett demonstrates this in his model of the service profit chain (Heskett et al., 1994) and it is shown in Figure 8.3.

This approach is at the heart of good business where internal management,

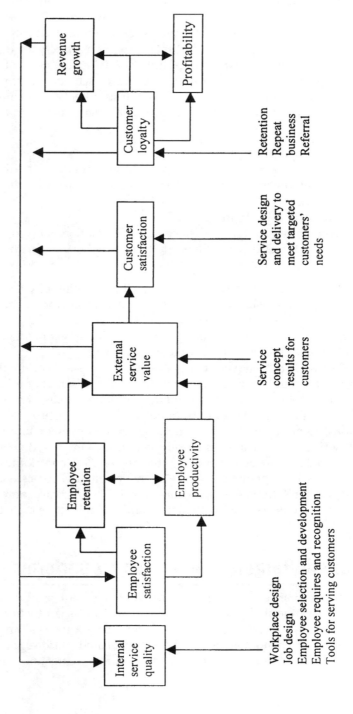

Figure 8.3   Links in the service profit chain (Source: Heskett et al., 1994).

process and systems are linked to external relationships. All parties benefit from the exchange and a matching between the offer and the customer is mutually agreeable rather than supplier-centric. Internal marketing can be extended to involve the customer as co-producer. It has been shown that for certain types of consumer product, for example reflex cameras and videos, that through better communication between supplier and customer, retention is likely to be higher and relationship quality is improved (Hennig-Thurau, 2000). This type of customer relationship management, unlike many loyalty card schemes (O'Brien and Jones, 1995), improves the relationship, not only the supplier's performance.

However, from a supplier perspective there are several benefits from effective CRM:

- more loyal customers;
- a higher share of customer spend based on understanding their needs;
- greater revenues can be shared with the customer who receives meaningful discounts;
- transaction costs are lowered;
- cycle times are reduced since new information is not required once obtained;
- the customer is more committed to doing business with a supplier who satisfies and delights them.

This creates a virtuous circle which links profitability to customer and employee loyalty and satisfaction. The complexity in a customer relationship management system can be daunting but no-one said it was easy. Figure 8.4 is one company's diagrammatic representation of CRM-enabling technologies. This shows that it is not only a vital but a highly complex process.

The need for innovation is pervasive and it is not confined to product or technology but extends to relationship innovation. CRM must find innovative ways to link with customers and involve them in different areas of the exchange process that create value. Profits come from customer relationships. The development of relationship marketing, broadening the customer contact, unbundling and rebundling of services to suit different requirements and increased enabling activity by customers taking an active part in the process, all contribute to the need for more complex management systems to ensure quality, consistency and customer satisfaction in relationships. The conclusion is that there are more intangibles, closer and increased complexity in interaction and an interactive logic between providers and customers.

Setting realistic targets and assessing performance

Strategic market relationships embrace the idea of service as a total business philosophy. Without doubt, relationships provide a competitive tool and a versatile concept that has important strategic consequences and opportunities. With advanced economies requiring sophisticated service and technology support, with more complex products, more out-sourcing and increasingly demanding

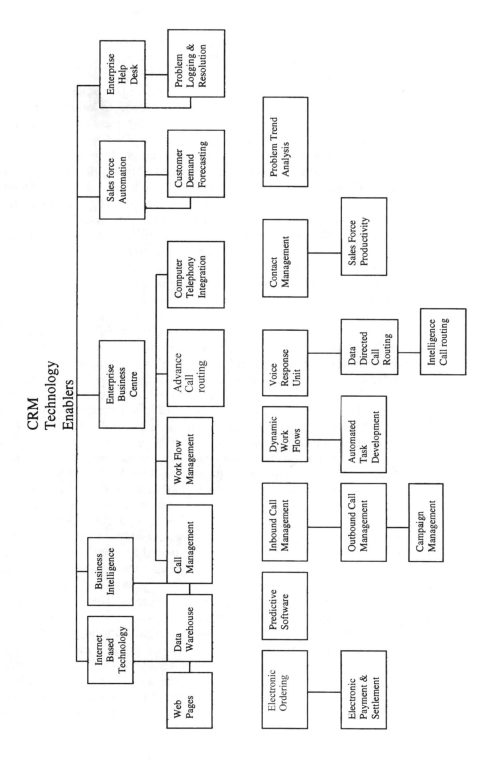

Figure 8.4   CRM in a multi-channel service business.

and discerning buyers, there is a need for a total customer care approach and greater relationship building between buyer and seller.

The relationship approach can be differentiated from any other business approach by its belief in satisfying customers as the number one priority, by investing resources to research markets and customers on a one-to-one basis and by taking a planned and joint approach to delivering customer satisfaction. At the heart of relationship management is service excellence. In most companies, a customer focus is strongly emphasised in their corporate mission or vision statement, e.g. Proctor & Gamble, Wellcome plc, Whitbread plc, Toyota, Tesco, etc. In these organisations specific personnel, departments and considerable resources are allocated to the service support areas of the business. This importance is confirmed by the number of seminars, training courses, practice manuals, textbooks and journal and newspaper articles, which have appeared in the last decade on the importance of being customer driven and how to implement customer care programmes. But it is important that this approach does not become empty rhetoric. It is a management activity and as such should be realistic and measurable.

Research on performance in relationships is still at an embryonic stage but many studies are now confirming that, in different contexts, relationships do pay. This has been referred to as the return on relationships or ROR (Gummesson, 1999). Part of the difficulty in measurement is to agree measures suitable for both parties. Sales, profits, shareholder value are all seller-centric suggesting, by definition, a win-lose relationship rather than a win-win. So far, we are capable of measuring customer satisfaction, customer retention and loyalty but are these appropriate for long-term relationship performance? For example, most firms measure customer satisfaction which we define as a measure of customer responsiveness to marketing stimuli in a given competitive environment. Customer satisfaction measures, e.g. very satisfied, satisfied, not very satisfied, not at all satisfied, are indicators but as a concept, satisfaction is not unidimensional and consists of various elements that may be different across customers. Satisfied customers often lead to repeat business and referrals which both greatly contribute to long-term profitability but studies show that satisfied customers are not always loyal (Naumann and Jackson, 1999).

Alternatively, customer loyalty can be used as a measure of relationship performance as it is a measure of repeat purchase probability. Unfortunately, repeat purchase does not, by itself, constitute a relationship. A customer may be loyal because of an absence of alternatives, a reality that many former public utilities are now experiencing. In today's competitive markets, consistently higher levels of satisfaction are required to drive customer loyalty, as shown in Figure 8.5.

While it is important to be aware of the difference between customer service, customer satisfaction and customer loyalty, all these aspects, important in relationships, should be monitored and measured. Organisations must have an understanding of what customers think about the different elements in its offering. It must then find out which elements are important to each customer. This is why the prime relationship can be enhanced by improved customer relationship management. CRM is not an alternative but a complement to the effectiveness of a business in delivering customer satisfaction. The firm can then redirect its efforts to real

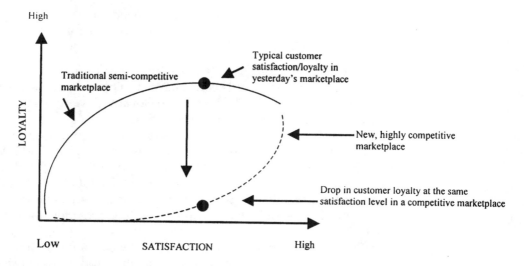

Figure 8.5   Loyalty vs. satisfaction.

customer needs and this has beneficial economic consequences. Reicheld (1996) refers to this as the loyalty-based cycle of growth, as shown in Figure 8.6.

True loyalty comes from a strong brand and the relevant market proposition combined with superior products, services and delivery. Accurate measurement provides factual information on which to build broader, deeper, long-lasting and more profitable relationships. We will return to relationship performance issues in

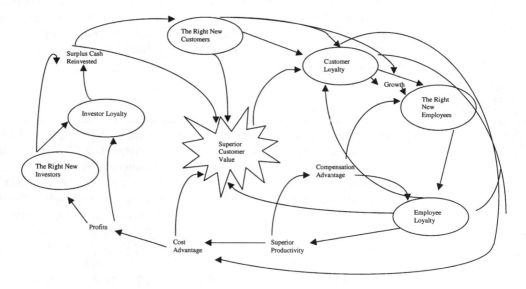

Figure 8.6   The loyalty-based cycle of growth (Source: Reichheld, 1996).

chapter 13. Key performance indicators must depend on the company, product and market factors relevant to that particular business but the following hard measures might be helpful as a checklist:

- Employee churn – if we are to walk the talk and ensure our people do matter, this is a crucial measure. Some call centres have employee churn factors in excess of 50%. Best in class is around 7%. If employee loyalty drives customer loyalty then this measure may be the most important of all.
- Customer churn – 100% loyalty from customers is, for most businesses, unrealistic and even undesirable. However, for those with a large and diverse customer base, a churn factor above 20% is likely to indicate a problem, although changes in the level may be a better guide than absolute levels in this measure. Remember too that higher value customers and those you choose to invest in relationships with should have a more exacting retention measure than the average.
- Share of customer – while revenue and profit by customer is important, a more significant measure is share of customer in the product categories than you compete in. Loss of customer share to competitors is serious. Product penetration or density targets should be set by customer.
- Lower processing and transaction costs – vicious circles of spiralling costs and increased churn should be replaced by virtuous circles which reduce costs and increase customer satisfaction.
- Higher margins and revenues – as relationships strengthen and deepen and more products are sold per customer, margins improve. Relevant to this is reinforcement of the brand or company loyalty figure.

CRM has been proved to improve supplier performance, enhance relationship quality and provide real benefits for customers. It can also offer, through information technology, new business models that change the buyer-supplier relationship in both business-to-consumer and business-to-business markets. Our end of chapter case can confirm this proposition.

Chapter summary

Nothing is more important than retaining existing customers, increasing the business they do with you and attracting new customers. It follows that CRM is not a passing fad but a key driver of business performance. This chapter looks at the gap model to identify key linkages between suppliers and customer or end user. Gaps exist between management and customer, management and staff and management and systems. Whilst staff and customer and staff and systems can also create problems these are also important management implementation issues. Leading firms focus on quality and embrace customer centric approaches to their products and markets. While customer satisfaction is an important issue, management activity must focus on drivers of customer's satisfaction rather than customer satisfaction itself. Leadership, coaching and commitment by management to reflect customer-based solutions are required. CRM benefits are clear and on an individualised, one-to-one approach is reflected in high retention rates and improved profitability. Key performance dimensions in CRM have to be measured and monitored.

POLAROID

Polaroid's name is synonymous with instant photography. The company enjoyed a long period of market domination as their unique process was patent protected but the technology and the market have moved on with digital imagining and processing and fun photography now key influences in a fast changing market place. Polaroid's traditional market was the professional user such as portrait photographers, scientists, doctors, valuers and estate agents looking for quality, immediacy and a specialised service. With a strong, dedicated sales force the company were committed to product, service and their existing customer base. Market and competitive changes have undermined this approach, first, as digital cameras become more affordable they threaten the traditional domain of Polaroid photography. In the passport photography sector, customers now have a range of suppliers offering a relative standardised product led by Fuji and Kodak. Gone are the days when Mr Land, the founder of Polaroid, could tell his engineers: "we don't have to do our own market surveys, we make our own markets." (Klein, 2000, p. 24).

The company's reaction to these changes has been interesting. They have implemented new product lines targeted specifically at young consumer groups and attempted to capitalise on the Internet by linking their products with others, redefining the company image and streamlining their business operations. In terms of new products they have focused on young buyers with a range of cheap, fun-based products that redefine photography as part of a dynamic life style. These products include *BarbieCam* targeted at young customers with decorative borders, *JoyCam* aimed at students and teenagers to make customer-tailored photographs and the *I-zone* instant pocket camera mainly targeted at teenage girls incorporating the ability to link photographs to documents, objects and, in particular, customise web sites with a 'where will you stick it theme' (Advertising Age, 2000). All of these developments are aimed at the young, fun and leisure market, rather than the professional user but the products will have a comparatively short life cycle.

Although not abandoning their traditional customer base whose purchase criteria were predominantly quality, these new, young customers require cheap and cheerful images reversing the requirements of traditional users who are now embracing digital imaging rather than print photography. The need for the traditional quality and service is less and less affordable. Similarly, these new types of product demand new retail outlets, different packaging and new forms of point-of-sales promotion. Products, channels and promotion needs to be constantly reinvented and repositioned to a fast changing market place. Recognising these issues, Polaroid has joined force with G&A Imaging in Canada to offer WebBadge which designs and creates personal identification badges which can then be printed as ID cards. Customers can use their own designs and choice of templates. This collaboration offers access to smaller customers and a new market and customer base, previously too costly to serve by personal selling.

Other types of collaboration aim to widen Polaroid's market share in the digital sector such as their collaboration with Olympus who provide the cameras and Polaroid the printer and paper. Such partnerships will become more frequent because they minimise risks and lower development costs while potentially speeding up the development process. Competitors become collaborators and offer wider market access and different product applications. For example, Polaroid are now in the office products market, in a venture with Avery Dennison, to provide photographs in folders and other applications.

Along with these product developments and new business relationships, the company is working to reduce transaction costs. Using e-commerce for business-to-business customers and only large dealers and wholesalers for more traditional markets, their efficiency in distribution and supply has improved. The company organisation has also changed with the traditional structure replaced with out-sourcing of finance, customer service and logistics. Marketing and sales processes have been realigned but the efforts to reduce costs have not been without customer resistance and an increase in customer complaints about deteriorating service levels.

Questions

1. What internal relationship changes do you envisage need to be made within the organisation to reflect the changing emphasis on fun, life-style products.
2. The key benefit that the company offers customers is 'instantaneousness'. Do you feel that this has helped or hindered its product development strategy?
3. The types of new products currently being developed and brought to market are fashion-based with only short life-cycles anticipated. How can strategic market relationships assist the organisation in this respect?
4. Critically assess the streamlining aspects of the Polaroid strategy. In particular, attempt to reconcile the conflicting demands of lower transaction costs with increased service demands. What practical solution can you offer for this managerial dilemma?

Further reading

Anton, J. (1996), *Customer Relationship Management*, Prentice-Hall, Englewoods Cliff, NJ.

Christopher, M. (1992), *The Customer Service Planner*, Butterworth Heinemann, Oxford.

Cram, T. (1994), *The Power of Relationship Marketing*, Pitman, London.

Griffin, J. (1997), *Customer Loyalty: How to Earn it, How to Keep it*, Jossey-Bass, San Francisco, CA.

Lash, L. (1989), *The Complete Guide to Customer Service*, Wiley, New York.

Lele, M.M. and Sheth, J.N. (1991), *The Customer is Key*, Wiley, New York.

Stowell, D.M. (1997), *Sales, Marketing, and Continuous Improvement*, Jossey-Bass, San Francisco, CA.

Winer, R.S. (2001), A framework for customer relationship management, *California Management Review*, Vol. 43, No. 4, pp. 89–100.

Chapter questions

1. Clarify the differences between customer service, customer satisfaction and customer loyalty.
2. Conceptualise the meaning of service quality. Using an example of choice show how it can be used to improve and manage relationship performance.
3. Select two examples, one where electronic transfer is more important than personal relationships and one where personal relationships are more important. Justify your selections.
4. Consider some of the specific measures and rewards that can be used to motivate people within the organisation to improve relationship performance.
5. Using one consumer tangible product and one industrial tangible product as examples, discuss whether product or service quality is more important to the customer.
6. For a product or service of your choice, identify specific aspects of poor service and suggest ways to correct the problems and recover the relationship.
7. You have identified a problem in the management-staff interface within your own organisation. What action would you take and why?
8. Your manager has asked for suggestions to implement a CRM system in your firm. Outline the proposal and highlight the benefits that you would expect to achieve with such a system.

CHAPTER 9

E-relationships

The objective of this chapter on e-relationships (electronic relationships) is to examine the impact of information technology (IT) on relationships. Given the pace of technology change, this chapter is probably out of date as you read it! However, the ideas and frameworks in the chapter and the core research questions will be slower to change. IT has had a huge impact on business in general but also has had major effects on the nature of how partners interact. These relationship impacts are the focus of this chapter. Information rich exchanges can be made at the touch of a button. Companies have been able to mass customise their products by selling them on the Internet. Organisations can use virtual transactions to maximise value, for example, finance people in organisations with large cash balances at the end of a day's trading can electronically lodge these balances with their bank to gain from overnight interest rates. Whole supply chains are interconnected by technology. Technology, through the routinisation of many operational processes, has minimised conflicts that arise with individual transactions, for example, product availability and delivery can be checked on-line. These are among some IT effects on relationships. Each core relationship variable has been in some way affected by technology. Its impact is pervasive. The chapter is entitled e-relationships to recognise the impact the Internet is having on relationships. Traditional inter-organisational systems (IOSs) are being transferred to the Internet. For example, in 2000, both Ford[1] and General Motors[2] announced the switching of their supply management system from electronic data interchange (EDI) to the Internet (Ford's system is Auto-Xchange[3] and GM's TradeXchange[4]). The attraction of the Internet over traditional IOS is its openness, flexibility and low cost. The sites can be accessed if a partner is connected to the Web. The impact of e-relationships is also seen through the effect e-mail is having in creating bonds across organisations and between individuals who otherwise would not communicate.

The e-relationship title is also apposite given the ongoing focus on the wider issues involved in electronic commerce. It is argued that e-commerce is changing market structures and the economics of competition. It is difficult to argue against this. For example, we see entertainment, media, telecommunications and Internet companies merging to create new ways of delivering communications and enter-

[1] *www.ford.com*
[2] *www.gm.com*
[3] *www.auto-xchange.com*
[4] *www.gmtradexchange.com*

tainment. The dot.com phenomenon has become a feature of most businesses. The fact that the e-commerce revolution will continue makes it necessary to focus on the electronic in relationships.

The chapter will examine the information technologies that impact most on relationship management. The Internet and databases are core here. We will also assess the value added by IT in relationships and argue that it can generate significant operational efficiencies through automation but to make relationships closer requires deeper inter-organisational commitment and responses to technology. Most companies have not used technology to transform their relationships.

After reading this chapter you should know:

- IT's role in relationships;
- how IT has developed over time in relationships;
- the managerial challenges to implementing IT in relationships;
- what academic research themes have been developed in IT and relationships, and have a critical appraisal of past research;
- the core e-relationships technologies in use;
- the value potential of e-relationships through communication and information.

The introductory case study focuses on the development of on-line relationships. In particular, that the growing power of virtual communities can act as a counterpoint to a company's activities, as the communities' sharing of information and developing of social bonds creates a new power base with which a company must deal. Internet communities may be giving consumers, who are relatively removed from each other, a new power base from which to negotiate with a company. Generally, organisations should pursue mutual information sharing with these communities as the preferred strategic route as it is nearly impossible to control who interacts with whom and the level of detail and emotion involved, so perhaps being proactive represents the only way to move forward with this channel.

CASE ILLUSTRATION   **ON-LINE RELATIONSHIPS**

The Internet is facilitating a whole new range of relationships. Consumers are able to form interactive special interest groups or virtual communities, employees can do the same thing, and members of a supply chain network can deepen and foster social connections between participants using Internet technologies.

Computer-mediated communication is a growing phenomenon. Previously, individuals or groups that were separated by physical or geographic boundaries or who simply did not know about each other can now find one another and create special interest groups on the web. These groups can be general or specific to a company's products and services. These new groups are creating relationships that need to be managed by companies. Virtual communities can develop strong social bonds by higher levels of interaction, i.e. by posting information on the web, responding to others, and participating in on-line discussion groups. A typical response by companies to the information seeking needs of their consumers is to transform advertising to be focused on gaining consumer attention on-line. For example, eyewear manufacturer

Bausch and Lomb[5] site was used as a competition site for an on-line 'the eyes have it sweepstakes' that involved on-line consumers in a trivia game in which they could win a cruise. In the course of the games players learnt more about Bausch and Lomb's products and revealed information about themselves.

The on-line world may create mechanisms for groups, especially consumers, to admire companies but also to resist and challenge them. Virtual relationships work both ways. This was particularly felt by Fox Broadcasting in the US when they tried to limit unofficial and free homepages dedicated to the Simpsons[6] by fans who were using the company's characters, music and symbols. Fox issued letters asking the sites not to use their material. Fans reacted on-line and organised a boycott of merchandise. Fox retreated from its actions. Trying to protect brand identity but to provide meaningful information to virtual communities is a challenge. Harley Davidson decided to host its owners' group (HOG)[7] web site for this reason. Software companies often allow their new product to be downloaded from the web for testing purposes. They gain a set of testers and enthusiasts for free.

Internet users often start with an impersonal search for information but will become more interactive when they discover groups who have similar consumption patterns and behaviours. The depth of experience and emotional devotion grows over time. Newsgroups are often used to discuss product attributes and worthiness of new product offerings making honesty and integrity of approach important. For example, coffee lovers exchange information on taste, source of supply and best ways to prepare coffee on special news sites. There are a huge number of sites devoted to interactive discussion on coffee, for example, smellthecoffee.com[8]. This type of empowerment was difficult in the anonymous world of the mass market and was limited to a few friends who had the same tastes. Now there is no limit to the number of people and types of interaction. By pursuing an open information strategy, companies can benefit from subtle lifestyle and psychographic research which they would never collect on a traditional database. Other examples and theories (which are becoming more common) on virtual communities can be found in Venkatraman and Henderson (1998), and Kozinets (1999), or in the now classic book by Hagel and Armstrong (1997).

Employees and trade unions can also create communities using the Internet. So too can members of supply chain networks. The nature of information flows between these groups using e-mail to date would indicate significant inter-group norm formation. The Internet is bringing people together who can organise cheaply and effectively to demand attention. Yet they can become the most loyal advocates for your business or can continue as a particular social network that the price paid to manage them could be worth it. Often company formed networks are task-based initiated by companies to solve problems but can also function as information and communication networks.

Federal Express[9], the US postal and logistics company, is positioning itself as the transport infrastructure of the web. It is aiming to become a core logistics partner to many organisations needing web enabled distribution. FedEx is seen as a partner that is part of the promise of its partner customer, supplier, and buyer organisations. Part-

---

[5] *www.bauschandlomb.com*

[6] *www.thesimpsons.com*

[7] *www.hog.com/home.asp*

[8] *www.smellthecoffee.com/community/chat/*

[9] *www.fedex.com*

nership enabled by web technologies cross competitive and geographic boundaries and have allowed 'best-in-field' companies to co-operate regardless of location. Few supply chains have remained unaffected.

Internal organisational relationships have benefited from Internet technology development. Key people who contribute to core company processes, regardless of function and location, have been able to co-operate for improvement using shared databases and high intensity communication networks. Consulting organisations such as Arthur Anderson[10] (now Accenture) and KPMG[11] are sharing project knowledge across their different locations to encourage in-company learning, knowledge transfer, and to speed up the learning phase of new consulting projects. They have created virtual practice libraries and information resources.

[10] www.accenture.com
[11] www.kpmg.com

The development of IT in relationships: research and practice

This section of the chapter will assess IT's role in relationships, how it has developed historically, present a critique of IT and relationship research, and outline the relationship management challenges of e-relationships.

IT's role in relationships

Information and communication technologies are having a profound effect on how business operates. Boundaries between businesses, cultures, countries are been made easier to cross with the developments in information and communication technologies. The marriage of both information technology and telecommunications, hereafter referred to generically as IT, has enabled firms to construct 'extended enterprises': firms without common ownership (Konsyski, 1993), or partnerships without ownership risks. IT has made partnering easier as co-ordinating information and communication flows have been made more accurate and free flowing (Buzzell and Ortmeyer, 1995). Instead of waiting for a customer service person to try and check the status of your order you can get the information direct from your partner's system. Federal Express, for example, allows automatic tracking of parcels by giving customers personal identification numbers to access the information from its system using the Internet. This type of use of IT creates many operational efficiencies as often there are frustrations in relationships caused by information and communication deficits. Benetton, the subject of the end of chapter case, is one such company who relies on a huge network of small suppliers linked to the company's highly efficient logistics system with a closely co-ordinated information system. From design to co-ordination, Benetton is reliant on IT to co-ordinate what is a network of vertically integrated partners.

IT's use in relationships has grown due to its multifaceted advantages in co-ordination. It has lowered transaction costs by making routine transactions electronic, thereby saving costs in order inputs, tracking, and invoicing. Holding stock has also been reduced as IT has facilitated matching individual items to demand more closely. IT controlled manufacturing systems have facilitated small runs and greater customer responsiveness. Demand management between manufacturers and channels using IT has made forecasting more accurate with attendant cost savings. Supply chain co-ordination has yielded dramatic savings from IT. Changing products and services through IT design has improved time to market with new products. We almost take for granted the effects of IT on relationships. Indeed, IT has created many new business relationships and has facilitated businesses to exploit their existing relationships. For example, supermarkets chains like Tesco have been able to exploit their brands by moving into financial services. Tesco Personal Finance had more than 1.5 million customers in 2000 with its own credit card and ATM machines. In 2000, it also launched an Internet mortgage supermarket. The Virgin brand, coming from a different industry, has also invaded the financial services business. Both companies used IT to set-up a market, traditionally seen as complex, but demystified by IT. Brand power has become a potent weapon in the e-relationship age.

Of course e-relationships can also be argued to depersonalise a relationship. This may be the challenge – to add personalisation to an IT relationship communication. For example, the Internet will enable companies to present their brand personalities in a more integrated way when compared to the limited message range available in traditional media. IT will also permit a fragmented consumer group to create virtual communities around products and services on the Internet. The creation of Internet markets can transform traditional marketing and distribution activities. There are no longer market places per se but market spaces within which partners interact. Potentially even high cost items such as cars could move to direct Internet sales transferring service and car dealers' responsibilities to the Internet. Carmakers such as Daewoo have begun such a transformation of distribution. Daewoo were the first carmaker to sell direct. Obviously companies with direct marketing expertise should have an advantage when it comes to the web. The consumer meanwhile will be able to validate web information by visiting independent newsgroups to check pricing and company claims. Establishing creditability in virtual interactions will be a central objective of all marketers in the future. If the car market became direct then car distributors might loose identity in consumer markets but many of the traditional distribution tasks will still have to be performed such as wholesale, service and transport (the loss of distributors or other intermediaries as a result of e-commerce is known as disintermediation). They may have to take on a business-to-business role. However, the efficiency of scale and speed of responsiveness may separate winners from losers. New types of intermediaries will also evolve who sort information and bundle our needs and wants on the web. They will act as 'hubs' to buyers and sellers. They will function as service rather than physical distribution companies. Hubs can also be called portals or search engines, for example, such as those of Yahoo.com or thebighub.com[12].

---

[12] *www.yahoo.com; www.thebighub.com*

None of our inter- and intra-organisational relationships will escape the potentially profound impact of IT. Interfunctional relationships can be strengthened through sharing information using intranets (an internal information system using Internet technologies to electronically share information among organisational members). Employee relationships to company can now include an emphasis on family life through the growth in home working or telework made possible with high speed connectivity through ISDN (high speed and thick content telephone connection). In addition, relatively new versions of mobile phones using WAP (technology that facilitates mobile phone users to access, interactively, information services including buying goods and services such as, for example, an airline ticket, using the web) technology will decrease costs of field sales communication to base. Field sales forces will be able to access vital information from computer systems using the mobile telephone. Consider the co-ordination effects of IT on the multinational corporation. Multi-site and multi-country and cultural interactions have grown in frequency and intensity. For example, video conferencing has enabled multi-country and cultural teams to function from different locations. These are but some of the relational effects of IT.

If we move to the micro level and assess IT's effect on the relationship variables outlined in the early part of the book, a similar impact will be evident. A weak member of a channel can increase its power by capturing more of the value added of another channel member, thus making itself more critical. For example, a small supplier might capture product design work as it can get the information needed to do this work electronically. IT can impact on trust. Sharing of information in a timely fashion can reduce relationship problems in areas such as order processing, customer service, investor updates, employee communications. Technologies such as e-mail can provide for richer and more diverse and dense communication across organisational boundaries. On the negative side, it is more difficult to control who and what is communicated across organisational boundaries. If multi-level electronic communication is permitted it requires internal and external trust. As outlined, most of the everyday interaction between relationship partners is impacted by IT. From product design to payment all can be, at least, in part automated. Technology in all its forms is likely to be the major platform for handling communication and information interactions in relationships. Of course, it could be argued that as well as a handling role, it will also have a shaping one. Our readers may have their own views on this.

Historical context

Research into information technology and relationships began in earnest in the early 1980s and is receiving renewed impetus today. The renewed impetus is due to the pervasive effects of the Internet on the conduct of trade.

In the early 1980s, authors such as Parsons (1983) and Cash and Konsynski (1985) viewed IT as the new competitive weapon capable of redrawing competitive boundaries. One way of doing this was through systems which linked independent companies together: interorganisational information systems (IOS) (Johnson and

Vitale, 1988). The early exemplars were companies such as United Airlines in the US with their Apollo reservations system, American Hospital Supplies placing on-line terminals for purchasing in hospitals, thus making it more likely for purchasing executives to use their ordering system, and, in the UK, Thompson holiday company introduced the TOP booking system to travel agencies, again giving its products advantage. It would be difficult to imagine going into a travel agent and not being able to check holiday availability on computer! Examples like these were found in many industries and today we take most of these for granted. In general, they created bargaining power which made it difficult to switch away from these systems, and created transaction efficiencies which forced other firms into similar moves in the market, albeit with significant time lags. Companies who owned or controlled such systems were seen as having a huge competitive advantage. Many argued that IT was facilitating the move to the use of relationships and markets to manage exchanges rather than doing this internally (Benjamin et al., 1990; Clemons et al., 1993).

By the early 1990s seeds of doubt had emerged about the potential of IOS to deliver competitive advantage (Senn, 1992; Galliers, 1993). In addition, technologies heralded as new competitive weapons were not universally adopted and the advantages easily copied by competitors. Banerjee and Golhar (1993) in an EDI study, found no strategic advantages from that technologies use. Stump and Sriram (1997) found only indirect effects of IT enhanced relationships. In our investigation of IOSs in the late 1990s we found low usage of these systems and among users they were seen as support in major UK industries and companies. The difficulties with such systems were often related to cost, seen as being pushed by larger partners with little obvious benefit to the smaller player, locked-in partners who had little wish to have this connection, and efforts to develop these systems seemed to be concentrating on 'push' rather than 'pull' factors. Powerful relationship players promised reductions in supply base, incentives for the use of the system rather than pulling in partners with benefits. Having said this the reader should be aware of the quiet revolution that has taken place in business-to-business markets where electronic connection is the norm.

The 'new age' for IT and relationship research is focusing on Internet technologies. The potential for organisations and relational partners to link has never been easier and cheaper. This potential will create winners and losers. We will argue that the key to exploiting inter-organisational IT will be through the relationships itself, its strength, and that technology will provide an additional platform for exploiting relational capabilities.

A critique of IT research in relationships

Much of the research into IT's impact on relationships centres around issues such as control of information, co-ordination of activities, cost saving and communication. These topics fall under the broad category of relationship governance: the study of how relationships are managed or the balance between the various parties to the relationship. Figure 9.1 depicts a range of research perspectives on IT and relationships.

Figure 9.1 categorises IT relationship research on two bases: the first is technology determinant, and the second concerns the strategic perspective of the research. Much prior research takes a systems perspective and focuses on transactions (along Line A in Figure 9.1). Emergent research streams take a relationship view and focus on the nature of information use (Line B). Researchers along Line A in Figure 9.1 concentrate on IT systems and concern themselves with the technology of IOS, for example, control/ownership of this technology, putting in safeguards to reduce the risk of gaining access into the system, out-sourcing relationship systems (Benjamin and Blunt, 1992; Bakos and Brynjafsson, 1993; Venkatraman and Loh, 1994; Ogbonna and Wilkinson, 1996). In addition, the research along this line often takes a transaction perspective. Chapter 3 compared a variety of theoretical approaches to the study of relationships. Transaction cost economics and agency theory have been commonly applied to IT and relationship research (Gurbaxani and Whang, 1991; Clemons et al., 1993; Brynjolfsson, 1994). The core ideas researched are transaction efficiencies (automating and streamlining existing processes using IT) at each stage in the value chain from supply to end user (Suomi, 1991; Riggins et al., 1994). This perspective applies a standard technology solution to all relationships. This risk of a systems-transaction viewpoint on IT and relationship research is that all firms will copy and the status quo will be maintained rather than additional value added to specific relationship types (Mata et al., 1995). A central point of this text is that all relationships are different and an aim of relationship management must be to exploit the uniqueness in the relationship. Line B in Figure 9.1 bases its research perspective on information and relationships. IT platforms can be developed to suit the unique information needs of the partners and the relationship type. In close relationships, sharing of high level information

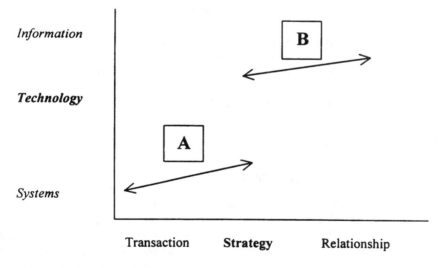

Figure 9.1   IT relationship governance research.

and dense communication patterns might be evident (for example, across-firm use of IT in new product development) in comparison to a more power based relationship where parties may only be willing to share the minimum necessary to complete transactions efficiently. Our key criticism of prior relationship research is that it was dominated by a transaction-systems position in its assumptions and design. This may explain some of the reasons why the initial phase of IOS research failed to live up to its promise. Many of the traditionally complex and costly problems of IOS represented along Line A in Figure 9.1 are proving easier to solve with falling technology costs and the adoption of the Internet as a standard IOS platform. The future research agenda will be dominated by Line B in Figure 9.1.

Cunningham and Tynan (1993), from a relationship management perspective, introduced the notion of electronic trading and emphasised the importance of electronic information sharing and communication between companies. They described high order and low order systems' tasks. The ability to complete these tasks electronically depends on the nature of the relationship between the partners. Some IT researchers have also tried to bridge the gap between IT and relationships so as to examine the technology issues posed by complex relationship structures (Nidumolu, 1995; Bensaou and Venkatraman, 1996). The era where relationship ability will determine any one organisation's ability to exploit the benefits of inter-organisational information technology connections is well and truly with us (Corbert et al., 1999; Lorenzoni and Lipparini, 1999). This will require application of relationship management assumptions and theory to the study of the impact of IT on relationships.

Possible avenues for future research are wide. Technology will impact on all relationships and most variables that underlie interactions between partners. In this section we have concentrated on reviewing research on technology's impact on relationship structure and governance. However, there are a variety of other micro influences to investigate. Parasuraman and Grewal (2000) outlined a research agenda on technology's impact on loyalty at a company, employee and customer level. If we just reflect on the impact that digital (interactive) television could have on consumer attention to advertising, or the effect of the potential growth in tele-working on an employee's relationship to the company (which is often reinforced by other employees) and to its customers, then we can appreciate the huge research potential in the IT and relationship field.

Managerial challenges of e-relationships

One of the core criticisms of IT implementation programmes has been that the benefits of it were not being realised because the investment is heavily biased towards technology and not towards managing change in how organisations work to gain the maximum benefits from the technology (Benjamin and Levinson, 1993). That is, there is a focus on technology at the implementation level. If this is applied to relationships, and it appears to be the case, then e-relationships face similar challenges. Indeed, because of the nature of the interactivity of relationships, the implementation problem is compounded with values and cultures other than an organisation's own to manage as part of the process.

Adoption of an e-business model is never confined to one business alone. For example, Ford and General Motors e-business supply chain will have knock on effects on an estimated 50 000 firms with whom they trade. To succeed in e-relationships therefore requires organisations to handle the relationship-specific aspects in their adoption and implementation process. Suomi (1994) suggested organisations must wait for benefits from an IOS to occur. This certainly applies to the benefits available through relationships – they will take time to build. Much can be learned from traditional IT implementation for the new generation of web-enabled systems. Authors such as Grover (1990) and Suomi (1994) presented a range of challenges: managerial (setting goals, providing resources, willingness to change systems and work with partners); systems development (technology issues including security of information). The managerial challenges have usually been found to be the most critical. Organisations that were technology orientated and had managerial commitment to the development were most likely to succeed. In addition, for systems based on relationships, a relationship orientation might distinguish between high and low performers.

A number of specific operational issues are worth highlighting here. E-relationships are information intensive. This factor places huge importance on managing volumes of data to best understand the relationship. Having systems in place to do this is critical especially well-managed databases (Khalil and Harcar, 1999). It is very easy to loose control over relationship information when business is electronic. There are many control issues when other independent organisations/individuals have access to your information. Risk of information abuse is always a factor. Obviously, relationships based on high trust may not perceive these risks to be great. However, many organisations aim to monitor and put in place safeguards to manage access problems. Security therefore becomes a major concern. To put this in context, if you consider the information that can be exchanged on e-mail across companies without any potential control you get the idea of the need for security. This is also true from a partner perspective. For example, consumers are always concerned about the type of information disclosed about them and the security of electronic monetary exchanges.

Another key implementation issue is managing back-office processes to support e-relationships. E-relationships must be linked to the business processes such as production, sales, service, and supply to be effective. E-relationships require people and processes to support them. Often, getting the back-office support correct requires considerable changes to current ways of working.

The combination of telecommunications and computing (for example, Internet, digital television) has opened up new modes of communication. Managing these communication channels can benefit relationships. For example, web site management is ongoing yet often the development and design are done up-front by external software providers. Therefore, there is no follow-up. The new types of communication channels are one-to-one which can lead to a splintering of messages. This poses huge risks for the marketing function in its contribution to

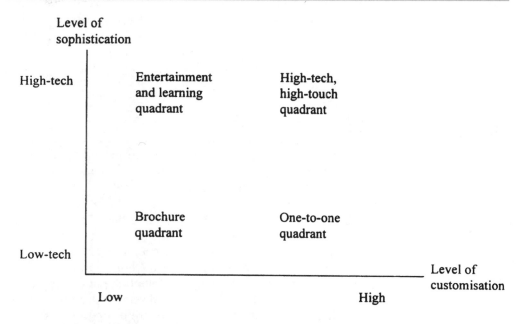

Figure 9.2   Four categories of internet marketing strategies (Source: Angehrn, 1998) *www.ftmastering.com/mk9.html.*

relationship management. Fragmentation of message and associated media (IT has opened new communication channels which is leading to a greater number and diversity of channels) makes it very difficult to communicate standard advertising messages and retain consistency in brand and product images. The splintering of mass media may present opportunities for smaller companies who do not rely on mass media as a prime vehicle for communications. Figure 9.2 presents four Internet marketing strategies. The first is mostly a web presence similar to a brochure but the others provide opportunities for web customisation including a range of high-content, high-interactive features. For example, banks initially started with electronic brochure type web sites but quickly moved to a high learning/information content provision and finally are aiming to provide highly customised personal banking solutions on the web.

The debate continues on whether e-relationships will reduce the inter-personal/social bonds prevalent in relationships. In the high touch setting of the service encounter, Bitner et al. (2000) reviewed the impact of technology and the service encounter and took a view that technology can enhance the service encounter. Technology usually improves the operational efficiency of a relationship and can, through this, result in higher levels of satisfaction. For example, when a customer calls their local telephone operator for service, it is possible for the service representative to have account details and service record on screen and be able to respond accordingly, or the call can be routed to a representative assigned to similar accounts. Added to this, technology facilitates further customisation and integration that may enhance relationships bonds but not necessarily personal bonds. Whatever the eventual outcome of virtual relationships, it is clear that e-relationships are identifying new operational hurdles and opportunities for the relationship manager. All parties to a relationship must be convinced of the benefits of the technology even if this process is difficult.

The e-relationship technologies

Information and communication technologies are providing the virtual space in which people, companies and processes within and between organisations can interact and mesh. There is a huge range of technologies that have impacted on relationships. We will only describe some here.

A few basic communication technologies have had a major effect on relationships, especially on relationships between people. These are telephone, fax and e-mail. The telephone is the basic tool of customer service and inter-employee communication. In fact, businesses have been able to link information services to customers and other stakeholders using the telephone and computer. The success of companies such as Direct Line, the financial service provider selling loans over the telephone, has been dramatic. The 1800 prefix or free telephone has made customer-company connectivity simple. Similarly, fax and e-mail with their in-built receipt of communication have facilitated many business-to-business processes.

Many technologies lie behind the Internet. Further than this, Internet technologies have allowed 'closed' systems to develop for certain types of relationship, for example, Intranets are internal web-based systems open only to employees, Extranets are external systems open only to certain customers or subsidiaries. Companies such as Oracle and SAP[13] provide the back-office communication and information systems which can be accessed via the Intranet or Extranet. These back-office systems provide the information for Internet approaches to communication and are built around core business processes in a systematic way, and are sold as total enterprise-wide communication and information systems. For example, Microsoft has put many of its key business processes on-line. The company used to have 18 different human resource locations where it could get information on employee employment status, length of service, skills and qualifications, etc. This information is now combined in one Intranet site that gives the entire human resource picture of the organisation. This Intranet site is supported at the back-end by a powerful information system. At the time of writing this book, the companies who provide these systems were riding a wave of stock market success in the face of problems with other technology stocks. Electronic data interchange (EDI) has been one of the most written about technologies in relationships. Basically, ordering, invoicing, and payment were linked on-line between companies using such a system – a form of Extranet. However, as the General Motors and Ford examples

---

[13] *www.oracle.com; www.sap.com*

at the beginning of this chapter seem to illustrate, this technology may be about to be subsumed by web-based equivalents. As outlined earlier, this is mainly due to the lower cost of web systems.

Most of the systems described so far in this section are applied to change or automate communication patterns or production and transaction processes. In the future, access to production and transaction processes and to the various web-based information systems described will be possible through mobile phones equipped with wireless application protocol (WAP). This will promote even further connectivity and will permit downloading of information using the mobile as well as the traditional landline that, in turn, will be capable of handling huge volumes and ranges of data at once. As a consumer we are faced with examples of technologies with relationship potential every day. From the ATM machine to the point of sale scanner, the use of technology to automate relational processes is firmly entrenched in our ways of working. Two additional technologies, not very new, that may play greater roles in our ability to manage relationships at work are groupware and teleworking technologies. Groupware technologies permit the barriers of geographic and physical distance to be broken down through facilitating teamwork to operate, regardless of the location of individual team members. Meetings then can take place using telephone conference facilities. This enables more frequency of interaction and this fosters bonds among individuals. The effects of teleworking, working from home using computers, on relationships has yet to be assessed. Whether it will result in a diminution of work-based relationships and thus filter into a firm's relationships with its other partners remains to be seen. Alternatively, it may result in a more satisfied employee who delivers more value to an organisation and its relationships.

Technologies that evaluate information are central to relationships. Decision support systems have yet, in the authors' view, yielded their potential. The idea that intelligent computers can aid, and even make decisions, about relationships is made possible through programming computers to have artificial intelligence. However, it is difficult to model accurately relationship processes so we think it will be a while before we are able to programme them! In the meantime, the existing relational systems have still to be fully exploited. The core technology behind relationship management is the database. Using databases to better meet customer, employee and other partners' needs is the key managerial challenge of e-relationships. The technology is relatively simple but the management of it to gain maximum benefits is more complex.

The database, as an information storage and handling device, is a feature of many knowledge management systems. One of these which is of particular relevance to relationships uses databases and other software tools and is being referred to as customer relationship management (CRM). CRM systems aim to integrate a company's sales, marketing and customer care processes with one easy to use software application. It is been haled as a customer-centric IT architecture designed to increase customer satisfaction and the bottom line. In essence, it provides the required transactional data at the point of service for customer query handling in addition to data that may help spot sales opportunities. CRM tries to integrate information from a company's multiple electronic channels into one customer-centred intelligent information point. Regardless of how a customer comes into contact with an organisation, his or her data is brought together and analysed at one point, including an analysis of account profitability. One major problem with database dependent systems is the accuracy and quality of information in the system. Getting the back-office behind e-relationships systems is therefore critical.

Maximising value in e-relationships

Much of the initial developments in e-relationships have been to automate existing transactional, production and service functions. This automation adds value in terms of cost reduction and possibly higher reliability in service operations. A lot of this value is probably relatively easy for other firms in any given sector to copy and, thus, is of a short-term nature. By taking a relationship management perspective to the study of e-relationships we can distinguish other levels of value created through the transformation of communication and information in the relationships. The potential to transform organisations with technology is real (Turner, 1998; Brady et al., 2000), but in relationships is dependent on another, at least one, partner. In the absence of absolute co-operation, maximising communication and information value using technology is limited. In one case, where a manufacturer of branded giftware had a close relationship with one of its large retailers, both companies had used IT to transform the relationship. Sharing of sales and customer data was made possible with a link to the retailer's point of sale who was also able to provide more accurate forecasting of the demand for the manufacturer's products. On the manufacturer's side, all order processing, inquiry, and service problems could be solved on-line within agreed time frames. Plus, the retailer was able to participate in the product design group on-line due to its knowledge of customers of the manufacturer's product. In other relationships of either partner, the IT integration is present but not as strategically used or pervasive. Linking technology strategy to overall relationship strategy is therefore vital. Holland and Lockett (1993) attempted to match relationship structures to IOSs in a supply chain management application. They define five forms of co-operation and their associated information flows.

Using e-relationships as a tool to manage better information and communication provides a myriad of possibility. Sharing of information can allow knowledge to be pooled for joint advantage (see, for classic treatment of potential for information sharing in an electronic partnership, Johnson and Lawrence, 1988; Konsynski and Mcfarlan, 1990; Glazer, 1991). Whether an individual employee or an external partner is part of an e-relationship, it requires a certain trusting culture for high-level sharing. Not all relationships may be worth this but there is considerable potential where it is judged possible.

Chapter summary

The introductory case study summarised the intent of this chapter which was to illustrate the impact of IT on relationships with a special emphasis on electronic commerce. The existence of virtual communities is made possible through the web. The impact of IT on most aspects of relationship management was delineated, as was the historical evolution of interorganisational information systems (IOS). The dominant approach to IT and relationship research is being replaced by a relationship strategy rather than a transaction strategy position, and by an information as opposed to a technical perspective. In addition, the managerial challenges in implementing e-relationships were outlined. An added dimension of e-relationship implementation is the relationship capacity of the partners. The final two sections concerned e-relationship technologies and the 'value added' by IT in relationship. A range of technologies were reviewed with specific emphasis on Internet facilitated information systems that incorporated back-office functions, and on databases with an application to customer relationship management. The value added potential of e-relationships is along two vectors – information and communication. Companies who can exploit these two vectors will be winners. But only if their partners are willing to play the game. The real difference in managing e-relationships to other types of e-commerce is its dependence on other independent partners with varying needs and objectives.

CASE FOR DISCUSSION   **BENETTON**

The Benetton group is made up of many brands including the United Colors of Benetton, the subject of this case, and other brands such as Sisley, Prince, Rollerblade and Nordica. Group sales are now running at around 4000 billion lire per annum. Benetton[14] is a vertically integrated company, not only in manufacturing, but also in other activities that make up the business system it operates in: styling and design, manufacturing, logistics and distribution and sales. The company relies on external partners for the major part of these crucial activities. The number of people it employs directly in proportion to its sales and industry is quite modest. Information technology plays a critical role in co-ordinating Benetton's network of buyers, suppliers, manufacturers, designers and distribution. Benetton has revolutionised an industry often seen as craft. Even though it has a highly developed network it maintains its distinctive 'United Colors' feel to all its knitwear by keeping dyeing in-house.

The styling of Benetton's products is done outside the company by a number of international free-lance stylists but the overall 'look' of the product is created by Benetton's in-house design team. Over 80% of the manufacture of Benetton's clothing is completed by subcontractors. Logistics and distribution activities are also performed, mainly, by outsiders who deliver the products on a global basis. External sales agents are used to manage the huge network of retail franchise stores world-wide, although Benetton is now creating its own managed superstores. To maximise efficiency in this system and to keep it competitive, co-ordination of the network is a critical issue. IT is

[14] *www.benetton.com*

central to this as it keeps costs low and allows the company to use this flexible mode of organisation.

The company's main plant is at Castrette in Treviso, Italy. It is totally automated and capable of handling 90 million garments per year. Beneton's distribution centre was built in the early 1980s and it handles warehousing, invoicing, payment and dispatch operations to 7000 points of sales throughout the world. The automated distribution system is capable of dividing consignments for transportation not only according to geographic area but also to individual clients, and an automated packaging system optimises the volume shipped. The centre is able to handle 30 000 incoming and outgoing boxes a day. This system has had a dramatic impact on cost reduction. Benetton's IT philosophy views IT as kernel to its operations and it is constantly trying to capitalise on the competitive power of IT in its business system. Benetton changed the structure of the knitware industry through its co-ordinating network approach and is further enhancing this using IT. Partnering is the core approach it uses to manage its system and IT its basic infrastructure for managing information, communication, rapid response to fashion trends, and costs.

The company's independent sales and distribution system is linked by a global database and communication system adapted to suit different language requirements. This system manages the relationship between sales, distribution, Benetton's retailers and the company through keeping the information of all groups aligned. This includes the commercial functions of order collection and management, order forwarding, shops and sales management. Orders are taken by the company three times a day and processed during the night, which makes them available for production the following day. The shops are promised to receive the goods within 8–12 days anywhere in the world. From ordering to Italian production to anywhere in the world in 12 days is some achievement. Clothing companies normally do not have the advantage of this type of vertically integrated system which means that they stock pile in the hope of anticipated demand or require their manufacturers to have a quick response. Benetton uses computer integrated design and manufacture allowing it to move a new item into production in a matter of hours. They even have developed software which allow them to produce a jumper without any seams! They also leave the dye process until near the end of the production process facilitating a change of colour at the last moment. Few companies have been able to copy Benetton's lead times even though they has been known for a long time. Add to this the costs of producing in Europe and it becomes apparent that Benetton's system is a uniquely managed approach of partnership using advanced technology. A franchise retailer clicks in a sale to a till in North America and this sales pattern becomes known in Italy and automatically begins forecasting and anticipating changes in demand patterns. The independence of the network yet its real-time integration through technology is a model.

Source: Authors research and for an interesting review and commentary on Benetton's partner system the reader is referred to Jarillo (1993). Benetton's web pages contain much information on its business system.

Questions

1. Examine the critical elements of partnership needed for close IT integration. In a class discussion, evaluate alternative modes of co-ordination such a system other than an integrated network.
2. Develop a set of core technology issues likely to have been encountered by Benetton

in implementing a co-ordinated IT business system. What roles would its top management and central IT group have played and continue to play?

3. Describe the communication and information processes that have been integrated in the business system, or in a part of it, using IT. Are these processes capable of being integrated in other types of partner situations?

4. Explain and evaluate the reasons other clothing and fashion companies have not been able to copy the Benetton way.

5. Discuss the potential long-term pitfalls in pursuing such an approach? What strategies would you put in place to minimise any potential pitfalls?

Further reading

Evans, J.R. and King, V.E. (1999), Business-to-business marketing and the world wide web: planning, managing, and assessing web sites, *Industrial Marketing Management*, 28, pp. 342–358.

Fletcher, K. (1995), *Marketing Management and Information Technology*, 2nd edition, Prentice Hall, London.

Figallo, C. (1998), *Hosting Web Communities: Building Relationships, Increasing Customer Loyalty and Maintaining a Competitive Edge*, John Wiley and Sons, New York.

Holland, C., Lockett, G., Richard, J.-M. and Blackman, I. (1994), The evolution of a global cash management system, *Sloan Management Review*, Fall, pp. 37–47.

McWilliam, G. (2000), Building stronger brands through online communities, *Sloan Management Review*, Vol. 41, No. 3, pp. 43–54.

Peppard, J. (1993), *IT Strategy for Business*, Pitman Publishing, London.

Peppers, D. and Rogers, M. (1999), *Enterprise One-To-One – Tools for Competing in an Interactive Age*, Bantam Doubleday, New York.

Suomi, R. (1992), On the concept of interorganizational information systems, *Journal of Strategic Information Systems*, 1 (2), pp. 93–100.

Storck, J. and Hill, P.A. (2000), Knowledge diffusion through strategic communities, *Sloan Management Review*, 41 (2), pp. 63–74.

Vlosky, R.P., Fontenot, R. and Blalock, L. (2000), Extranets: impacts on business practices and relationships, *Journal of Business and Industrial Marketing*, 15 (6), pp. 438–457.

Chapter questions

1. Examine how the emergence of virtual communities can impact on the way a company manages its relationships with that community, be it a customer, employee, or other community. Develop a plan for managing such a relationship.

2. Taking any relationship process of your choice, consider the impact of IT on it. What actual and potential benefits does the technology give the company? Are there any risks involved?

3. Discuss the following statement: information and communication technologies are having a profound effect on customer relationships.

4. Figure 9.1 presents a critique of relationship research. Develop three hypotheses or research questions that would fit along Line A and Line B in this figure. In a class discussion, brainstorm ideas for research along Line B.

5. Evaluate the managerial challenges in implementing e-relationships. Which in your opinion is the greatest challenge and why?

6. Taking a company of your choice, describe their e-relationship activities and present a critique and a set of recommendations for developing them.

7. As a longer-term project identify a company who uses databases as a significant part of an information system for a particular relationship partner, for example, customers. Analyse the actual and potential information generated from such a system.

8. Information and communication are argued to be the two key components of the 'value added' by e-relationships. Examine the rationale behind such a statement.

9. Describe how the nature of a relationship (the degree of co-operation) impacts the depth of electronic integration between partners.

CHAPTER 10

Innovation and strategic market relationships

Introduction and objectives

Traditional approaches to management are often inappropriate for many of today's markets. The speed of change, the instant availability of information and the need to find not only customers but create opportunities are some of the reasons. While the also-rans are fighting over share of declining markets, innovators replace the market with alternative product/service combinations. Many of today's markets and a number of high-performing companies did not exist 10 years ago. To be fair, many incumbent companies have kept pace by redesigning business processes incorporating total quality management (TQM), just-in time (JIT) manufacturing and computer-aided design (CAD). Unfortunately, these improvements become basic requirements to compete and any temporary advantage is eroded quickly by the sincerest form of flattery – imitation. No sooner have companies embraced these concepts that they can be imitated by competitors.

Innovation is the life-blood of an enterprise but it is a costly, difficult and risky process. We would argue that relationships are a potential source of differentiation and of comparative advantage, particularly in new and improved product or service development. Traditionally, product development and improvement has been the domain of marketing as a function. However, the written, usually annual, marketing plan is often rendered obsolete by new information, changing markets, changing customers' tastes and preferences and by the activities of competitors. Even the research and development department will have made many of the assumptions on which the plan is based redundant. Geoffrey Moore refers to this as tornado marketing because it sweeps away old approaches, disrupts markets and crafts new ones (Moore, 1995).

So, how do relationships fit in this new-world order in product and service development? In this chapter we adapt the active user and network approach to new product development (NPD) by showing how relationships and a relationship-based approach impact on this process. We then, by classifying six different contexts, examine how strategic market relationships can influence innovation and product or service development within and between organisations. It is not our intention to cover the subject of new product and service development in detail (we offer some reading suggestions to do this at the end of the chapter). Instead, we aim to show how a relationship approach can offer new and exiting ways to develop products and services and in finding alternative routes to market them. After reading this chapter you should:

- appreciate the limitations of the traditional management models with regard to innovation and NPD;
- be aware of the change drivers influencing innovative activity across firms and markets;
- assess the impact of different contexts on NPD activities and processes;
- be able to decide how to achieve competitive distinction through a strategic market relationship approach to NPD activity;
- be aware that different forms of market relationships may create different routes to market and ways to innovate.

CASE ILLUSTRATION   **NETWORKS INTERRUPTED AT MOTOROLA**

Motorola has grown from a producer of car radios in the US in the 1920s to its current position as a leader in communications, semi-conductors and advanced electronic systems. Motorola is a global player with an impressive growth record. With revenues in excess of $30 billion, R&D expenditure of $3 billion and over 140 000 employees worldwide, the company are an important presence in the markets and locations where they operate. Approximate sales by product segment are shown in Figure 10.1 and sales by geographic region in Figure 10.2. With over 1100 locations in 45 countries and 65 manufacturing facilities worldwide, Motorola can be classed as a truly global company. They have grown this way through world class technology and in 1997 alone were issuers of 1208 US patents.

The difficulty for such a diverse group is to link their different divisions in a coherent and unified way to compete in the markets in which they operate. For example, their personal communications sector includes consumer and retail businesses, cellular subscribers, personal communications, messaging systems and consumer solutions. In their telecom operations they operate with business customers to facilitate the development of end-to-end communication solutions which include satellite communications, aviation applications and smart card solutions, in addition to their portable and mobile radio networks and products. Their major markets include transportation, government, military, construction, utilities, manufacturing, financial services, heath and education.

Motorola are almost unique in that they hold an almost full spectrum of communications applications. The company has a growing presence via the Internet and a plethora of networking groups. For the future, Motorola's objectives are to:
1. obtain global leadership in their core business;
2. proceed up the value chain to provide total solutions;
3. embrace technology platforms that provide future technology leadership;
4. achieve operational excellence.

Motorola presents an interesting paradox with what follows in this chapter. By any standards Motorola is a success story and a well-managed company. They are a fine

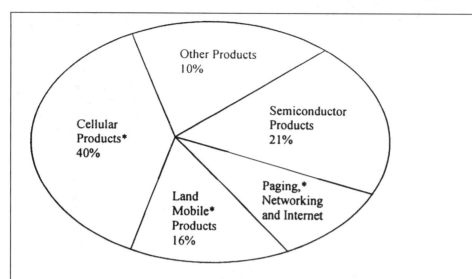

Figure 10.1 Motorola sales by product segment. *Grouped under communications enterprise.

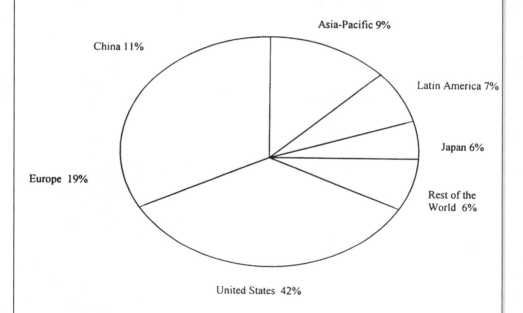

Figure 10.2 Motorola's global presence sales by market region.

example of building upstream and downstream relationships with both suppliers and customers. Their procurement policies and supplier contracts provide an industry benchmark and their customer focus and service delivery is world class. They are previous winners of the prestigious Malcolm Baldrige award[1]. Yet the company also follow a US-based, almost imperialistic approach to expansion. As a result they have lost ground in semi-conductors and although the world leader in mobile technology they have been losing market share to Ericsson (3rd) and, in particular, to Nokia (1st) in terms of mobile phone sales. Would a more co-operative approach to developing markets, rather than manufacturing product, have been to their advantage? The answer is, apparently, yes. Motorola now have a number of joint venture initiatives, some of which are reported in this chapter, in an effort to expand on several fronts in related telecom areas.

Sources: www.motorola.com

[1] The Malcolm Baldrige National Quality Award is a US prize awarded to companies who epitomise world class quality performance.

NPD – active users and networks

The Motorola case study demonstrates how complex business life can be in a high technology, fast-changing market. Any supplier to, or customer of, Motorola knows how important relationships are but life becomes tougher rather than easier in relationship mode. This is because close relationships require greater commitment, more flexibility and increased complexity to succeed and prosper. In chapter 5 we introduce the concept of networks and it was suggested that network analysis provided us with insights into interactions, their composition, strategic potential and different relationship forms. In this chapter, we examine some of these ideas and their effect on new product development.

We subscribe to the view that "...relationships help put technologies into a context where they can create value" (Ford et al., 1998, p. 227). There are many influences changing the agenda for what firms have to do to deliver new products and services. The case illustration places innovative activity in a relationship context that results in new ways to develop products and services and in finding new routes to market. The role of context in this is crucial and this must be a main area for future research to focus upon in the NPD area. We suggest how, and in what ways, relationships might influence NPD processes and outcomes in the development activity within firms.

Traditionally, the recommended way to minimise the risk and to enhance new product development has been to follow a systematic process, create an effective organisation to handle this process and employ the best means at your disposal at each stage of development. This process is outlined in Figure 10.3 and comprises several sequential stages.

The user active paradigm for developing new products has a long lineage (Von Hippel, 1978; Biemans, 1991). We are demonstrating and providing amplification of this with examples in this chapter. However, it is not just about users but other network partners as well. Co-operation in the process is vital. We provide further examples of relationship product development in different contexts and refer to

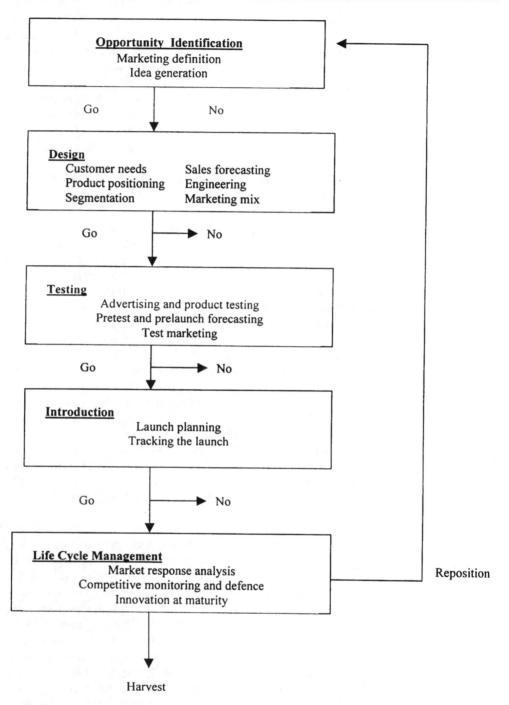

Figure 10.3   The five phases of product innovation process (Source: adapted from Urban and Hauser, 1993).

some of the literature on relationships in NPD. However, we do not attempt to cover the many themes that investigate the influences users and other partners have on the complexity of this process (see, for example, Hakansson, 1987; Ford and Saren, 2000). There are many important issues including the number of users, partner selection, formality of partners' interaction, social processes (developing trust being found as key), mechanisms for communication, number of meetings and leadership. The level of co-operation required varies but the greater the innovation, the higher the risks and, potentially, the closer the integration. Different partners will have varying levels of involvement at each of the stages but the key to success lies with the management of the process.

Before considering the impact of relationships on each stage of the NPD process, an example of the new order, referred to in the introduction, should be helpful. IBM is changing its strategies to become a 'direct' vendor using the Web. The company is moving from supplying hardware via intermediaries to providing enabling technologies and information solutions. The competitive advantage is not the technology but how you help your customers use that technology in customer relationship management and IT services. Sales are not solely PCs but items like personal digital assistants, web-enabled TVs, screen phones, smart cards and a host of other products and services, some of which are not yet developed. IBM will collaborate with others on product compatibility of standards and communicates jointly with others on pre-announcements of new technology. Hence, IBM is forging alliances with Cisco, Intel, Siebel and others to achieve the necessary expertise and market coverage. The added value for their customers is in the consultancy advice and solutions provided and not in shifting boxes. This kind of transformation can be achieved by the management of different types of relationships and variable levels of co-operation with multiple partners.

Using the process outlined in Figure 10.3, it is our intention to show that relationships can be conduits for NPD by overcoming some of the problems associated with in-house development and a formalised process. In a way, what has been argued in the NPD literature for years, that functional integration is crucial to success, is supported here but extended from intra-organisational networks to inter-organisational networks.

Stage 1 Opportunity identification – Traditionally, having set out the strategic purpose of the business this has to be translated into a product development strategy. This reinforces the idea of a core benefit proposition that you can offer to the customer which has value and competitive superiority. At its core is a clear definition of the market that is being served. Ideas can be developed from a variety of sources but there is conflict here between the need and opportunity for creativity and the nature of the organisation which, to be efficient, also has to be focused and coherent in terms of the product offering. To stimulate new ideas and products requires creative people, an environment receptive to new ideas and the use of creative problem solving techniques. There is empirical evidence that the sources of ideas and methods for generating them has an effect on success rates for new products (Cooper, 1998). While cause and effect are difficult to measure, established firms spend significant resources in an effort to find product winners.

Of the various sources available to generate new ideas, most of these are market-derived from customers, salespeople or competitors rather than technology-derived from laboratories, technical groups or supplier sources. In one study, only 3% of companies were found to liase with research laboratories (Hakansson, 1989). The same study emphasised that the essential relationship is between members of the company and the market. Encouraging employees to build relationships with customers and external bodies is recommended but large numbers of separate collaborators can cause major problems if they are not co-ordinated. Surprisingly, the same study showed that 29% of companies had no development relationships at all. Techniques for developing new ideas such as lead users, delphi forecasting, brainstorming, creative groups, etc. can be enhanced if they are relationship-based. However, rather than use eclectic groups, many firms employing these technique do so internally and the problem of group dynamics is likely to inhibit the outcomes (Prince, 1970). Although most new product ideas are market-based it cannot be denied that market sometimes follows technology and there are still many technical breakthroughs that arise from inner-driven R&D. Relationships offer one way to achieve good product ideas yet is an under-used approach. This is particularly so in industrial markets where the customer-active paradigm has been proved an essential ingredient in NPD success (Urban and Von Hippel, 1988).

The Sony Walkman is a classic example of inner-driven belief in an idea, yet the Sony Betamax video system proved a costly failure. Digital television, to avoid another Betamax/VHS conflict, is a good example of how relationships are now essential to product development in technology-based product areas. Digital is not really a product but a technology shift. One company developing ' digital' will fail since all other firms have a vested interest in the existing technology. What is required to achieve a market position and customer acceptance is to develop this concept into a 'must have' technology. This can only be achieved within a relationship context and it is no surprise to see a consortium of collaborators and competitors combining to achieve the desired shift. The BBC, SKY, Sony, Philips and other parties, including regulators and government, combine to offer a new solution for the market that is digitally based.

These new opportunities, facilitated by technology, seem to cry out for new business models. Evidence of factors for success in NPD show that understanding user needs, proficient marketing, top management support, efficient NPD processes and speed to market are differentiating factors (Hart, 1996). However, the process starts with market focus and idea generation. Another key issue is the quality and speed with which information is collected and acted upon. As well as the idea itself, information drives this new agenda in product development. McKenna (1991) argues that technology and marketing have now not only fused but have also begun to feed back on each other. This information on both the technology and the product is reshaping both the customer and the company and the interaction between the two.

Technology permits information to flow in both directions between the customer and the company. It creates the feedback loop that integrates the customer into the company, allows the company to own a market, permits customisation, creates a dialogue and turns a product into a service and a service into a product.

(McKenna, 1991, p. 78)

According to McKenna, knowledge-based and experience-based marketing will change and supplant the old approach to marketing and new product development. This means that integrating the customer into the design and development process, new approaches to segmentation and positioning based on re-assessing your value-added proposition and developing supply chain infrastructures to deliver the unique proposition. The other half of this new marketing paradigm is experience based marketing, which emphasises interactivity, connectivity and creativity (McKenna, 1991).

Therefore, information is adding a third category to the classical product/service classification dichotomy. The value of information lies in its unique properties in that information can be consumed at a distance from its production site, has very low tangibility and very high reproducibility in various modes and media forms. Information may form the basis for competitive strategic advantage, in contrast to traditional market-share versus differentiation strategies. This is because information assumes various functions in facilitating transactions: it can be a marketable product itself; it may not be part of the offering but be critical to the marketing effort.

The key difference between the physical and virtual value chains is that the virtual value chain treats supporting information as a source of value in itself, not just an auxiliary element of the value-adding process.

(Hoey, 1998, p. 33)

It is this distinction that is relevant to NPD in a relationship context. Information flows using the gatekeeper network and personal contacts can overcome communication problems but distance and physical location still create barriers in innovation. The need to communicate and build relationships with lead users is crucial to subsequent market success (Urban and Hauser, 1993).

Stage 2 Design – If a firm is successful in generating ideas some means of translating the concept into a reality is required. Various systems and techniques have been used and in the early stages, evaluation is necessary to establish key success factors including:

- a product or service based on real customer needs;
- realistic sales forecast based on market size and growth prospects;
- market position based on the strength and vulnerability of competitors to establish market share and sustain it;
- the resources and investment required in engineering, capital and people;
- the rewards and risk, particularly the expected profit margin and return on investment;
- the most appropriate marketing mix to exploit the opportunity.

In relationships, product, services and information combine with supply chain processes as part of the innovation. Rayport and Sviokla (1994) who coined the phrase 'marketspace' contend that in an information-defined arena the dimensions of content, context, and infrastructure can be mixed and matched in ways that may at first seem unrelated to the core transaction. Thanks to these almost endless combinations, the marketspace bears new business opportunities with the creation of 'virtual value chains'. This phenomenon was also observed by Ghosh (1998) who branded the Internet as a platform for innovation. Some examples may illustrate these three dimensions. In terms of content, information about cars – rather than the cars themselves – become the new element in an electronic car exchange system. This can be two-way as shown by BMW who use their web site to generate information and ideas from customers and enthusiasts as well as provide information in a sales sense. Context may refer to the content-rich environment the on-line service provider America Online (AOL) created, in which "people consume, communicate, and transact" (Rayport and Sviokla, 1994, p. 149). Computing and telecommunication equipment – the traditional hardware, may fall under the umbrella of infrastructure.

The link between information, internal structures and external relationships is vital to achieve the breakthrough required but also important is the co-ordination of internal linkages in the NPD process. Firms build teams, often in parallel, thus using relationships in multi-faceted ways. Parallel processing means multifunctional, multidisciplinary inputs with different activities being undertaken in different parts of the firm concurrently rather than in sequence. This means co-ordination and integration between departments and often with suppliers and customers and end-users. However, the approach to the development of a new shampoo is radically different to an integrated machine tool. Both developments benefit from customer input at all stages but in vastly different ways in terms of relationships.

Some contexts, pharmaceuticals for example, cannot rely on the customers to say what they want. A cure for aids, cancer or asthma will not come from customer or market research but from investment in scientific and medical research. Nevertheless, the history of NPD is littered with technological solutions that the market simply did not value. For this reason, there are many variations of organisational solutions in NPD ranging from suggestion schemes to matrix organisation. Networking across functions, companies and industries must also be encouraged. This can be done in different ways. For example, when Intel develop a new microprocessor the existing technology becomes redundant overnight. All computer suppliers Compaq, Dell, IBM, etc. have to have this new technology with the result that there is a shift rather than a gradual development process. Part of this process is to acknowledge that the product is not enough. What is required today is a combination of product, service and information to drive winning business solutions. Of course, the technical merits of the product are necessary but not sufficient. Knowledge of using the product, being able to increase productivity by employing new and better products, systems and processes, the ability to grow your own and your customer's business are the drivers of customer adoption. We do not buy products, we buy benefits in the form of total solutions. This is the challenge for relationship management in the future. You will be known not by your product alone, but by your ability to offer customer solutions.

Stage 3 Testing – Bearing in mind our proviso with regard to the type of product or context, fast moving consumer good versus jet aircraft and so on, it is at this stage relationships can be vital to market adoption and ultimately product or service success. Following the screening of ideas and prior to any large-scale investment, a feasibility study involving both commercial and technical evaluation should be undertaken. Throughout the process and even at this initial stage, market evaluation needs to be undertaken to establish customer acceptance. Various ways can be used to test acceptability of the product idea, prototypes and real products. Concept testing can evaluate the initial idea, product testing can be used to ensure the product works in the way intended and test marketing can assess the commercial viability prior to national or international launch. Although these evaluation measures involve additional expenditure, they are crucial in reducing the costs and risk of failure and also ensuring that the product meets the customers need in the way intended. However, an ongoing dialogue between the innovator and various role partners can be surrogates for the traditional evaluation measures. As costs begin to rise dramatically and this scale of input is matched with highly uncertain outcomes then relationships help spread risk. Internally, departmental integration is important in a smooth development process and is enhanced by frequent communication among members within the organisation. Internal group cohesion helps product innovation performance and studies have found that when communication, co-operation and harmony are high between departments in an organisation success in NPD is greater (Gupta and Wilemon, 1988). Sometimes these developments and the relations that span them take many years to come to fruition. In a study of electronic devices in the motor industry it was found that some firms had committed funds up to 30 years before profits finally emerged (Albach et al., 1993). Firms that are future oriented and build relationships internally and externally over very long periods are likely to succeed in innovation. However, contrary to this long-term view, others have suggested a more short-term approach to achieve success and accommodate market changes using a process of continuous NPD (Downes and Mui, 1998). Either approach needs efficient relationship management but evaluation is often problematic.

Therefore, many companies are pursuing multiple strategies embracing new products, product improvements and service enhancements. They achieve feedback by entering into a dialogue with their customers and in some cases their customer's customer. For example, Bosch Power Tools target the professional and the DIY market. They maintain top level after sales service, a team of on-line experts, an Extranet, an education club, education material for retailers and the Bosch DIY academy with over 800 courses. Such a service provides feedback and stimulates an on-going relationship with a widespread customer base yet reduces the emphasis on product testing alone.

Stage 4 Introduction – Eventually products that survive this process make it to launch stage. Adopting a marketing-led and customer-focused approach is essential for success (Von Hippel, 1988). The platform for this success must be based on building the existing and new customer base by creating value, the outperformance of the competition and differentiating the product in the mind of the customer. Information as a marketable product itself also comprises customer databases. These enable companies "to target their most valuable prospects more effectively, tailor their offerings to individual needs, improve customer satisfaction and retention, and identify opportunities for new products or services." (Hagel and Rayport, 1997, p. 64).

An example of this is Dell. Founded in 1984, the company grew in 8 years to become a Fortune 500 company selling computers. Equally impressive is that today the company sells over $50 million per day via the Internet. It achieves this in a number of ways - by forming alliances, such as the Dell/Ariba alliance to develop inexpensive tools for developing B2B e-commerce capabilities. This is a vital but radical change in their strategy. In Dell, relationships with customers are backed by the 'Resolution Assistant' a customer-based, Internet system for management and support for software. It therefore moves from a product-centric company to an Internet-centric focus and builds new forms of relationships. Its' expert services group includes partners such as Andersen Consulting, Gen3Partners and others, selling to many types of businesses. Using Internet technology in this way enables the company to collect profiles about consumers' preferences, transactions, activities and log behaviour. The Internet creates a valuable memory that enables marketers to address customers on a one-to-one basis and a "a database of transaction histories will be the primary marketing resource of many firms" (Kiani, 1998, p. 187).

In the business-to-business arena, the idea of linking distinct businesses electronically is not new: EDI (electronic data interchange) has been around for more than 40 years. EDI is complex and expensive to set up, and the type of data to be exchanged is restricted and inflexible. Using Internet technology in the form of Extranets (the combination of internal networks of selected business partners), all kinds of data can be exchanged cheaply, such as sales contacts, product brochures or engineering drawings (Reinhardt, 1998). The greatest benefits are derived from streamlining the supply chain, customer involvement and speed to market. Adaptec, for example, reduced the time between order and delivery of its chips from 16 weeks to 55 days, saving $1 million in costs (Reinhardt, 1998). General Electric and its Trading Process Network (TPN) is another successful example of business-to-business e-commerce: It links about 1400 of GE's suppliers, doing $1 billion-worth of business a year through TPN (Economist, 1997). NPD in a relationship context must account for this new business process model.

What seems to be happening is that a new marketing paradigm emerges whereby management activity aimed at manipulating their resources using the traditional four Ps, or doing something to, or in some cases for customers, is replaced by a model of working with customers incorporating one-to-one contact, negotiation and customer fulfilment. Kiani (1998) concludes, from the works of various authors, that marketing in the marketspace is dominated by:

(a) many-to-many communication model (marketplace: one-to-many communication model);
(b) individualised marketing (mass marketing);
(c) dialogue (monologue);
(d) communication (branding);
(e) demand-side thinking (supply-side thinking);
(f) diversity (megabrand);
(g) decentralised market (centralised market);

(h) customer as partner (customer as target);

(i) communities (segmentation).

Information and relationships transform business supply chains.

Stage 5 Life cycle management – Traditionally, following the product launch and initial market acceptance there has been no guarantee of market success. Studies in the US suggest that a marked percentage of new products fail in the consumer, service and industrial markets despite following this sequential process and methodological approach (Booz et al., 1982). Despite a vast literature on success and failure in NPD, failure rates in new product introductions remain high. For industrial products, over half the projects fail to meet the objectives set by the firm (Cooper and Kleinschmidt, 1991) and one reason for this is a failure to mange the product launch phase. One conclusion from this may be that the stage-gate NPD process is too simplistic a formula. Information and relationships will be influential and, in many cases, crucial to success. This is so because information, in addition to being a product itself and a critical part of the marketing effort, plays a crucial role in the purchase decision-making process and in the NPD process. Somewhere, somehow, there is a failure between supplier and customer in effecting routes to market. Collecting fast, accurate information at this stage is critical to NPD success.

This is important for virtual or net-based companies in the consumer sector in the way they communicate with customers and receive feedback. They must ask:

(a) What information is required?

(b) How can it best be disseminated to relevant parties?

(c) What are the sources of income?

How do organisations cope? In part, the answer is to re-think your future in different scenarios and partake in the art of strategic conversation (Van der Heijden, 1997). You have to introduce a dialogue that changes the mind-set to find ways of looking and anticipating the future differently to that which is currently conceived to be the way the world operates. Evidence on organisational structures to achieve and realise such change tends to be thin. However, it can be suggested that organisations that are hierarchical and formalised are less amenable to change than other forms. Hence, there is a move to delayerment, empowerment and in NPD various forms of organisation have been suggested incorporating cross-functional teams, venture groups and separate business start-ups.

What often emerges from this relationship way of thinking and managing is a new conceptualisation of product linking buyer, supplier and the object in what has been described as a 'pluri-signified' product in which "the key unit of analysis... is the relationship between the actors rather than any inherent characteristics of the actors themselves" (Saren and Tzokas, 1998, p. 451).

Relationship-based NPD activity in context

In our relationship world we would advocate that firms require a matching process to manage the development and marketing of new products and services. This is best achieved in conjunction with others rather than by internally-driven processes alone. There is evidence to support this not only from our experience but from others who are suggesting this to be the way to compete in a global economy. For example, in a global study it was found that speed to market was the outcome of a matching process (Eisenhardt and Tabrizi, 1995).

Others point to the importance in establishing standards "for everything from part numbers to security" (Reinhardt, 1998). With this in mind GE's achievement seems even more impressive, having integrated 1400 suppliers in their trade net. In some cases this technology has the potential for giving the business a clear competitive advantage over its competitors. Forrester Research estimates that businesses will exchange $327 billion in goods and services by 2002 over the Net. This compares to $250 billion worth of trade using EDI. It has been forecast that within 5 years equal amounts of trade will be done through the Net and EDI (Gartner Group report quoted in Reinhardt, 1998). These figures are already out of date!

New product development in a relationship mode, similar to other areas of the business, requires internal co-ordination and managing external linkages. This has been referred to as the voice of the customer (Griffin and Hauser, 1993) and the voice of the engineer (Hutt and Speh, 1998). The work of Von Hippel et al. (1999) re-enforces this point. Most commercially important innovations are developed by product users rather than by the manufacturers that were first to bring them to market. Further, leaving the customer out of your product development process is almost a guarantee of failure regardless of its technical merits. In the relationship arena, the priority should be customer needs expressed in terms of benefits that the new product or service has to offer. Depending on the concentration in the market, a representative selection of customers must be chosen to evaluate the product concept, the product and the implementation plan. Particularly important in this is the 'leads users' within an industry and these are the people and organisations where relationships are important. Von Hippel gives us an excellent example of how this works in medical imagining. Using a series of 'pyramids of expertise', project teams network … "to identify lead users and experts, first in the target market then in other key fields" (von Hippel et al., 1999, p. 50).

Therefore, traditional value chains are fundamentally changed on the information highway with a huge impact on stakeholders. For example, consumers are expected to benefit from greater choice at lower prices. Producers and retailers incur lower co-ordination and distribution costs. The result is that while some companies' profit margins might be squeezed, this can be offset by higher volume. For NPD the implications are as follows:

- greater focus on existing relationships based on using and sharing new information rather than on winning or creating new relationships;
- by positioning itself as a value-adding intermediary, one company leads the supply chain to effect lean distribution;
- new ways can be found to add value based on re-structuring processes and systems. For example, Cisco has provided the value chain model for business-to-business marketing in the digital economy;
- goods and service are created, designed and delivered by sharing knowledge

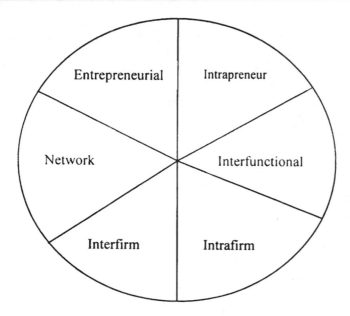

Figure 10.4   New product development context.

and experience. This is not always financially motivated but is based on risk sharing. For example Linux software is distributed among partners for mutual benefit rather than self-interest;

■ new forms of distribution networks emerge which facilitate information exchange, as well as products and service exchange.

Continuing our theme in this book that relationships are a different way of viewing business problems, nowhere is this more evident than in NPD. Traditionally, as we have observed, NPD has been seen as the result of an internally driven process through the stage gate concept of screening, concept development, testing and so on. Success was, in part, dependent upon customer involvement in the process but, in reality, success is dependent on the relevance of the approach to the context in which it is applied. Using a previously established framework of context (O'Dwyer and O'Toole, 1998), we attempt to support this assertion that NPD activity is situation and context specific. We have identified six different contexts for NPD activity as shown in Figure 10.4. Using these contexts we will examine how and in what ways relationships might influence NPD processes and outcomes in development activity.

Context 1 Entrepreneurial

In this context we refer to individuals who create and develop new products. They invest their own time and effort and assume the financial, physical and social risks associated with such activity. However, it is they who also reap the rewards of monetary and personal satisfaction. Being entrepreneurial means that research/

development skills and marketing effort are combined in the same person – the entrepreneur. Perhaps the role is combined in a partnership or in a group of entrepreneurs. The problem is that skills in one area such as technical know-how are not necessarily available in knowledge of another area such as market and specific customer knowledge. Therefore, to overcome uncertainty or ignorance, it is preferable to operate in a relationship mode. Working with others such as collaborators, customers and competitors can yield rich rewards in a spirit of co-operation. Given the vast body of knowledge about customer involvement in NPD (Von Hippel, 1988) entrepreneurs should, at least, modify their enthusiasm with a degree of market feedback and customer involvement.

In some economies, Scotland and Ireland being good examples, government-backed agencies sponsor 'entrepreneurship' using a network approach. This encourages business start-ups by providing connections to sources of finance, in some cases business angels, with other related businesses with similar interests and to partners with different skills and abilities. This provides support in information, marketing expertise and finance to those with the good idea or technical development. These tend to be small companies where the skills and abilities necessary to compete cannot all be found in one or two people alone. The Scottish Executive 'Proof of Concept' fund is one such scheme. They fund grants of five and six-figure sums of cash to academics that have come up with innovative ideas. The aim is to turn university-based research into new products and services. Businesses in biotechnology, computer games/software and even service-related areas have emerged as real growth prospects from such schemes.

Context 2 Intrapreneurial

This context differs in that there is company involvement to support innovative ideas, usually with financial or other resources. Organisations try to cultivate this in various ways such as suggestion schemes or specifically allocating an individual's time to NPD activity. 3M, one of the leading-edge companies in NPD, encourage its technical staff to devote 15% of their time to developing their own ideas. A key factor in the success of many products and projects has been the role of one or more individuals usually referred to as product champions. Although this person may reduce uncertainty, they can also create difficulties within the organisation with a desperation to succeed that is not based on sound commercial judgement. The skill is in combining R&D skills with marketing know-how. Again, we would argue, a relationship approach is necessary to combine the skills required to get the product or service to market in conjunction with the technical back-up to achieve winning product solutions. Relationships still require leadership but of a different form and kind to traditional management models.

While the sole entrepreneur can still emerge with the 'big idea' to achieve a route to market requires some form of relationship-based strategy. Dyson, a UK company, was launched in 1993 to make vacuum cleaners based on the design inspiration of its founder John Dyson. Within 4 years the company had achieved 52% market share in the UK and now employs 1200 people with a turnover in excess of £200 million. It produces 10 000 vacuum cleaners per day. According to John Dyson "design matters, design sells" and their success is led by technology, design and innovation. What is impressive is the internal relationships that have been achieved at the 'heart of the business' between research, development and engineering. Although the company works closely with intermediaries their product orientation is noticeable in their success. This confirms that relationships are multi-faceted embracing internal and external contacts.

Context 3 Interfunctional

For more mature firms, the predominant focus in NPD would be in the context of interfunctional co-ordination whereby different functions within an organisation need to be combined, such as the sharing of resources and information, to achieve successful product innovation. To successfully manage NPD, reduce the risk of failure and enhance the chances of success requires that the interface between functions, especially marketing and R&D to be managed effectively. Therefore, the focus has been on the role of management, project structure, leadership and communication effectiveness in management of the product development system. Management has a significant role to play at all levels, especially in interfunctional co-ordination. Strategically, this means engendering a shared belief amongst employees in the need for team effort and in facilitating this team effort to produce the required result. The role of project structure in enhancing cross-functional integration is critical to success although the nature of this structure may vary. Organisational forms such as cross-functional teams, matrix organisations and venture groups are variations that have been employed. The role of project leader is crucial in enhancing this functional integration. This person is most effective if they have in-depth knowledge or expertise of their specific area and of the business as a whole. This will be influential in the team achieving their objectives. Equally important is the need for a continuous flow of communication and information, especially in larger organisations. Location is an important factor in this respect. As the organisation grows and expands, the need for improved communication and co-ordination across functions becomes greater. In our research, a continuous flow of information was seen as a means of reducing uncertainty and establishing credibility among disparate functions. Integration and team effort in this context is important in achieving a successful outcome.

Tetra Pak, the Swedish based packaging group has three divisions in cartons, plastics and processing. Each division works in partnership with 70 market companies to produce the best solutions for customers and end consumers in over 150 countries. The divisions work on the technical innovations and NPD for global solutions yet they have to work closely with their market companies and vice-versa. In addition to its own NPD and production developments the company also pursues take-overs such as its acquisition of Swiss company Dynaplast and global alliance including Graham Packaging in the US. Some competitors see this as an attempt by Tetra Pak to dominate and monopolise the market while an alternative view is that this is relationship-based strategy. Motives behind these relationships are important but the outcome is a network-enabled proactive and interactive process both up-stream and downstream in the supply chain. This encourages a partnership approach within the company between market units and technical divisions and externally where the buyers are involved in product development, delivery and service enhancements. As a result customer relationships are strong.

Context 4 Intrafirm

Firms today are seldom one product or one-unit operations. Many firms have multi-products, divisions and subsidiaries. In terms of new products, intrafirm co-operation between parent and subsidiaries is not uncommon. Traditionally, this may have been seen as an 'us' and 'them' between head office and plant or subsidiary. In the international or global company, elimination of duplication of effort and spreading of risk is a necessary and realistic option. Companies look for, and form, centres of excellence for particular product technologies and organisations need to access resources and skills on a transnational basis. For some firms, and for some product areas, the idea of growth clusters such as Silicon Valley, determines location and investment across their organisation. NPD can be multi-disciplinary and multicultural using global teams. In some cases these are referred to as virtual teams although this is a misnomer in that the people concerned do exist albeit in different localities. The cultural dimension can be a highly successful source of differentiation in the product development process.

The Adtranz Signal Group is one of the key players in the European rail network. Their Automatic Train Protection (ATP) system is an advanced embedded computer system that provides the interface between driver and track control equipment. Although of Swedish origin, Adtranz operates in several different European countries providing ATP systems. Their difficulty is that the traditional rail monopolies of each country have chosen different ATP systems. For example, a train running through the Channel Tunnel must be equipped to understand both British and French signalling standards. Their origins in Sweden were based on a monopoly buyer purchasing from a single supplier and their natural instinct was to work closely together. When entering other markets, e.g. Finland, France, Norway and Portugal, Adtranz have had to adapt in several ways. First, they have to co-operate with local partners in some cases via acquisition, in others in some form of alliance. Further, price had to be competitive and investment costs had to be absorbed to achieve long-term benefits. Finally, the product had to be adapted to take account of different traffic conditions which had much higher levels of intensity than that which existed in Sweden. Adtranz collaborated with Alcatel, Alstom and Siemens to develop a European Train Control System (ETCS) which allowed trains to run between countries without being double equipped with expensive equipment. Pilot orders were placed in the Netherlands and Switzerland to achieve the standardisation, thus enabling the industry to compete on the same basis. Though this reduces costs for the customer and opens the supplier to a much larger market, there is increased competitiveness. The result is predictable. In 1985 there were ten companies competing, today there are six. Adtranz have responded by attempting to have one customer in each country, rather than only one customer (*http://www.adtranz.se/ signal*).

Context 5 Interfirm

The importance of customer involvement in the NPD process is now well documented. It follows that it may not require a quantum leap in lateral thinking to realise that pooling knowledge of suppliers and other intermediaries is a rich vein of untapped potential. In consumer goods, innovation in this context comes from pooling supplier knowledge of production and distribution. Along with expertise in logistics and information technology and the intermediary's know-how of marketing to their customers, innovation is achieved. The rise of own label products enhances this need for collaboration. Retailers in particular are proactive in the type and range of produce that they supply. Inherent in this process is the importance of the brand. Retailers need to manage their branding operation often between different price positions. In the UK, Tesco have their own label products and a low value range. M&S and Sainsbury have tried to enhance the quality of their own label. This market power forces the retailer to be active in developing the specification and analysing market trends and customer needs for their products and services.

Important in this context is whether the business is a brander or supplier. Branders are strong leaders in brand management, product service and design. They own and manage their brands through technical innovation, design and creative positioning. They also exercise strict control over product/service specifications, the customer interface and their communication message. Suppliers focus on operations and look for profit in value engineering and manufacturing efficiency. They do not have brands of their own, their interface is with the brander rather than the end customer or user and their operations are the equivalent of a sub-contractor. Their business is therefore volume but low margin.

Nike is a brander. They do not manufacture but they control rigidly, the specification and development of products under their brand name. This is akin to our dominant partner type of relationship but this approach may be necessary to maintain the integrity in their brand and the need to maintain their market position in the future. To achieve this, Nike has three different categories of supplier – volume producers who have economies of scale as footwear producers; developed partners who are exclusive to Nike and produce advanced designs; developing sources who can produce at very low cost (Donaghu and Barff, 1990; quoted in Ford, 1998).

Although the relationship is as a dominant partner, Nike shares its knowledge and resources, including personnel, to ensure beneficial outcomes. Thus, by managing its activities in a co-ordinated way, sharing its resources and providing personnel expertise, Nike manages the relationship. The supplier can also manage this relationship to acquire skills and competencies that they otherwise would not have or be able to use as a manufacturer. There is a clear need to manage this process with the utmost care and integrity. Inter-retailer and supplier relationships are perhaps the most significant and potent form of product and service development in today's markets. Again, it can be observed that by working together, transaction costs and risk can be greatly reduced. In business-to-business markets the need for collaboration is even greater if costs are to be reduced.

Context 6 Network

Although relationship clusters are most visible in Silicon Valley, California, this is a concept that can work in many shapes, sizes and geographical areas. By linking university research and new businesses with the relevant expertise accompanied by active government backing, new growth industries can develop. The idea is to combine competencies of compatible firms with others to create new market leaders of tomorrow. Firms must identify these opportunities for collaboration and realise that thinking in conventional product terms may inhibit rather than create innovation. For example, an IT supplier and a pharmaceutical company. The pharmaceutical player identifies that their product is a crucial but low value item with the result that customer service and supply issue dominate their customer's thinking. The requirement is to find ways to add value. Based on technology from the retail sector, the IT supplier recommends bar coding so that pharmaceutical companies can easily replenish stocks based on instant read-out from users. For one company the cost of this process improvement may be prohibitive and may undermine the viability of the scheme. However, the IT company can see an opportunity, not only to service the pharmaceutical company's needs better but to offer this solution to all pharmaceutical suppliers. The result – first mover advantage and opportunity identification for business growth.

Almost all businesses can be represented in a network and excellent examples have been published in recent years describing and analysing different network scenarios (Achrol and Kotler, 1999; Hakansson, 1987). Perhaps it would be appropriate to conclude with an example from the financial services industry.

We have advocated that relationships have to be situation specific. The Bank of Scotland (BOS)/Halifax merger indicates a relationship imperative in financial services resulting in a formal collaboration. Having attempted but failed in two major take-overs – NatWest and Abbey National which were lost to competitors, Royal Bank of Scotland and Lloyds, TSB, respectively. BOS finally succeeded with Halifax. This demonstrated that relationships in this industry are important to future prosperity. The BOS is Scotland's second largest bank with pre-tax profits of £540 million in 1999 and total assets in 2000 of £58 billion. The bank operates in the UK, Ireland, Australia, New Zealand and the USA. Basically, the products are retail banking, card services, mortgages, factoring and its traditional clearing services. It operates via a branch network, telephone, PC banking and with others such as Sainsbury's and Centrebank. The main problem for banks is how to use new technology to drive the business forward and achieve economics of scale via Data mining, the Internet, and other high-tech developments. These developments will be crucial to future growth and development. In terms of BOS's relationships we can observe that banking is increasingly telephone-based and staff are having to become interactive salespeople. Where they do not have distinctive capability in the

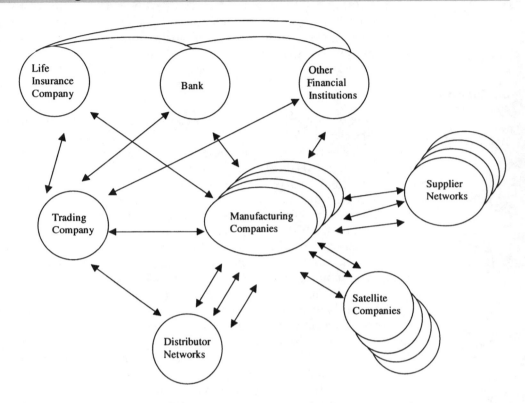

Figure 10.5   Organisation of transactions in the intermarket network (Source: Achrol and Kotler, 1999).

new technology they will have to out-source or acquire via merger. The high cost, labour-intensive branch network is becoming a liability although it does offer the potential for cross-selling. As an example, call centres grew by over 50% in 1998 with over 4 million calls recorded. They are now selling mortgages by telephone and have built the alliance with Halifax, in factoring, motor-based loans and, of course, mortgages. Using the Intermarket network framework (Achrol and Kotler, 1999), shown in Figure 10.5, provides an ideal framework to develop strategic options for the bank.

Yet, alliances are proving highly difficult and complex. BOS have recognised that they do not have distinctive competencies in all areas of financial services and therefore are trying to build relationships, formally or otherwise, to bridge these gaps.

Chapter summary

Relationships offer a new and different way to develop products and services that is more in line with customer needs and wants. Organisations somehow have to create and manage synergy to encompass concurrent processing of information flows with organisational cross-functional integration. Organisations must find new and innovative ways to incorporate the voice of the customer but avoid the incumbent's disease of failing to react to a changing external environment. What is required is creativity, control and customer feedback rolled into a new strategic market relationship. The main issues are therefore speed to market, customer involvement and feedback, creativity versus control and mobilising resources to achieve objectives.

To survive and prosper information management is crucial. The need for instant information across the world demands accurate responses from customers and sources of data on market trends and competitors as and when it is happening. New knowledge-based thinking involving customers, suppliers and other role partners is a pre-requisite for successful innovation that creates new value propositions and enables companies to compete, despite rising development costs and shorter product life cycles. Organisations have to respond and relationships, appropriate to the context in which the firm operates, can provide significant advantage.

However, we would guard against the idea of a panacea for all types of development. Six contexts were suggested and indicate that some variation in approach is warranted. These six contexts are entrepreneurial, intrapreneurial, interfunctional, intrafirm, interfirm and network, each of which presents different challenges to compete in the NPD and relationship arena.

CASE FOR DISCUSSION **HUGHES NETWORK SYSTEMS**

Hughes Network Systems (HNS) is a subsidiary of Hughes Electronics (HE), acquired by General Motors (GM) for over $5 billion in 1985. Hughes Electronics is a huge concern with interests in TV, satellite, cable and digital communications and other forms of entertainment. Originally, HNS was involved in selling their satellite business networks to GM, Ford, Amoco, Wal-Mart and other Fortune 500 companies. Their main business was providing private satellite links integrating very small aperture terminal technology (VSAT), allowing businesses to link up many small sites such as petrol stations, retail outlets and dealerships through a central hub in the customer's data centre. This was very much business-to-business selling, primarily through sales and technical staff. Often there would be a specific software build for that particular customer's hardware configuration. HNS's competitive advantage was its leadership in VSAT technology. With the takeover by GM, this technology was backed by the reliability and reputation of the world's largest company. Although this was relationship-based marketing the company was very much product oriented.

However, with technically based products the value of the relationship lay in the nature of a technical lock-in between HNS and its customers. To run a VSAT system was a complicated process requiring sophisticated functionality between proprietary hardware and customised software that required significant training for even the basic shift operators. HNS provided this training and support service, adding value for the customer, with the result that customers naturally looked to HNS for existing and future purchases. HNS's success proved the value of this approach but it also led to an arrogant attitude by sales and marketing staff, especially from the directors of the company. With approximately two-thirds of the market, this confidence was perhaps understandable but a major competitor, Gilat, won the US Postal Service contract in 1998 suggesting that the position of HNS was beginning to be less secure than hitherto.

With the emergence of the small office, home office (SOHO) Internet market, the opportunities for HNS and its associated technology was immense. The new multi-media home entertainment environment offered huge potential for the company and its related products. In 1996, HNS targeted individual consumers with its new product DirecPC. This product/solution allowed a home user to access the Internet using both a conventional modem and a high speed satellite feed to receive high volume content direct to their PC. This provided each home user with download speeds of up to 400 kbps. HNS sold the dish, hardware and installation through major retail chains but the service itself was bought directly from HNS. Their target market, according to Paul Gaske, executive vice president of the newly created Broadcast Network Division of HNS, was what they called the "upscale technophiles". This translated into those seeking Internet services faster than those of current analogue modems of 28–56 kbps. In other words, they (HNS) appear to have assumed, like their business customers for VSAT, that customer choice would be for one system based primarily on its technical merits.

Although HNS felt that they had the right product and price they did not achieve as many subscribers as was projected. Eighteen months after launch a hastily compiled $10 million advertising and promotion effort was launched in an effort to win new subscribers. Retail outlets, used to selling hardware, had less experience of selling telecommunications services with little or no on-site technical specialists. Nor did HNS have a technical support back-up, a fact criticised by many who had purchased the system. Sales of DirecPC were around 40 000 compared to the DirecTV service of over 9 million. Although these are two different markets, the intention was that many TV subscribers would follow into the arena for Internet access. To overcome this lack of penetration, HNS began selling a product called DirecDUO that shared the same satellite dish but the service was operated separately, the TV service from San Diego and the PC service from Washington. This did not work. Another problem was that there was not enough bandwith to supply everyone with the 400 kbps offered and heavy users were forced to reduce consumption under the fair access policy to avoid accusations of discriminatory tactics by HNS. DirecPC was panned in the media, in journals, computer magazines and the like, despite favourable product reviews. Recent new technologies such as digital subscriber lines (DSL) and cable modems suggest the future for DircePC is rather ominous. For example, DSL subscribers have risen from just over 1 million at the end of 1999 to an estimated 2.1 million at the end of 2000. Cable in the USA has 85% of the multi-channel TV market in 66.6 million homes.

HNS is now pursuing a policy of partnering with AOL to offer AOL plus and DirecPC is seen by AOL as a vehicle to achieve their subscriber target. This is a great boost to DirecPC but AOL are also pursuing links with cable and DSL service providers. AOL's priority is, apparently, subscribers regardless of the technology used.

Questions

1. Critically evaluate the strategy of HNS in terms of the bilateral relationship model.

2. In terms of its relationship with consumers how is this similar or different to that of HNS's traditional business customers?
3. To what extent do you agree that technology is a necessary but not sufficient condition for market success?
4. Do you agree that the initial target market should have been "upscale technophiles"? Create a profile for such a customer and suggest ways to develop an ongoing customer relationship for retention as a customer in the future.
5. Be more explicit as to the benefits of a product such as DirecPC and its value to potential customers.

Further reading

Gruner, K.E. and Homburg, C. (2000), Does customer interaction enhance new product success? *Journal of Business Research*, 49 (1), pp. 1–14.

Hart, S.J. and Baker, M.J. (1994), The multiple convergent processing model of new product development, *International Marketing Review*, 11 (1), pp. 77–92.

LaBahn, D.W. and Krapfel, R. (2000), Early supplier involvement in customer new product development: a contingency model of component supplier intentions, *Journal of Business Research*, 47 (3), pp. 173–190.

Milson, M.R., Raj, S.P. and Wilemon, D. (1996), Strategic partnering for developing new products, *Research-Technology Management*, 39 (3), May/June, pp. 41–49.

Tushman, M. and Nadler, D. (1986), Organising for innovation, *California Management Review*, 28 (3), pp. 74–92.

Wynstra, F. and Pierick, E. (2000), Managing supplier involvement in new product development: a portfolio approach, *European Journal of Purchasing and Supply Management*, 6 (1), pp. 49–57.

Zagnoli, P. and Cardini, C. (1994), Patterns of international R&D cooperation for new product development: the Olivetti multimedia product, *Research and Technology Management*, 24 (1), pp. 3–15.

Chapter questions

1. Given the importance which many companies place on getting new product to the market as quickly as possible, to what extent would you agree with the view that the sequential approach to new product development is no longer effective? Use examples to support your line of argument.
2. Your company has just survived following unwise investments in new product activity. Write a memo to your managing director explaining how to avoid another costly failure and improve the process.
3. The Product Life Cycle (PLC) concept is suggested as a useful marketing planning tool. Assess the PLC in terms of buyer-seller relationship.
4. Elaborate on the idea of a dialogue which could change NPD activity from proactive to relationship-based.

5. In the Intrepreneurial context how might relationships enhance the interface between marketing and R&D within an organisation? What practical measures would you recommend?

6. In the Interfirm context, using your own examples, show how relationships can bring the customer into the product or service-development process.

7. Select one example of a brander and one of a supplier. Differentiate between them based on their approach to relationship building in NPD.

8. Imagine you are to launch a new digital TV channel for business. Make a list of potential collaborators and outline your approach with each.

CHAPTER 11

Relationship internationalisation

Introduction and objectives

This chapter takes a relationship and network perspective to some of the central decisions made by international business managers. Implicitly, throughout this book, companies with international dimensions have been cited as examples. Much of any company's activity is global or, at least, crosses country boundaries. Examining key international decisions from a relationship and network position is different to the traditional dominant sequential assessment. This chapter therefore will present further opportunities for organisations to gain from relationships, by looking at their international activity in a different way as well as to introduce an important area of relationship study. The international dimension of the environment is difficult for most business to ignore. Trends towards growing internationalisation of business activity and the complexity of different cultures merits a chapter concentrating on this topic. New insights have been found using a relationship approach. Traditional presentations on international business (see, for example, Root, 1994), take a sequential view of a firm's international growth and development. In this view, firms operate as independent actors making rational analytical choices about which markets to entry, the optional method of market entry, and modes of operation in particular countries. The relationship reality is rather different. The international business choices and decisions made by a firm are impacted by its relationships and the existing relationships in the foreign market. For example, markets may be entry-blocked by existing relationships and firms; entry and location decisions may be forced by customer firms; personal contacts may inform smaller firms about which market they might enter; relationship failures may force exits from particular markets; close intra-cultural relationships may mean your business is always on the outside track in particular countries. Existing international management approaches do not sufficiently emphasise the relationship dynamic of international operations. This chapter will present this.

The chapter will examine the added dimensions a relationship perspective to the study of the development of a firm in the international market can make. To achieve this, the trends towards international inter-firm relationships being forged by forces such as technology, globalisation, and hypercompetition will be examined, and a brief theory presentation of the international relationship approach will be made. However, the main emphasis will be on a review of international managerial decisions. Specifically, four critical international decisions will be scrutinised using a relationship perspective. These are the decisions about market selection, entry, expansion and organisation. The chapter is organised to avoid over concentration on any one firm type. The material is applied to both multinational and smaller international firms. Finally, the chapter assesses the managerial implications of a relationship approach to the study of international business. The end of chapter case focuses on Statoil's internationalisation in Estonia using a relationship approach.

After reading this chapter you should know:

- the trends placing a greater emphasis on forging international relationships;
- how a relationship approach adds to the study of international business;
- relationship approaches to market selection;
- market entry from a relationship position;
- how markets can be expanded using relationships;
- relational impacts on the organisation of an international company;
- the managerial implications of an international relationship strategy;
- have a view about the impact of national culture on relationships.

The case study demonstrates a unique cultural relationship, that of personal relationships or Guanxi among Chinese business people. This form of cultural-specific relationship may inhibit outside competition from being successful in the market, and may help develop overseas markets for Chinese businesses. However, favouring such relationships may also hinder change and objectivity in decision making. Guanxi has been found to be a key feature of Chinese business success overseas (Kiong and Kee, 1998; Yeung, 1998; Lovett et al., 1999).

CASE ILLUSTRATION   **GUANXI: CULTURE-SPECIFIC RELATIONSHIPS**

Many business networks are culture-specific based on underlying forms of social organisation unique to particular groups. These networks can be based on personal ties that connect individuals based on their race, gender, family connections, business associations. One such example is the way Chinese business people cultivate personal relationships (Guanxi) for doing business. The ties developed are often based on family and seem to transcend the size of any organisation in that these ties do not seem to break down as the business enlarges internationally. That is, the businesses grow through Guanxi. Guanxi is an informal way of doing business that has developed Chinese business through South East Asia and globally. In fact, it parallels the trend towards relationships in Western business or, at least, to the growth in importance of the social structure of business interactions, now a feature of western business. It also parallels similar forms in other countries such as Keiretsu in Japan and Chaebol in Korea. Due to the growth and sheer size of the markets in China and other Asian countries, the need to pay attention to cultural-specific networks of relationships is of paramount importance in doing business in these countries.

The rules and procedures for establishing and maintaining Guanxi are complex and subtle and require a deep cultural understanding. For example, Yang (1994) describes the process of asking for favours and gift-giving to establish Guanxi. Firstly, it is necessary to target the correct person (an intermediary may be needed here). Then where one hopes to establish Guanxi by giving a gift, it is necessary to be very sensitive in finding out what gift to give, and whether gift-giving is acceptable. For westerners it would be very easy to offend. This gift-giving is probably separate from simple bribery in that it has reciprocal obligations and, in some cases, return of favours implies a bigger favour is done to demonstrate respect. In business the friendships created through Guanxi provide security and comfort that come from dealing with someone whom you know. This Guanxi develops through reciprocal dealing and interpersonal trust. Maintaining Guanxi through continual social interaction is important. There are many bases of Guanxi such as the older forms of shared locality/dialect and kinship. Today, family remains important but bonds developed through working together, trade associations/social clubs, and friendship are also critical. The common feature now being nationality. Sometimes the Chinese abroad, often for their very business success, have faced hostile race-related discrimination. It is perceived that Guanxi helps guard against hostile action by individual or states.

It is often difficult for us to accept that business might be done on the basis of personal relationships rather than objective hard-heartedness. Cultures that have a high concern for people and group harmony can be seen to be corrupt and inefficient on Western, especially, American and UK standards. However, given the complexity of conducting transnational business and the degree of uncertainty surrounding it, it is becoming difficult to place every aspect of an international business deal within a legal framework. This implies trust is becoming a co-ordination mechanism for many business dealings. Adapting business process to deal with trust and understanding it is now a reality for western business. So we are moving closer to Guanxi. It in turn is moving closer, as Chinese business becomes more internationalised, to some universalistic norms of business dealing based on trust. There are efficiency limits which are changing Guanxi bases – too much reliance on trust and personal friendships may lead to choices that, over time, favour inefficient and inferior quality and a subsequent loss of competitiveness. International business competition, and the move to an urban society with less an emphasis on family connections than on business relationships established on ability, is tempering Guanxi.

Trends forging international relationships and the international relationship approach

In this section we will argue that a relationship approach can add significantly to our understanding of how a business enters and develops its international markets. Using a relationship approach provides an alternative way for dealing with the traditional export barriers such as lack of knowledge of the foreign market and the uncertainty associated with it. This alternative is through partnerships that can bridge the knowledge gap and reduce uncertainty. This section begins with an examination of some of the factors that are pushing an international relationship approach to the fore. Among these are the international outsourcing by multinational firms, the flexibility afforded by relationships, the shortening lifecycle of products which requires partnership to get to the market quickly, and changes in technology making international partnering and communication easier.

Many studies on international business activity have shown that international business-to-business relationships have significantly long duration, that these customers represent important sales percentages of the selling firm and that critical adaptations and investments have gone on in the relationship indicating the development of learning and experience between the companies (Turnbull and Valla, 1986; Johansson and Mattsson, 1988). These findings illustrate the usefulness in using a relationship perspective to study international business. In addition to these findings, many other trends in the international business environment of today are providing fertile conditions for the use of relationship to cement and develop international business. While many barriers to free flowing trade between countries still exists, a growing globalisation of demand patterns is evident in some product categories. Whether it is created by international television or technology is arguable but a certain homogeneity in demand is emerging for products in luxury, fashion and entertainment markets. However, the ability to exploit a global market requires global coverage and the ability to keep up with rapid changes in trends demands nimble competitors. Both of these are provided in relationships and networks of connections between companies. It is becoming so easy to make incorrect international choices as changes in demand patterns and delivery modes are constant. These changes are often a feature of technology. Rapid technology change has facilitated the growth of new industries that require networks to survive. Large established multinationals need a network of smaller companies to keep in touch with new ways of doing. These new industries require global presence that is only achievable through partnering with existing networks. For example, Keeble et al. (1998) found that technology-intensive small and medium sized enterprises in the Cambridge and Oxford regions of England were forced to gain entry into international networks at an early stage due to the market for their products being essentially global. Internet technology, as explained in a previous chapter, is creating communities of consumption across the world whom, through communication, are challenging how companies provide services and any cross-cultural differences in their strategy. Even mass market relationships need to be carefully managed as consumers have access to knowledge and to other consumers via technology.

Access to knowledge is a core driver of success in international business. Firms with access to superior knowledge are able to offer more innovative products and services, delight their customers, and deliver at lower costs. Knowledge does not need to be transferred as part of a proprietary system but can be added to packages offered by other firms which fosters further co-operation and specialisation and makes firms more dependent on relationships. Knowledge is not owned by any one firm and the 'best' knowledge system might arise through the cross-fertilisation of ideas across companies and in markets. To gain access to this knowledge source requires active relationships. It is not only the regulatory environment that favours relationships through, for example, restrictions on ownership but also the inherent pace of change in the international environment and the diminution of importance of location brought about by information technology. However, local culture and the requirement for a company to be embedded in a local culture is also a factor that supports a relational approach. Some of the forces mentioned here may be used to argue that the role of culture is declining. However, to the extent that all business requires trust and interpersonal interaction, then local relationships will be a prerequisite for competing in local markets. This will require partnerships or a highly adapted local presence.

The traditional sequential method of making decisions about international markets is represented in the following set of decisions (Root, 1994, p. 23):

1. assessing products and foreign markets: choosing the target product/market;
2. setting objectives and goals;
3. choosing the entry mode: export, contractual arrangements or investments;
4. designing the marketing plan: price, product, distribution;
5. the control system to monitor performance.

This set of decisions and actions are implemented by an individual firm acting alone. Our assumption is that firms are interdependent on other firms and therefore, cannot control the series of entry decisions outlined above. Completing the above set of decisions is likely to provide a checklist of factors rather than a comprehensive entry strategy as it ignores the role of interdependencies in the market.

Axelsson and Johanson (1992, p. 221) suggest the following questions might be relevant to a network or relationship assessment of foreign markets:

1. Who are the main players in the foreign market – customers, suppliers, competitors, public agencies? Which are the important relationships? Identify the strength of the ties between the actors – social, technical, economic, legal or other ties.
2. What are the relative positions of each of the firms in the network? What are the roles of the firms and what power do they have in the network? What constraints does the network impose on the firm regarding, for example, possibilities of relating to other actors, areas, fields of application, suppliers, etc? What possibilities do specific potential partners in the network offer to the company as regards access to suppliers and resources controlled by others?
3. What are the relations of the focal firm to actors in the potential country market? Which are the direct relationships? How can they be used? Are there any indirect relations to actors in the potential host market, for example, through contacts with partners in other local markets who in turn have direct relationships with the entry market?
4. How can the resources of other actors be mobilised in support of market entry? What people, which technical and financial resources?

The relationship view of markets leads to a very different set of questions than the traditional sequential approach. The strength of international relationships a firm can expect to have and its position in the international market will determine its entry success in the foreign market under a relationship approach. Without such an analysis it is very difficult to predict how a firm will perform as its performance is constrained by the power and actions of others.

Once entry has been considered, attention turns to the growth and development of the firm or the internationalisation of the firm. This has often been studied from a transaction cost perspective and from a stages of development approach. The transaction cost model has been applied typically to the multinational firm to explain its exploitation of its unique competitive advantage and search for lower production costs as key motivators in its internationalisation (Buckley and Casson, 1979). A multinational firm internationalises as it has unique advantages that it can exploit in the export market and, in turn, can take advantage of lower production costs overseas. Transaction cost economics can be used to help explain multinational location and international product cycles. The stages theory of internationalisation, associated with Uppsala University in Sweden (Johanson and Wiedersheim-Paul, 1975; Johanson and Vahlne, 1977), focuses on the experience gained by firms as they gradually develop internationally. Typically, firms go through a series of stages as they internationalise. Both approaches concentrate on the individual firm determining its choices and pathways in international markets. Larger firms obviously have the resources to do this. However, many of the explanations based on transaction costs were found using data on large US firms who were the pioneers of international market development. The international market place today is more competitive and it appears that without some type of relationship international growth and development is more difficult to achieve – witness the growth in international alliances. The stage models, while applicable to smaller firms, assume a gradual incremental learning and development, again using the individual firm as the main influencer of its international development. Whilst both of these approaches are widely used and act as powerful explanations of international business development, the dynamic of relationships and networks adds to further understanding as to why and how businesses internationalise. For example, Durr[1], the German World leader in manufacturing paint shops/systems for car plants, internationalises by locating its staff and operations where their customers are, and indeed, where the company's staff actually do their job. Durr's business, because of its relationship approach, has evolved from being a systems supplier to the automakers to being a service consultant in this important process as well. Through locating staff where its business is, the company also performs a major service role. Over 35% of the company's sales are outside Europe, as are its staff. This philosophy has benefits for Durr: with engineers and sales staff in customer plants solving problems, these staff are also able to feedback ideas to the mother company. This has allowed the company to continually innovate into areas such as paint robotics. Indeed, Durr relies on sub-contract relationships for many paint jobs where it cannot be price competitive as it continually evolves to being a value added close relational service partner cum manufacturer.

Relationships and international market selection

Hollensen (1998) provides an approach to market selection typical of the method presented in most leading textbooks on the subject. Market selection, under this

[1] *www.durr.com*

approach, is about screening potential markets/countries using a set of predetermined criteria/filters and matching the result to the characteristics of the firm. Taking a large sized company, an analyst would start with broad macro economic filters such as income statistics, demographics, geography and language, and then would move to market specific factors such as competition and product adaptation. As this process proceeds the number of suitable markets or countries reduce. The actual selection pattern of most firms does not follow this sequential pattern and often tends to be less planned and based on other factors such as the existence and availability of contacts in the target market. The relationship approach would accept the objectivity of this sequential process but would add a strong element of relationship assessment at all stages. A large firm could begin with macro level relationship assessments such as those with governments and state agencies in the countries targeted. A small firm might begin a relational assessment by looking to its contacts across the following domains: any international connections in its current network of buyers, suppliers, and competitors. This may represent an access point for the firm. In addition, knowledge networks such as other exporters you know, people you know overseas, and home country export trade promotion agencies represent an important source of ideas and contacts. A larger firm might look to its internal subsidiaries or, as with the small firm, its external partners. Often potential distribution relationships overseas are blocked or taken up by existing competitors. So it may not be choice of market, but ability to develop relationships in the foreign market that will determine success. That is finding pathways into international markets through a firm's set of present and potential relationships and networks.

Selecting markets through relationships facilitates organisational learning about foreign markets. The information collected might be first hand contact, factual information, or qualitative information gained from comments your networks make about the market. Learning from relationships might be relatively cost-less when compared to other forms of market research such as international surveys. Relationship learning is more highly involved when compared to the alternative screening process. Both can be linked as learning from relationships also facilitates information search on the main criteria used in the sequential process. This is especially true of markets in developing countries where secondary sources of information may not be that reliable. Once a potential set of partners has been identified the firm must begin planning for entry into these foreign relationships. One of the key aspects of this will be establishing credibility and trust. This can be done through recommendations from partners or contacts connected to the sourced relationship, through contact with the potential partner, and by being flexible with trial orders, etc.

Ghauri and Holstius (1996) used a relationship assessment of entry patterns of three case companies who where entering Eastern European markets. They showed how the case companies, one of which was Statoil, the Norwegian oil and gas company that is the subject of our end of chapter case, used relationships to solve problems and develop entry contacts and partnerships that ultimately established their success in new markets. The opposite can also hold true of course.

Table 11.1 International market entry modes (Source: Root, 1994)

Export entry modes
   Indirect
   Direct agent/distributor
   Direct branch/subsidiary
   Other

Contractual entry modes
   Licensing
   Franchising
   Technical agreements
   Service contracts
   Management contracts
   Construction/turnkey contracts
   Contract manufacturing
   Countertrade arrangements
   Other

Investment entry modes
   Sole venture: new establishment
   Sole venture: acquisition
   Joint ventures: new establishment/acquisition
   Other

Axelsson and Johansson (1992) described the length of time it took, Scania[2], the Swedish truck maker, to establish a position for itself in the Australian market. It first entered the market in 1971 but it was the early 1980s before its sales took off. In 1985, Scania was awarded truck of the year in Australia. Scania's initial choice of relationship did not work out for a variety of reasons including lack of trust and communication between it and its host partner, responsiveness to the market, and perhaps ultimately due to a less than optimal entry match. Scania's initial entry partner only met half of the company's entry criteria. It was not until the company appointed a Swedish local manager that it began listening to the market, and teaming up with a number of Australian technical partners that helped it adapt the product for the market. Selecting the right networks can be a powerful stimulant to foreign sales in so much as a bad selection can make for foreign market stagnation.

Relationships and international market entry

Once a firm begins exporting, it has begun using some market entry mode. These range from the quite passive use of an agent to the more involved use of an invest-

[2] *www.scania.com*

ment in a new plant in a foreign market. Market entry methods have been commonly classified into groups (see Table 11.1).

The entry methods listed in Table 11.1 have varying levels of risk, commitment to the foreign market, and control over foreign operations. It is usual for firms to evolve to more risky and highly committed forms over time, that is, towards investment entry modes. Smaller firms start with the direct agent/distributor mode. There are many advantages and disadvantages to each of the methods listed in Table 11.1 that are obvious from their levels of risk, commitment and control. By taking a relationship approach to the understanding of these methods we become interested in the process rather than the method. That is, to what level can we develop a relationship with our host partners? In other words, we assess the potential to embed ourselves in the foreign market through the entry mode choice. We build our entry operations on the relationship we want to build in the foreign market rather than on a decision about entry mode.

Referring to earlier chapters of the text, any one of the market entry modes can be governed by a close or a more distant relationship. For example, we can be in an alliance that can be power based with each partner jockeying for position or in an alliance that is mutually based and intent on delivering joint value to both partners. It is what is done in the entry mode that is emphasised when a relationship approach is taken. For example, Hyder and Ghauri (2000) found that strong joint venture relationships led to more resources being committed to the partnership that enhanced its success. Often joint ventures fail through lack of commitment to the partnership. By understanding the relationship development prospects of our entry mode many possible problems can be sorted out in advance of entry. The potential social and economic structure of the relationship should be suited to the long-term expectations of the exporter and this should be clearly understood by the partner. Once a foreign market entry choice is made it can determine a firm's flexibility in a market for a long time as these arrangements can be difficult and costly to change.

Some entry methods have evolved on the principle of relationships. However, these principles can be applied to all the modes. The growth in international outsourcing has led to an explosion in international sub supply as a contract entry method. This is where a multinational company sources from foreign countries thus bringing foreign suppliers into the export net as it would with its domestic suppliers as it moved into foreign markets. The role of a sub supplier can be very complex and demanding with high specification requirements. This relationship is based primarily on a relationship contract rather than any other form of entry mode. Similarly, organisations and firms that come together to organise joint marketing/promotion/distribution in foreign markets also do this activity on a strong degree of relationship co-operation. In practice, they even may be competing but see benefits in being able to offer a broader range, or simple to afford foreign market entry. One familiar co-operative brand is Sunkist[3]. It was created by Californian fruit growers in the 1840s as a marketing and distribution agency to gain

---

[3] *www.sunkist.com*

better prices but is still successful today. Another example is the Kerrygold[4] brand, a leading dairy brand in Europe. It is owned by the Irish Diary Board and was set up in the 1960s to overcome the small size of individual diary firms. The Board is owned by a combination of State and diary producer interests in Ireland. It aims at developing overseas markets and distribution for Irish products and has developed the Kerrygold brand in Europe. The only entry mode that does not require a relationship approach is foreign direct investment. However, it does require strong intra-organisational relationships and indeed managed relationships with many partners, including the host government in the foreign market.

Relationships and international market expansion

Expanding a company's position in a foreign market or aiming to reach a critical mass is the core challenge in the post-entry phase. The competitive dynamic of the international market and the tensions between the home and host parts of the business are two central issues in evolving a firm's position in the international market. Normally, expansion would see a change in a firm's entry mode. In this text we view relationships as a key way of managing competition and expansion in foreign markets. Competing through relationships regardless of entry mode is part of a relationship strategy. This might be the easy part when compared to organising for international relationships. International organisation is a major theory and practice challenge even outside the relationship field. Relationship structure is one of the 5-S of implementation. The pervasive influence of relationships on international organisational structures is the subject of the next section of this chapter. Ensuring cross-cultural learning transfer between the partners is a necessary element for growth. If learning does not take place, then the home company is not developing experience of the foreign market or a true understanding of it and will, due to this, be able to offer less to its foreign partners over time.

Three strategic decisions face the expanding international company. These are: whether to enter a huge range of international markets simultaneous, particularly apparent where there is a short lifecycle for a product, whether to concentrate resources in a few markets or to diversify, and the managerial and organisational implications of whichever strategy is chosen. The latter will be the focus of a further section of this chapter. Rather than review the merits of rapid entry versus a concentration strategy, we choose to focus on the additional insights provided by a relationship approach. A firm can choose to rapidly expand by developing through its international networks. However, embedding into any network may take time and it might be wise to see how existing networks could be further developed rather than to enter new ones. Many international markets are huge in size so there may be further relationships and network opportunities within a market. Whilst we may favour slowing growth to develop relationships, particular industry or product categories may place time pressures on a company, for exam-

---

[4] *www.kerrygold.ie*

ple, software with high obsolescence. In this case, networks are usually more open to rapid diffusion and new relations.

Many business people prefer to diversify their international market portfolio rather than to concentrate all their 'eggs in one basket'. Reasons cited include changes in economic conditions and in currency requiring a company to have a diverse portfolio. The authors tend to believe it also has something to do with approach. If you do not see relationships as being important, or only want a minimally involved relationship, then a diversified portfolio might make sense. However, if close, enduring relationships are the focus, then the need to put time and energy into developing international relationships might favour a concentrated strategy. In fact, to be oriented towards international markets should require your relationships in these markets to be as embedded as those in the home market. How many firms can say 'we are' to this question! Being involved not just in the micro relationship but in industry networks within a country should be an aim of those wishing to pursue a close relationship strategy. Overall, the use of relationships and networks is an alternative strategy to expand in international market but is an involved one.

Relationships and international organisation

The optimal organisation structure is difficult to obtain. Trying to balance flexibility with control is a central dilemma in organisational theory. Co-ordination and control of an organisation operating in more than one country adds an additional dimension of complexity. Usually, the same organisational types used in the domestic market are applied to the international one, for example, functional, divisional, product and geographic structures. We have reviewed the characteristics of relationship organisation forms in other chapters, such as the need for team based approaches and managed interaction across organisations. Relationship organisation is a fertile area for academic and practice research. As with the other aspects of international business covered in this chapter, relationships and networks are providing additional insights into the study of international organisational relationships. Looking at the pattern of relationships as opposed to the formal organisation and control structure has provided new insights into how an organisation grows. The attention to the management of relationships and in particular to interpersonal relationship development is important to international relationships. An example of how relationships and network insights are changing how we view organisations is provided in the work on multinational organisation by Nohria and Ghoshal (1997). Through focusing on relationship patterns they likened the structure of a multinational company to a network. The work was based on studies of companies such as Philips, the Dutch consumer electronics company, Procter and Gamble, the American consumer products company, and Swedish electronics giant, Ericsson. As part of the study the authors also sought the views of over 300 managers. Normally such a study would focus on the degree of formalisation of a company's rules and procedures and the degree of centralisation of decision making in corpo-

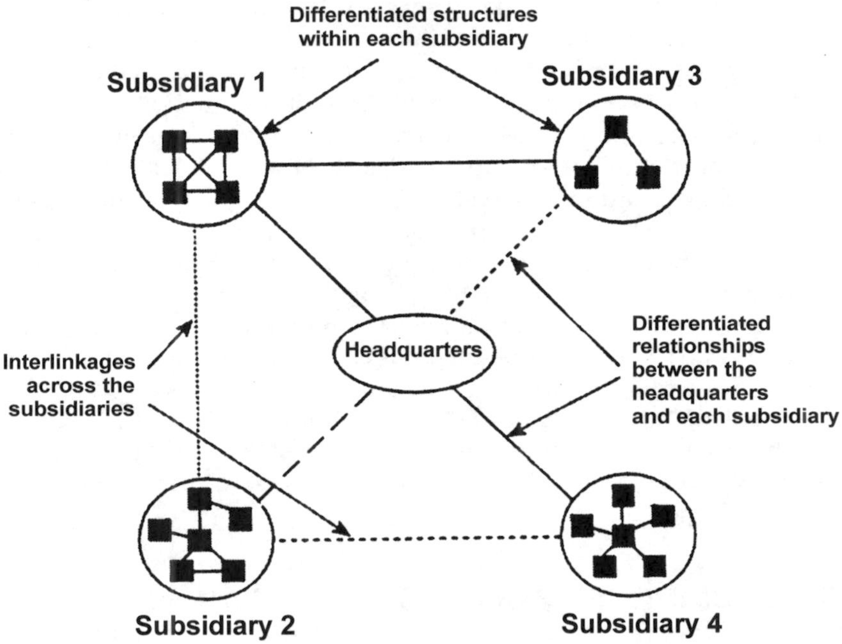

Figure 11.1   Multinational networked organisation (Source: Nohria and Sumantra, 1997).

rate headquarters. However, by focusing on relationships the authors developed the following network form of organisation of a multinational company.

Figure 11.1 shows how network characteristics can mirror the complexity of a multinational organisation which does not seem to follow any of the traditional patterns but is a criss-cross of many structural types defined by the nature of intra-organisational relationships. Relationship and network characteristics of the companies in the study were:

- A differential pattern of resource flows (human, technical, capital) and intensity of resources across subsidiaries. The resources used in each subsidiary and the transfer pattern across subsidiaries varied widely.
- Organisation structures varied in each subsidiary (see Table 11.1).
- The relationship between headquarters and subsidiaries varied. Technically one would assume that headquarters has all the power and control but, in practice, many subsidiaries operate semi-autonomously and have considerable power.
- Variation in social structure across and between subsidiaries was found that might imply differences in organisational cultures and values across the company.
- Communication flows in the multinational company can be quite differentiated – intensity of communication patterns varied across the individual companies in the study.

Characteristics of the network approach seem to offer unique insights into how multinationals actually work. Much of the activity was influenced by resource transfers patterns, actor behaviour, and how activities are performed in the group. The linkages between different parts of the multinational company can be significant sources of value. Managing the network becomes a key source of advantage for the firm. Nohria and Ghoshal's (1997) research has illustrated the benefit of using the relationship and network approach in the analysis of international organisation structure.

Managerial implications of international relationships

The reality of trading for many companies is international. Volvo car company[5] of Sweden buys over 60% of its components abroad, albeit much of this is in close-by countries. This would compare to other European car manufacturer's average of between 10 and 20%. Therefore, Volvo has to take a cross-cultural perspective on its relationship with suppliers and customers. For example, many of its procurement staff are multilingual and may have up to four extra languages including Dutch, English, German and French. Culture obviously plays a role in managing international relationships. Cultural differences impact on relational processes and attitudes such as sharing of information, openness, communication patterns, attitude towards risk and adaptability and flexibility. Managing relationships across cultures requires these differences to be assessed and incorporated into strategy. We do not attempt to review differences in national culture and organisation in this text as it is a subject in its own right (Hofstede, 1991; Trompenaars, 1993; Usunier, 2000). Our focus is on relationship internationalisation but we hope that the critical role that culture plays in relationships has been emphasised throughout this chapter.

The success of many international ventures depends on managerial effectiveness. This is especially the case in international relationships and networks. Managers bred on a competitive and hierarchical management philosophy require a different set of skills for co-operation and consensus. In advance of making international decisions it is important to consult partners before you act and involve then in the decision process. Often international relationships require commitment up-front. This might, for example, be in support structures that cost the exporting company's margin but can have considerable relationship benefits and lead to increase in business over time. One important relationship skill is the ability to negotiate across cultures. Managers used to getting their own way need to develop negotiation skills that are relevant in the cultural context in which the negotiation is taking place. Negotiated outcomes in relationships represent compromises based on 'win-win' outcomes for both partners. It is this joint benefit that represents relational practice. Obviously, to continue to develop the social structure of a relationship through meeting and information share is of major importance. In close international relationship, the

[5] *www.volvo.com*

more the social structure can be made dense through multiple contact points throughout the organisation the better. This may be harder to control but provides a bond difficult to break. This type of bond facilitates problem solving and information transfer. It is also optimal for senior managers and managing directors to have good social relationships with their counterparts as this provides a smoother path for business being done at lower organisational levels. In any international business settings, remaining flexible to partner needs is vital. Openness to change is not often a feature of business done where contracts and prices are stuck to rigidly. Flexibility to solve problems and help partners demonstrates trust and commitment to the international market that can be a useful asset in long-term international relationship stability.

Finally, we must emphasise the role of learning in international business relationships. The value added from relationships is often the learning that occurs between companies. This learning is more difficult to achieve across cultures. Partners can fall into the trap of leaving each partner to what it is good at. The relationship becomes a sharing of skills rather than a learning organisation. To facilitate learning, routines must be built into the relationship – formal and informal mechanisms for communicating and sharing new knowledge. Cultural learning facilitates understanding of the partner but also of their markets. This learning is very difficult as we tend to look at problems and issues from our own cultural perspective and the little information we have about a foreign culture can be rooted in stereotypes that represent a very simple one dimensional understanding. The debate in the international literature about developing international managers capable of transcending cultural barriers remains, as does companies' efforts to create such super-people! We can only suggest a continued openness and willingness to learn. Perhaps after each visit to or from our partner we could ask what did we learn that is different from the way things are done in our culture. We never stop learning about another culture because its nuances go deep. Trying to challenge cultural assumptions is not only a challenge at the top of the organisation but most go further down. Hoecklin (1994) described how the British company ICI[6] (Imperial Chemical Industries) managed to develop cross-subsidiary cultural understanding between a group of British and Italian workers who, when working together, found communication difficulties even though English was used as the language of communication. Each group with the help of consultants made explicit its perceptions about the other. On this basis, both groups then recognised the behaviour identified was perfectly legitimate and professional in each respective culture. The challenge became to integrate the best bits of both cultures to add value to the business that can come from cross-cultural teams. The case illustrated the need to bring cultural learning through the organisation to ensure smooth relationships. Identifying and challenging cultural stereotypes at all levels in an organisation can facilitate the adaptation to and understanding of the foreign partner.

---

[6] *www.ici.com*

Throughout this book factors critical to the management of relationship have been presented and analysed. These apply equally to international relationships. The added dimension here being cross-cultural understanding which is often underestimated. Cumulative learning in any society can be difficult for an 'outsider' to understand and become part of. Relationships, particularly close ones, require strong social and structural bonds. These necessitate an adaptation, not only to another organisation and as individuals but to a national cultural as well.

Chapter summary

The chapter began with a case illustration of culture-specific relationships, that of Guanxi in China. The overall aim of the chapter was to present the insights and the usefulness to be gained from using an international relationship and network approach to study the international activity of a firm. The trends forging close cross-border ties and the comparison between a relationship and a sequential view of analysing international business decisions were presented. The additional perspective brought by relationships to four key international business decisions was described. These were selection, entry, expansion, and organisation. Relationships provide opportunities for sourcing new markets and for expansion through partnering. Indeed, any of the market entry modes can be governed by close or more distant relationships that may predicate the very success of market entry. The implications of close relationships for market expansion that may lead to a narrow portfolio of markets and a concentrated strategy were examined. As a firm develops and grows so to does its organisation. The relationship between the different parts of an international organisation may be quite differential. International organisations were likened to a network. Finally the managerial implications of a relationship-centred international strategy were examined. The emphasis was placed on the need for cultural learning to aim, in a close relationship, to know and treat the international partner in the same way as a domestic one. Gaining an international relationship orientation requires adaptation by an organisation but critically by its managers. A lack of cross-cultural relational skill and orientation could impede a company's growth in international markets.

CASE FOR DISCUSSION   **STATOIL RELATIONSHIP APPROACH TO MARKET ENTRY**

Statoil[7] is the Norwegian State owned oil, natural gas, and petrol company who refines oil and gas in the North Sea, and elsewhere, and is also a petrol retailer. It employees over 19 000 people throughout its operations and is a dominant player in many of its markets. This case traces Statoil's selection, entry and expansion into Estonia in the early 1990s as detailed by Ghauri and Holstius (1996). Estonia, at that time, was emerging from Soviet rule, and would therefore, have a Soviet-style administration. This means that the economic and business decision making would be centralised and the concept of western business practices and ownership virtually unknown. No business

---

[7] *www.statoil.com*

legislation as we know it would have existed and therefore trust would be paramount in reducing the uncertainty caused by this, for both the local participants and for the foreign entrant – Statoil in this case. Companies entering other transitional economies or less developed countries would have some experience of the differences and challenges posed by entering such markets. The infrastructure and level of technology would not compare to the home nation nor would the political, legal and cultural climates. Estonia (population 1.5 million), at that time, was looking west for investment and at becoming a member of the European Union. It aims to gain membership of the European Union sometime in the early 2000s and its transition to an open economy is a necessary part of this process. In the mid 1990s Estonia would have attempted to harmonise its laws along the lines of western Europe and have done much to reform its banking system. In 1991 Statoil was the first western company to establish a wholly-owned subsidiary in the Baltic States that were part of the Soviet Union – Eesti Statoil. It set-up petrol stations in the port and capital city of Tallinn and is committed to building Estonia's infrastructure in this area and to transfer management know-how to its subsidiary.

In the selection phase Statoil negotiated with the central and local authorities responsible for foreign firms. This helped exchange two-way information that was critical in establishing credibility in the market. The central Soviet authorities were also important in that phase as Soviet laws were still in place. Estonia became independent of the Soviet Union in 1991. Statoil's objective in the selection phase was to build up a good contact network of both state authorities and industry actors. Since Soviet laws were still in place and Estonia was not independent of Soviet control, approval to establish in Estonia had to be sought from Soviet authorities. However, the central Estonian authorities were important mediators in this process. Statoil would obtain the information needed from the central Estonian authorities to deal with the Soviets and with the local authorities that they were dealing with in Estonian. As Sweden is geographically closer to Estonia than Norway and has close historical ties with Estonia, the responsibility for developing this market was transferred to Statoil's Swedish subsidiary. At a Governmental and Agency level, the Nordic countries had in place a Baltic Investment Programme financed by the Nordic Governments and by the European Bank for Reconstruction and Development (EBRD). In addition, to improve regional co-operation, the Council for the Baltic Sea States was established in 1992 by the countries surrounding the Baltic Sea. As well as the Nordic agencies, the World Bank, the International Monetary Fund and the European Union were also involved in providing finance to the Baltic States, and loans at low rates of interest to companies setting up in the region. Companies that could bring these sources of finance together and have a local contact base had a clear advantage in entering the market. Statoil was able to do this and use its home nationality and ownership to advantage in assembling its contact and finance network to enter the market. The Norwegian government has also established trading agreements with the Baltic States as would have other Nordic countries. As part of its entry negotiation, Statoil also donated some petrol and diesel to demonstrate goodwill in the market. Statoil project management team would have invested considerable amount of time on the project.

Statoil had important contacts in the Foreign Trade Department and other Estonian authorities. The Swedish ambassador, executives from the Swedish Export Council, and the Swedish Foreign Minister helped in developing contacts with the Estonian authorities. The Norwegian ambassador also helped, especially with negotiations about building sites for service stations as Statoil had to rent these sites from the local Estonian authorities. The Estonian authorities would be very risk adverse and would not wish to make mistakes. Their negotiation characteristics would be typical of a centralised state or of hierarchical buying behaviour. Therefore, information meetings arranged by Statoil where the company would discuss its plans and problems were particularly important when Statoil was entering the market. Statoil's multi-level contacts were vital to entering the market but also necessary to develop the market. Statoil was bringing its knowledge of service station management and its commitment to transferring this knowledge to Estonia. To this end, Statoil has sent Swedish employees to train local Estonians but also to transfer information about the market back into the company. The company has had to overcome many problems on entering this market with the lack of established oil distribution network and the initial problems with currency (Estonia now has its own convertible currency) being two key operational problem encountered by Statoil on entry. It also aims to establish itself further in the market by sourcing products for its service stations in Estonian as it develops a supply network, thus integrating itself further into the economic networks of the country.

Postscript: Statoil had, by the end of 1999, 31 service stations in Estonia and the headquarters for the Eesti Statoil subsidiary was in Riga, the capital of Latvia. It is the largest player in the Estonian market and its entry has clearly been a success and has acted as a beachhead for the company in the Baltic States. By the end of 2001, Statoil aimed to have 110 petrol stations in the Baltic States of Latvia, Lithuania and Estonia.

Questions

1. The application of a relationship approach to assessing a market in transition seems very appropriate in this case when compared to a traditional sequential assessment. Comment on this statement. As a class assignment, examine whether you believe a relationship approach is characteristic of Statoil's expansion overseas using an analysis of their web site or newspaper archives.
2. What additional insights did a relational market selection approach achieve in this case when compared to a traditional screening assessment? How much, if any, did Statoil's selection approach contribute to its successful entry into the market?
3. Statoil used an investment entry mode to get into the market through the establishment of Eesti Statoil. This was a risky approach. How was the risk reduced in this case?
4. Examine the importance for Statoil of ensuring its Estonian subsidiary is embedded in its local market. What further steps can it take over-time to achieve it?
5. Many companies were unsuccessful in their entry to Eastern Europe at the time of this case. In the light of this, discuss the managerial applications of the approach to entry taken by Statoil.

Source: Author's research, company web site, and for the research on the internationalisation of Statoil into Estonia: Ghauri and Holstius (1996).

Further reading

Bartlett, C.A. and Ghoshal, S. (1995), *Transnational Management: Texts, Cases and Readings in Cross-Border Management*, 2nd edition, Irwin, Chicago, IL.

Dyer, J.H. and Chu, W. (2000), The determinants of trust in supplier-automaker relationships in the US, Japan, and Korea, *Journal of International Business Studies*, 31 (2), pp. 259–285.

Financial Times (1997), Regional perspectives: Keiretsu, Chaebol, and the Bamboo network, global opportunities in eastern Europe, *Global Business Series*, 3rd April, Part 10 of 10. (www.ftmastering.com/gb10.html)

Griffith, D.A. (2000), Process standardisation across intra- and inter-cultural relationships, *Journal of International Business Studies*, 31 (2), pp. 303–325.

Holm, D.B., Eriksson, K. and Johanson, J. (1996), Business networks and co-operation in international business relationships, *Journal of International Business Studies*, 27 (5), pp. 1033–1053.

Holmlund, M. and Kock, S. (1998), Relationships and the internationalisation of Finnish small and medium sized companies, *International Small Business Journal*, 16 (4), pp. 46–63.

Johnston, W.J., Lewin, J.E. and Spekman, R.E. (1999), International industrial marketing interactions: dyadic and network perspectives, *Journal of Business Research*, 46 (3), pp. 259–271.

Karunaratna, A.R. and Johnson, L.W. (1997), Initiating and maintaining export channel inter-mediary relationships, *Journal of International Marketing*, 5 (2), pp. 11–32.

Lu, Y. and Burton, F. (1998), Reflections on theoretical perspectives of international strategic alliances, in Buckley, P.J., Burton, F. and Mirza, H., editors, *The Strategy and Organisation of International Business*, Chapter 9, Macmillan Press, Hampshire, pp. 149–172.

Sadler, A. and Chetty, S. (1999), The impact of networks on New Zealand, in Dana, L.P., editor, *International Entrepreneurship: An Anthology*, Entrepreneurship Development Centre, Nanyang Technological University, Singapore, pp. 51–70.

Segal-Horn, S. and Faulkner, D. (1999), *The Dynamics of International Strategy*, International Thomson Business Press, London.

Chapter questions

1. The changing nature of the global marketplace is forcing companies to co-operate in international markets. Discuss.
2. Compare and contrast the relational and sequential approaches to making decisions. Refer to selected reading, if necessary.
3. Describe how a company might go about selecting international markets using a relationship approach. How would this vary between a small and large company?
4. As a class project, select a company and examine the impact relationships and networks had on its choice of entry modes and subsequent success in the foreign market.
5. Assess the drawbacks in using a concentrated strategy to expansion in foreign markets with the objective of developing close relationships.
6. Evaluate the impact of a relationship view of organisation on the structure and management of a multinational firm.

7. Write down the key cultural characteristics of two countries of your choice. How will these characteristics impact on your ability to manage business relationships in these countries? How would you challenge stereotypes held about other countries in an organisation and promote cross-cultural learning?

8. Examine the role culture plays in international business relationships. How important is this role?

CHAPTER 12

Relationship performance

Introduction and objectives

Relationships can and do have performance implications. In this chapter, we attempt to synthesise the agenda that strategic market relationships represent a different approach to management. This is an alternative form of exchange behaviour and a potential source of differentiation and hence, competitive advantage. Our approach is to examine the performance differences, if any, between a variety of relationship types and to describe any discernible patterns that might emerge for each of the different relationship structures. We begin with a review of the literature on relationship performance, dividing it into two camps. First, there is the retention/profit performance camp based on economic measures borrowed from finance and accounting. Naturally, this is favoured by investors and traditionalists owing to its specificity. While useful, these measures are retrospective and based solely on outcomes. As such, they can be misleading as predictors of relationship performance since they do not anticipate future interaction. In the second camp, there is the wider but less specific performance dimensions of the relationship, based on inter-organisational evaluation such as satisfaction. However, relationships differ, performance is not uniform or unequivocal and there are merits and disadvantages to both approaches, depending on the context and purpose for which they are used.

Results on relationship performance, from our own research and other sources, are presented and discussed. Although the results are promising, considerable work needs to be done to develop a structure-specific performance metric or scorecard that will prove beneficial across firms and industries in the longer-term.

After reading this chapter you should:

- be aware of the evidence from the literature on relationship performance;
- understand the need for a more comprehensive definition of relationship performance;
- appreciate the performance implications of different relationship types and be able to assess the impact that structure can have on inter-firm relationships;
- be able to work towards identifying and developing a more appropriate set of relational performance measures.

The banking industry illustration that follows is indicative that markets are volatile and unpredictable. Banks have operated for centuries in a very static and traditional mode. This is now changing. This, therefore brings in to question the nature of relationships among different role partners and also poses serious questions about transactions. Different relationship types will influence performance outcomes in this industry in the future.

UK BANKING

Traditionally UK banks have operated in a conventional way whereby they accepted deposits from customers and investors, lent money and operated extensive branch networks to facilitate their transactions. Relationships between customers and their branch were personal, strong and enduring. However, the industry has been going through substantial change in the past several years and this has been transforming the way that financial service are delivered. The boundaries between distribution channels, product categories and types of institutions are now less clear and, in some cases, non-existent. Customers are becoming more sophisticated and time poor. They are less loyal to their banks and more likely to evaluate their options when looking for financial products. Financial services are primarily information based and with de-regulation, the lowering of entry barriers and the capacity of IT to facilitate transactions, intense competition has emerged. Perhaps, more than any other industry, the dual challenge of IT and relationships will affect financial service providers in a dramatic fashion within the next decade. New ways will have to be found to reach and service existing customers, attract new ones and decide on the nature of the relationship that providers have with their customers.

The major distribution channels are currently:

- The branch network
- Automatic teller machines
- Telephone
- PC/internet based home banking

Added to this is the entry of supermarkets as bankers and the widespread availability of cash-back facilities. The changing cost of transactions is shown below:

Distribution channel	Cost per transaction
Branch	£1.07
Telephone (operator-based)	£0.40
ATM	£0.20
Telephone (independent voice recognition)	£0.15
PC transaction	£0.12
Internet transaction	£0.07

(Source: Datamonitor, 1998).

The Internet has already had a profound effect on the delivery of financial services and is likely to bring more radical change (Morgan Stanley Dean Witter, 1999). The intangibility aspect of financial services make them well placed to exploit advances in technology. Core products can be digitised. Customers attribute value to such dimensions as improved communication and enhanced customer service (Booz-Allen and Hamilton, 1999). Benefits to providers include customer loyalty, better targeting of customers and more rapid response. A 1998 study by Ernst & Young predicted that by the year 2000, banks would be spending the same amount of money on Web applications to develop their on-line presence as they currently do on branch networks (Ernst and Young, 1999). At that time only 34% of European banks believed the Internet would help them maintain existing customers. By July 1999, that is in a period of 6 months, the number of Internet banks has doubled.

According to Datamonitor (1999), European banks are spending the equivalent of $1 million per day on e-banking and the total will increase by 2004 to a spend of $1.4 billion per annum, of which $850 million will go to external contractors. Current high set-up costs, telephone charges and security issues are hampering growth but the trend is undeniable since there are advantages for both customers and suppliers in this new relationship. These include:

- cost savings – online transactions are up to 15 times cheaper than traditional branch operations (Datamonitor, 1999);
- the customer will have peace of mind knowing the transaction is done the way they want it;
- increased customer reach with cross-selling of financial products;
- increased customer service and convenience or what has been termed any place, any time, any how banking;
- improved communications and information targeting.

Therefore, customer interaction changes in character and type. Figure 12.1 shows these based on the product and interaction style:

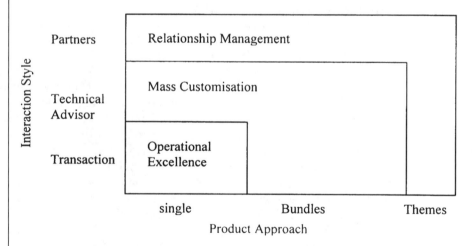

Figure 12.1   Styles of customer interaction (Source: Ernst and Young, 1999).

(a) Transaction level where institutions offer single products at a low price and convenience. For instance, insurance providers deriving customers from their brand and efficiencies by linking with other providers in strategic alliances or partnerships. The AA is an example of this. Performance is retention and loyalty-based.

However, most traditional banks are moving away from competing in single product areas and into higher value product/service combinations.

(b) Technical advisor by combining transactions and cross-selling either directly, or with others, to provide a range of products and services. Virgin Direct are an example of this approach. By being customer focused they are successful in cross-selling products and services and developing the one-to-one relationship based on the appeal of a strong brand and relevant customer service.

Partners where the institutions are trusted third parties that take single products and combine them with added service and information flows. Banks see themselves in this role, as do some building societies and insurance companies. Relationships with others, such as universities and trades unions and other distribution channels such as the link between Tesco and Bank of Scotland, offer new relationship opportunities in this sector.

These different types of relationships between financial service providers and their customers are both a response to, and an ability in, the use information technology. this ability is enhanced by using the internet as part of the relationship. What we appear to be witnessing is that a relationship with a customer, based on the Internet, follows one of three types. Firstly, those with a web presence who provide information via their web site (*www.cbonline.co.uk*). Secondly, those who are web enhanced who, in addition to a presence, offer products and services on-line (*www.royalbankofscotland.co.uk*). Third are the new-comers who are web centric (*www.egg.com* and *www.cahot.com*).

Relationship performance overview

Relationship performance measurement is at its early stage of development. While all business performance is measured in a financial way in the long-term, there is little agreement on how to measure relationship performance in the long-term. Some believe we should concentrate solely on the cost of the transaction in the relationship. For example, by considering the cost of negotiation we can come up with a measure of cost which we could subtract from revenue that will give us a measure of return on a relationship. Others, from a non-financial standpoint, argue for assessment of more behaviour-based (non-financial) outcomes such as satisfaction with the quality of products/services, or with the contribution to problem solving in the relationship. However, many related disciplines use an integrated approach, which we support. The strategic management literature has long supported combining financial and non-financial measures of performance into an overall performance metric (Eccles, 1991; Ketchen et al., 1996). Indeed, this perspective is also reflected in the accounting discipline through, for example, the classic balanced scorecard that stacked a range of measures across key activities in the business into an overall score (Kaplan and Norton, 1996). The development of such a metric might be useful and we would advocate some evaluation or audit of activities to assess the contribution of business value made by relationships.

We see three major problems in the relationship literature to date. First, the remarkable lack of a performance dimension in many of the main theoretical models of relationships. There seems to be an assumption, by many, that relationships are good per se. The second problem is the narrow nature of performance that emerges from many of the relational theory schools that include performance measurement. The schools seem to adhere rigidly to a narrow performance definition that suits the purposes of their theoretical assumptions. These assumptions are usually economic or behavioural based. The final problem is that the main contributors to the relational performance theory literature borrow concepts and measures from other literature. While this theoretical borrowing is welcome, it should be complemented by theory research specific to the area itself. Based on these issues and on the relationship performance literature, several themes relating to relationship performance emerge.

Theme 1 – exclusion of relationship performance from models

Relational performance is often excluded from models of relational development, interaction and indeed, networks. The assumption is made that relationships improve performance. The seminal Industrial Marketing and Purchasing Group's dyadic interaction model (Hakansson, 1982) does not contain a performance dimension but implicitly assumes the performance enhancement quality of relationships. Jackson's (1985) model of account behaviour ignores the performance implications and evaluations of buyer-supplier relationships. Further, Dwyer et al.'s (1987) model of relational development neglects performance motivation while recognising the importance of performance management. Recently, Morgan and Hunt's (1994) classic contribution to industrial marketing relationship theory failed to include a performance dimension in their commitment-trust model. However, these relationship models concentrate on relational processes, which may determine relationship performance. Other authors who include relational performance in their models do so on a limited number of dimensions, such as Mohr and Spekman's (1994) model of partnership success, or Anderson and Narus's (1990) model of distributor-firm and manufacturing-firm working partnership. We assess that performance needs to be addressed in its own right to determine its effects on relationship structure and strategy.

Theme 2 – relationship theory schools pursue a narrow definition of performance

The empirical domain of research into relational performance has been limited. A selection of studies is listed in Table 12.1. Studies were evaluated based on the performance dimensions included. That is whether performance was the major focus and the theoretical base, if any, for the performance dimensions. We did not find a huge number of studies on inter-firm relationship performance and therefore, some of the studies are from other, albeit related, areas. Therefore, there is an obvious need for more research into inter-firm relationship performance. As can be seen from Table 12.1, the amount of studies with a specific theoretical background cited for the performance dimension is rare. Where a theoretical background is given, transaction cost economics (TCE) is the main field of reference. This means that the cost of making the transaction is the main performance item

Table 12.1   Empirical studies on relational performance

Author(s)	Types of relationships studied	Number of respondents	Performance dimensions included	Performance main aim of study yes/no	Relational perspective	Theoretical perspective of performance measures	Business discipline
Heide and John (1988)	Manufacturer-agent	199 agents	Sales, costs	No	Agents	Transaction cost economics (TCE)	Channels
Noordewier et al. (1990)	Buyer-supplier	140 OEM buyers	Acquisition costs	Yes	Buyer	TCE	Industrial marketing
Kumar et al. (1992)	Supplier-re-seller	2 suppliers, 223 re-sellers	Multi-dimensional	Yes	N/A testing scales	Multiple	Channels
McNeilly and Russ (1992)	Manufacturer-dealer	145 dealers	Profit, sales, satisfaction	No	Dealer	Not specified	Channels
Sako (1992)	Buyer-supplier	3 buyers, 36 suppliers	Transaction costs	No	Buyer-supplier	TCE and industrial economics	Industrial markets
Mohr and Spekman (1994)	Manufacturer-dealer	102 dealers	Satisfaction, sales	No	Dealer	Objective and subjective measures – not specified	Channels
Evans and Laskin (1994)	Manufacturer-buyer	276 buyers	Satisfaction, loyalty, profit, quality	No	Buyer	Not specified	Industrial marketing
Boyle and Dwyer (1995)	Distributor-supplier	314 buyers	Task completion	No	Buyer	Not specified	Channels

			Transaction-related				
Heide and Stump (1995)	Manufacturer-supplier	155 buyers, 60 suppliers		Yes	Buyer-supplier	TCE	Industrial marketing
Joseph et al. (1995)	Manufacturer-distributor	221 distributors	Satisfaction, profit, organisational time, effect on other relationships	No	Distributors	Not specified	Channels
Kalwani and Narayandas (1995)	Supplier-manufacturer	152 suppliers	Sales, inventory costs, prices, profits	Yes	Supplier	Economic outputs – not specified	Industrial marketing
Leuthesser and Kohli (1995)	Buyer-supplier	454 buyers	Satisfaction, share of business	No	Buyer	Not specified	Industrial marketing
Dahlstrom et al. (1996)	Buyer-supplier	189 buyers	Transaction costs	No	Buyer	TCE	Channels
Dyer (1996)	Buyer-supplier	5 buying companies, 152 suppliers	Speed of new product development, quality, inventory costs, profit	Yes	Buyer-supplier	TCE	Industrial marketing
Young et al. (1996)	Buyer-supplier	509 buyers	Satisfaction, productive, worthwhile, carried out objectives	No	Buyer	Not specified	Industrial marketing
Artz (1999)	Buyer-supplier	393 buyers	Negotiation costs, delivery, satisfaction	Yes	Buyer	TCE	Industrial markets

being assessed. This limits the conceptualisation of relational performance to a financial definition and to the perspective of one partner – often outcomes are jointly maximised in a relationship and we would prefer to embrace other theoretical schools as discussed in chapter 3.

By developing and testing a wider definition of performance, research can develop and expand the relational performance domain. TCE, a cost perspective, assumes performance is optimised in transactional efficiency and through the performance maximisation efforts of a firm acting alone (Williamson, 1985). Agency theory, like transaction cost, examines the outcomes of relationships between principals and agents in terms of economic costs, particularly, the cost of potential relational abuses and the monitoring of a partnership (Ross, 1973; Bergen et al., 1992) and this is predominantly a risk perspective. The channel literature also sees economic benefits as the main outcomes of relationships with a particular focus on costs and profits of relationships (Heide and John, 1988; Noordewier et al., 1990). In particular, it concentrates on the power-dependency relationship and the outcome balance of any change in this relationship, hence this is a more political perspective. Again, performance is viewed from the perspective of the individual firm. While these benefits are important other schools see more non-financial performance outcomes as being beneficial. The social exchange school of relationships (Blau, 1964; Cook and Emerson, 1978; Macneil, 1980) includes wider benefits of relational co-operation. Areas such as flexibility and satisfaction become important outcomes of inter-firm relationships, thus a conflict resolution and satisfaction perspective.

Much research on relationship performance concentrates on output performance, that is, on the result of a relationship. Others concentrate on how well the interaction process is performing – input measures. Either approach has its merits but most of the empirical work is conducted using output measures. Ganesan (1994) empirically examined the determinants of long-term marketing orientation and is one of the few studies to concentrate on input-based measures of industrial relationship performance. The relationship audit and relationship orientation are two approaches to relationship input performance measurement that have great potential. These could be developed using, as a base, the measures developed by strategy or marketing. In fact, Gummesson (1999) suggests a possible outline for an approach to the development of a relationship audit using the marketing audit as a reference.

Theme 3 – theoretical borrowing

Table 12.1 illustrates that performance is not the main concern of studies that include a relational performance dimension. Performance research in industrial relationships is often as a tag-on to a study with another focus or is assumed to be an outcome of ongoing relationships. This finding relates back to the lack of a performance dimension to the main models of relationships. All the studies cited in Table 12.1 include performance solely from a financial perspective except one. Of the six studies that have performance as the main focus, four take a transaction cost perspective (Noordewier et al., 1990; Heide and Stump, 1995; Dyer, 1996; Artz,

1999), one a financial perspective from figures reported in two US financial data-bases, COMPUTSTAT and Compact Disclosure (Kalwani and Narayandas, 1995), and only one study uses a multidimensional view in its research, combining both financial and non-financial elements of performance (Kumar et al., 1992). Clearly, this broadened perspective should be the place to begin inter-firm relationship performance research.

The three themes identified in this section provide an impetus for research into the inter-firm relationship performance domain. We would argue that this perfor-mance domain has been neglected in research on business market relationships to date. This would also appear to hold true when compared with consumer market relationship research where concepts such as loyalty and retention have been used to measure performance.

Relationship performance in context

Relationship performance research is still at an early stage and has developed with a focus on consumer markets and on the concept of customer retention. However, managing and implementing market relationships is becoming increasingly impor-tant in management for all businesses. In an effort to integrate some of the previous and current work on relationship performance, we attempt to learn from the services, retailing and business to business contexts, starting with context one.

Context 1 – lessons from the service sector

In service-based businesses, particularly business-to-consumer, specific attempts have been made to calculate the lifetime value of customers to demonstrate the importance of customer retention and loyalty (Reicheld, 1996; Heskett et al., 1997). In chapter 9, we stressed the importance of measurement in implementing relation-ship-based strategies. It is vital to measure performance in any management activ-ity but hard measures alone may be too supplier-centric in a relationship context. Realistically, firms must profile their service performance based on their customers' perceptions of the importance of product, service and support criteria, with any shortcomings providing a clear guide for managerial action. As such, this bench-mark approach will highlight interesting considerations for the firm's positioning in the market and form the basis for a relationship enhancement programme, but are not complete measures of relationship performance.

To recap, we do know that measurement in terms of customer retention rates is crucial to profitability. Work by Bain and Co., management consultants has suggested that a 5% swing in an organisation's customer retention rate levers profits by between 25 and 85% across a broad spectrum of industries (Dawkins and Reichheld, 1990). Zero defection by customers, i.e. retaining every profitable customer, is therefore a performance measure and profit indicator of utmost impor-tance (Reicheld and Sasser, 1990). However, all relationships are not the same and not all customers are profitable to the same extent. Relationships imply that custo-mers are treated on an individual basis but these measurement schemes do have merits. Measures of customer satisfaction and customer retention are the key to long-run profitability and help management evaluate whether their strategy is working or not. It is now accepted that it is five to eight times less expensive to retain loyal customers than to attract new ones (Knauer, 1992).

The pursuit of customer loyalty and measures to evaluate it is therefore deemed to be a profitable marketing practice. Increasingly, firms accept that a co-operative approach to trading is preferred to an adversarial one. Hence, strategic market relationships is a driver of improved corporate performance. This is a virtuous circle that management must encourage. Customer satisfaction drives customer loyalty but care must be taken that customer and competitive forces do not drive the market place back into a highly price-sensitive mode. If the vendor is to protect its market position, strategies that emphasise account management, product augmentation, and customer service must, at some point, give way to a strategy based at least partly on price. It is important to continually monitor performance and moderate the value offered to your customers.

An organisation's service performance cannot be determined without measuring it. Only by comparing organisational opinions with those of internal employees and customers can confirmation or refutation of a service effect and its performance be made. Deciding on the basis of appropriate measures is not an easy task (Goodman, 1995). The lessons here are that measuring satisfaction and retention is important but these do not, on their own, measure relationship performance. Input measures of service performance are useful but they seldom take into account different customers and contexts. Further, the satisfaction-loyalty connection is not always explicit with many satisfied customers not remaining loyal (Jones and Sasser, 1995).

Context 2 – lessons from the retail sector

The characteristics driving increased service performance are part of the trend by buyers to be more explicit in their needs, the increasing trend to relationship building and the pursuit of quality and excellence by suppliers. Higher service is found in the better performing companies and is a continuing process whereby organisations strive for competitive advantage, customer satisfaction and loyalty. Leading companies measure and obtain comments on service performance, pursue superior quality service strategies and have meetings to discuss these issues. These firms are doing most things and doing them well. These 'things' are customer based (Donaldson, 1995). UK retailers, despite their need to pursue economies of scale, have been successful in relationship building with customers using a similar approach.

From a managerial perspective, it is essential to separate that which can be controlled, measured and managed from that which is the overall result of the organisation's endeavours. Many sales promotions and customer retention schemes have been called loyalty programmes but what do we really understand customer loyalty to be? Some on the high street, including supermarkets and petrol stations, have been using 'loyalty cards'. When a certain level of expenditure is achieved, prizes, mostly in the form of discounts on future purchases are awarded.

Research has shown that such schemes attract already existing customers, but do not encourage new customers (Mintel, 1998). With some of the schemes there is evidence that if the rewards are not sufficiently attractive, they may even cause customers to defect to alternative suppliers. Taking as an example Marks & Spencer (M&S): they have a charge/credit card where members receive mailshots, magazines, invites to fashion evenings and occasional special offers. Their customers use their cards frequently, some very heavy users may be considered loyal. Again, research has shown that M&S have higher levels of customer satisfaction and customer loyalty than other retailers do, yet their sales and profit performance in recent years has been relatively poor. Most M&S customers buy food from other outlets and clothes from other stores, so its customers are not 100% captive. There is some form of relationship in these situations but our definition of customer loyalty needs re-appraisal and some alternative measures of relationship performance need to be introduced.

Measures of service performance, satisfaction and loyalty need to be used cautiously. In the M&S case, there is evidence that high ratings in customer satisfaction encouraged complacency among some managers (personal interview sources). In terms of up-stream suppliers, the sudden decision by M&S to terminate some long-term supply agreements came as an unpleasant surprise. Terminating agreements of long standing, for example with Bairds and Courtaulds, has spoiled M&S's reputation and left the company to be seen as resorting to increasingly desperate measures. Relationships are not one-way but a co-ordinated approach as a way of doing business.

In other cases, the loyalty schemes have been so successful, as a promotion, that they have become separate businesses in their own right. The British Airways sponsored loyalty scheme 'Airmiles' which subsequently incorporated, among others, BA, Hilton Hotels, Shell, BT was one such case. Schemes such as British Home Stores (BHS) with its choice card, Tesco, Sainsbury, and others have introduced similar customer retention schemes but most of these so-called 'loyalty' programmes are a form of sales promotion under a different name. If this promotion is effective, customers will be retained and business increased, but only for as long as the promotion is run. There is every chance that the customer will go back to their preferred product and so the loyalty is to the promotion itself rather than to the brand or the outlet.

The lessons here are that a real loyalty programme gathers information that distinguishes between different customers and then offers them benefits tailored to their individual needs. This is the relationship approach. Whilst there is much contention and debate and many unresolved issues about relationship performance, a customer facing strategy, product performance and service delivery form the basics for relationship performance. The problem is that relationships are more difficult to define and to measure than loyalty measures alone. Indeed, many companies use measures of customer satisfaction as a surrogate for customer loyalty and measures of loyalty as surrogates for relationships but these are not the same. Measuring customer satisfaction is problematic because it measures perceptions and a state of mind, not actual behaviour and certainly not future behaviour.

Likewise measuring dissatisfaction, for example via complaints, does not confirm that those who did not complain are satisfied. Customer satisfaction does not therefore automatically lead to customer loyalty. A better measure of customer loyalty is to measure customer defections through some form of lost order analysis and repeat purchase behaviour.

To recap, customer retention is a phenomenon whereby a customer uses a particular product or service regularly and shows signs of being loyal to that company. What we are witnessing with most loyalty schemes and loyalty measures is an assessment in transaction mode only. The loyal customer will view a product or service in a particular way and the retention comes from the customer themselves rather than from the supplier's actions. As a result, customer loyalty is difficult to measure and of course will be dependent on contingent factors such as the type of product or service and the time span over which purchases are made and repeated. The degree of loyalty and the point at which loyalty develops from retention is different for every customer. The customer may only become loyal if something extraordinary, or beyond the call of normal practice occurs or because the supplier has done something extraordinary. Therefore, customer loyalty is impossible to measure and manage in a conventional way and this also applies to relationships.

Context 3 – business-to-business relationships

Successful relationship based organisations, in both services and retailing, show that companies need to be both mass customisers, efficiently providing goods and services at economical prices in a way that customers require them, and also one-to-one marketers that are responsible and flexible to each customer's special needs and preferences. To really cultivate learning relationships with customers, an organisation must have a desire to listen to, collaborate with each customer, and turn this into products and services that provide benefits. Information technology has made this combination of efficiency and customisation not only possible but cost efficient.

The search for competitive advantage is relentless. Although some Western economies and some prestigious organisations may have reached an 'age of contentment', firms operating in competitive markets must constantly invigorate themselves to remain competitive. Successful companies do a number of things and do them well, but such activity and the prosperity it brings requires constant renewal, innovation and often a degree of luck. The literature on what it is that makes a company successful and keeps it there is first fashionable, then fashionable to knock, as companies find it difficult to adapt or change to new circumstances, competitors and external conditions. Customers, on the other hand, often portrayed as fickle, irrational and susceptible are much more consistent than is generally acknowledged. With the exception of passing fads and trends in selected consumer goods, customers still seek price, quality and service in their purchases. In most organisational buying situations for repeat purchase products, price and quality can be defined, measured, explicitly stated, related and with a reasonable degree of objectivity, evaluated. Given this, both suppliers and buyers have focussed on service-related aspects to differentiate between competing alternatives with the aim of assisting management to identify what to measure, how it can be done and with what effect. Our review of the literature and our recent empirical research confirms that a relationship approach is the way forward for many firms across different markets and product categories.

Where different relationship types are introduced they tend to be the polar opposites: the extreme cases of discrete versus relationship exchanges (Jackson, 1985). Thus, the benefits of having a relationship are compared only with the traditional independence model of marketing. This concentration may underplay the variety in the degree of relational elements present in many situations. Indeed, even a traditional arm's length approach may have considerable relational elements, as standards of prices, quality and delivery may be a minimum expectation of all relationship types. In addition, these relationships may be long in duration as this could suit both parties. The lessons here are to treat customers as individuals but be clear what type of relationship is appropriate. To achieve superior returns for any relationship type a separation of the performance dimensions and the variety of governance structures is needed. In essence, relationship performance may vary across relationship types and this performance may be quite different. Firms in relationships that have a long-term element to them will have different performance outcomes depending on how they are governed.

The link between relationship governance and performance

These contexts suggest the need to be aware that the relationship type will impact on performance and it is necessary to differentiate between relationships. The four common relationship forms labelled bilateral, discrete, dominant partner (hierarchical), and recurrent introduced in chapter 6 are repeated here and used to assess relationship performance (Figure 12.2).

By focusing on the different structural forms of relationships, a realistic performance management programme can be put in place. For example, if a broad range of non-financial performance outcomes is preferred, then close relationships will be needed but it may be difficult to move to this type from more antagonistic positions. Management culture and style may preclude the leveraging of maximum performance outcomes under any given type. To recap, bilateral relations are co-involved, mutually co-operative structures. Discrete relationships represent the market type but with realistic minimum levels of relationship activity to facilitate the exchange. A dominant partner or hierarchical-based relationship is where the partner unilaterally uses its decision making power. Recurrent relationships represent the archetypal just-in time (JIT) relationship – close but not strategic enough to be bilateral. Any of these structural types can be found in long-term relationships.

As already outlined, few empirical studies attempt to link a range of governance structures to performance but one exception is Dahlstrom et al. (1996) who, in a logistical industry study using three of the forms, found their antecedents to impact on performance. However, some authors have used one or two of the four types and linked them differentially to performance. For example, Sako (1992) linked

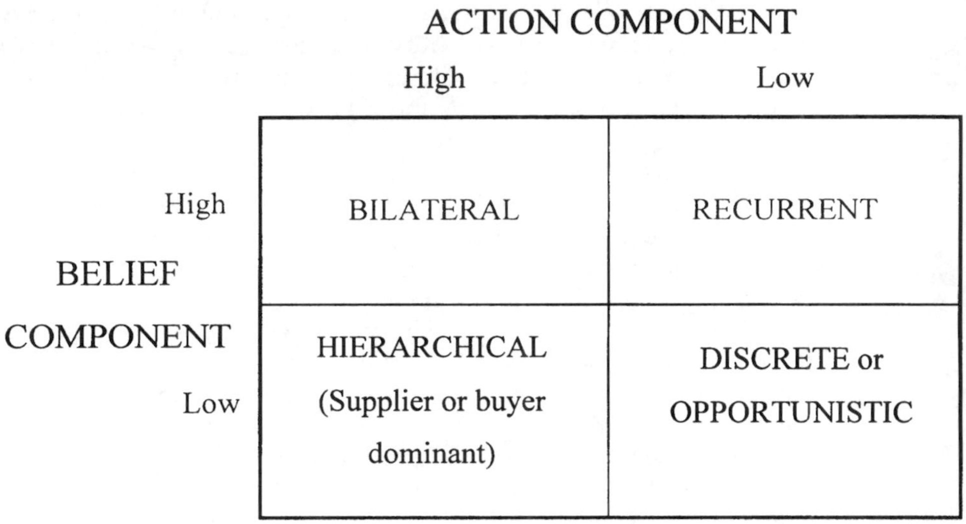

ACTION COMPONENT

	High	Low
High	BILATERAL	RECURRENT
Low	HIERARCHICAL (Supplier or buyer dominant)	DISCRETE or OPPORTUNISTIC

BELIEF COMPONENT

Figure 12.2   The relationships matrix.

bilateral (obligational) and discrete (arm's length) relationships to the performance of buyer–supplier relationships in a study of British and Japanese companies.

Understanding relationships and the development of suitable metrics is an essential focus of business exchange behaviour. Unfortunately, models of business-to-business relationship performance are often descriptive and, if measured, are limited to a few dimensions reflecting a narrow theory or practice assumption. Our own research investigated inter-firm relationships that incorporated both non-financial and financial output dimensions of inter-firm relationship performance (Donaldson and O'Toole, 2000). In particular, we assessed what it is that was being sought and delivered within relationships and thus increased our understanding of relationship performance[1].

Using a range of performance measures (see Table 12.2) we assessed not only for differences but for the effects of different relationship types.

Bilateral relationships perform significantly better than the other relationship types across most of the non-financial performance measures. Using bilateral firms as the comparison group, our research shows them to be significantly different to dominant partner and discrete firms on all except one non-financial outcome (design involvement for dominant partner). In addition, dominant partner types also perform at a low level comparatively, even to discrete relationships. Being in a partner dominant relationship, with the partner using its power, produces lower

[1] The results are developed from seven qualitative interviews followed by a postal survey incorporating the views of 200 industrial respondents in the UK. To examine the relationship among the performance variables, factor analysis was conducted on 21 dimensions of performance included in the research. On this basis, key dimensions of relationship performance are grouped and implications drawn for defining relationship performance and its measurement.

Table 12.2   Performance evaluation statements

Non-financial performance statements:
"The overall benefits of the relationship are better in comparison to other relationships we are in"
"The lead times for this supplier are shorter than for others"
"The quality of this supplier's product is higher than others"
"The speed of response to problems by this supplier is quicker than others"
"We are happy with this relationship"
"One of the main advantages of this relationship is its stability"
"A lot of value that is difficult to quantify has been created in this relationship"
"One of the main advantages of this partnership is its flexibility"
"We are constantly working on joint value added projects in the relationship"
"The supplier is involved in the design of our products"

Financial performance statements:
"It would be difficult to switch to an alternative relationship"
"The more interdependent we are in this relationship the better"
"The relationship makes it easy for an abuse of confidence to happen" (reversed)
"The relationship has meant we have to share a lot of information and knowledge that we would normally resist" (reversed)
"The costs we have avoided in this relationship are less than in similar ones" (reversed)
"The prices we pay in this relationship are lower than in comparable ones"
"Return on investment (ROI) is higher in this relationship than in others"
"The long-term profitability of this relationship is higher in comparison to alternatives"
"The bought volume in this relationship is higher when compared to others"
"More costs are shared equally in this relationship when compared to others"
"The overall costs of running this relationship are lower in comparison to others"

outcomes than a discrete relationship. In an overall sense, non-financial performance divides the dominant partner and discrete types from the other two.

Bilateral firms also perform better than other relationship types across a range of financial performance measures. From a financial perspective, the costs of running all the relationships would seem similar as would price comparisons except for dominant partners who probably pay higher prices due to their weaker power position. Similar responses across the relationship types on bought volume was expected as they represented main supply relationships. However, it was not as significant as discrete types where it was easier to switch. Confidence abuse is only a significant outcome in dominant partner relationships when compared to other types. This is probably an outcome feature unique to the dominant partner form. Being more interdependent and sharing costs are performance outcomes unique to bilateral relationships. Both they and dominant partner types cannot easily switch. A similar pattern emerges for information asymmetry which is a choice in bilateral relationships but not so in dominant partner ones.

Performance does vary across the four relationship structures included in the research for main supply relationships. This supports existing research which links relationships to performance and extends it to a variety of governance structures. The multi-faceted nature of relationship performance, including both financial and non-financial items, is needed to access the scope of the performance possibilities of buyer-supplier relationships. However, the results also have some conflicting theoretical implications. Transaction cost economic (Williamson, 1985) predictions of higher costs of closer relationships were not borne out. These costs, if incurred, must be leading to greater cost saving elsewhere. This implication has received much support in the studies, cited earlier, which link long-term relationships to performance (see Kalwani and Narayandas, 1995, for example).

A consideration of those performance dimensions relevant to each structural type, as well as an idea of the weighting attributed to these in performance evaluation, is needed before conclusive metrics for each relationship type can be established. Also, an evaluation of both sides of the relationship divide may be necessary to understand the dynamics of the performance variables. It is likely that performance will be maximised where both parties have agreed on outcomes and understand the nature of their relationship. Whilst the performance of bilateral relationship in this study is noteworthy, each of the four types may be effective if managed in their ideal forms. Considering the length of the relationship was not significant, it may be that a range of relational types can be effective and stable, provided that management can cope with the diversity.

Managers need to be aware that the relationship type will impact on performance. It is necessary to differentiate between relationships and their performance. By focusing on the structural forms, a realistic performance management programme can be put in place. Fundamentally, the nature of the relationship will impact on the performance. If a broad range of non-financial performance outcomes are preferred, then bilateral and recurrent relationship may be needed but it may be difficult to move to these types from more antagonistic positions. Management culture and style may preclude the leveraging of performance outcomes maximised under any given type.

The performance of close relationships was a feature of this research. Bilateral relationships seem to offer a broad range of performance possibilities. Whether this can be translated into superior performance and thus, competitive advantage is a challenging research issue.

Chapter summary

In this chapter, we have reviewed some of the literature on relational performance. Criticisms concerning some previous work focussed on the lack of performance dimensions, being too restrictive in theoretical assumptions and representing either financial or non-financial, seldom both. However, context is crucial. Significant gain in understanding about relationships have emerged from services, retailing and business to business contexts. Our own research, in the business to business context, suggests that relationships are seen as having positive links to performance but little is known about the nature of this performance. Relationship performance research that investigates the dimensions and relationship-specific attributes of performance can provide researchers and managers with further justification to implement relationship management strategies. This work keeps the management of relationships as a strategic issue within and between organisations. If research into the performance of relationships remains neglected then, by default, relationships may be in danger of becoming a mere fad, or regulated to a tactical rather than strategic weapon in a firm's competitive armoury. For the longer-term, we would also like to be able to link performance to individual relationship structural types. Academics and practitioners alike can gain much from knowing that different forms of relationships can yield different performance outcomes for both parties in a relationship.

CASE FOR DISCUSSION   **LANDIS AND STAEFA**

Landis and Staefa (L&S) is a global company divided into three regional corporations based in Europe, Asia and America. It is a US $1.8 billion company, employing 12 700 people in 55 countries. The company is a leading supplier in building and energy efficiency for commercial, residential and industrial building using the latest building control technology. This includes computer-based building management systems, field controllers and devices such as sensors, valves and actuators. Valves and actuators are the core components of any control system in the field of heating, ventilation and air conditioning. In addition, L&S offer services to engineer and commission projects, as well as providing facilities management and performance contracting services. However, their business is mostly through indirect channels as shown in Figure 12.3.

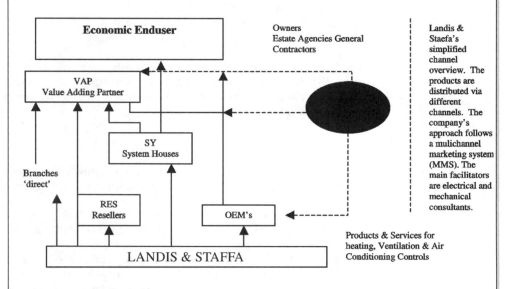

Figure 12.3   Channel overview.

The channels shown can be described as follows:

- Original Equipment Manufacturers (OEMs) – buy different products and integrate them into their own manufactured product. The OEM's customer receives the single bundled product solution designed, tested and guaranteed. Special discounts and specialised products can be provided based on volume.
- Wholesalers – buy products and resell to other customers. Depending on volume, variable discounts apply. Ideally, L&S are looking to grow with the distributor in a specific geographical area and look for long-term financial and commercial viability.
- System houses are control specialists who can offer complete hardware and software solutions to control the heating, ventilation and air conditioning (HVAC) systems in buildings. They buy a range of products from different suppliers and create their own systems and prices for solutions.
- Value added partners cover a wide range of customers with various skills relating to the installation and service of HVAC devices and controls. They may be installers, contractors or panel builders and will work closely with building authorities, HVAC consultants and project managers. They are important intermediaries but require a lot of support from branch level operations.

The business is very profitable with strong growth in the building management systems division. L&S's comprehensive range of products means that the company can offer an appropriate solution whatever the application. In an effort to maintain growth and increase sales and profits of valves and accentuators, the company have:

- created demand with end users via advertising and PR activity;
- increased service and support;
- increased the level of training for planners and contractors, their main facilitators;
- developed more added value distributors;
- strengthened relationships with wholesalers;
- opened new channels with performance contracting and facilities management systems.

However, by selling through this variety of channels, their only means of control is via price and discounts. Each channel partner or intermediary has a different position in the value chain but control and consistency is difficult. Relationships do vary and management must adjust for different contexts.

Questions

1. Using the distribution model in Figure 12.3, can you classify the different types of relationships using the matrix from Figure 12.2? Discuss the suitability of the model in this context.
2. Given that relationships are important with all intermediaries, what performance measures would you advise? How might these measures differ between types of intermediary that the company use?
3. Although service is important to all customers, the type of services and the cost of providing them put a strain on profitability. Some projects with profitable customers lose the company money. What are your recommendations with regard to added value services? Do you price them separately at cost, as a profit revenue earner or incur the cost in the overall total order?

4. Given the importance of the supply chain should L&S attempt to become the essential link in this chain and provide solutions for their customer's customer?
5. How do you see the internet changing the distribution system and relationships in this business?

Further reading

Doyle, P. (2000), *Value-Based Marketing: Marketing strategies for corporate growth and shareholder value*, Wiley, Chichester.

Gale, B.T. (1994), *Managing Customer Value*, Free Press, New York.

Jaworski, B. and Kohli, A. (1993), Market orientation: antecedents and consequences, *Journal of Marketing*, 57 (July) pp. 53–70.

McQuiston, D.H. (2001), A conceptual model for building and maintaining relationships between manufacturers' representatives and their principals, *Industrial Marketing Management*, Vol. 30, No. 2, pp. 165–181.

Oliver, R.L. (1997), *Satisfaction: A Behavioural Perspective on the Consumer*, McGraw-Hill, New York.

Peppard, J. (2000), Customer relationship management (CRM) in financial services, *European Management Journal*, 18 (3), pp. 312–327.

Woodruff, R.B. (1997), Customer value; the next source of competitive advantage, *Journal of the Academy of Marketing Science*, 25 (2), pp. 139–153.

Chapter questions

1. Examine your own personal reasons for choosing a bank/building society. Consider the benefits you were seeking and describe your normal means of contact. Anticipate how your method of contact may change over the next 10 years. Do you envisage that all your banking could be done from a hand-held device? What are the relationship implications of your analysis?
2. Explain some of the difficulties in relationship performance assessment.
3. Compare and contrast financial with non-financial dimensions as measures of relationship performance.
4. In some financial service organisation it has been estimated that it costs 5, 8 even 20 times less to retain a customer than to acquire a new one. What reasons can be given for these ratios?
5. How do you assess costs in relationships? What elements do you rate as crucially important and which less important and why?
6. The managing director of your firm has asked you to recommend measurement of customer loyalty. How would you respond?
7. Research seems to show that, in some situations, bilateral relationships outperform other type. Explain why this may be the case.
8. Firms are in business to make money. It follows that return on investment and profit on sales are far more important measures of success than assessing relationship performance. Discuss.

CHAPTER 13

Strategic market relationships: conclusions and further reflection

Introduction

This chapter brings together the key ideas of the book: it sums up its main themes. The core idea in the book is that relationships are strategic and should be managed as such. We believe relationships can be managed, i.e. we take a managerial approach to the study of relationships. However, this task is complex as there are a wide variety of relationship types and strategic avenues. We concentrated, primarily, on close relationships. The material can be adapted to suit alternative relationship strategies. Managing close relationships requires co-operation from participating partners. In this sense, management is a joint activity. However, relationship strategy can be understood and planned for by an individual firm and this activity should be at a strategic level. Individual firm can make relationship choices and implement them.

In the text we brought the study of strategic market relationships from strategy to implementation. This structure involved consideration of how to analyse relationships, formulate a relationship strategy and implement it. We have covered such topics as relationship planning, relationship classification and electronic relationships. The structure of the book has also helped us to achieve another key objective – to integrate the relationship literature into a cohesive course of study for the relationship manager, strategists, or marketer, or indeed, researcher. We also hope that we have provided students of relationships with a starting point for research through the provision of ample references and selected further reading for each topic area. The constraint of writing this book has meant leaving out topics in favour of others. In this final chapter we introduce some further issues to the reader, especially in the areas of relationship ethics and researching relationships, and add some future relationship trends.

In common with many of the writers that have received multiple citations in this text, we believe relationships represent a different way of doing business. They can be seen as a 3rd way – governance that is not reliant on the market or on an organisational hierarchy. We presented mainly win-win type scenarios that revolved around the decision-making assumption of the benefits and realities of interdependence and long-term horizons. Our perspective is a strategic one, founded on the view that relationships do indeed represent a paradigm shift.

Relationship strategy

The first half of this text was devoted to relationship strategy and presented the tools and techniques to define, analyse and develop a relationship strategy. Strategic market relationships are a way of looking at business that questions the independent action model of a firm typical of many business strategy texts. Clearly we view a relationship approach as a philosophy for doing business. The focus of the book is on an interactive, close relationship structure and we see this form as an ideal governance mode but, in practice, only available to a few, and some would argue only wanted by a few! Therefore, the strategic focus of this book is on cooperation as a means of competing. However, relationships do involve risk and even in close relationships some of the greatest risk can be inertia and reluctance to change. The strategy developed to manage risk depends on the relationship type. Co-operation in antagonist, forced relationships has huge information and dependence risks. Much strategy in these situations might be about reducing dependence or placing safeguards to avoid abuses in the relationship. Perhaps an unhelpful development in relationships is the fact that the term itself has become generic, applying to all relationship. We have tried to avoid this by concentrating on the beliefs and actions in a relationship which determine its underlying nature, so instead of discussing a generic relationship we can discuss a discrete versus bilateral relationship. Beliefs about the nature of relationships can be strongly held and the range of actions that a firm is willing to take in the relationship limited by its worldview. Yet these beliefs and actions can differentiate among relationships and provide a range of opportunities for trying to implement a relationship development strategy. Changing beliefs may require a cultural change and a change in actions possible in a range of activities including customer service levels, and in investment and adaptation patterns. We re-produce our relationship classification matrix here (Figure 13.1) to emphasise the focus of strategy on a variety of relationship types, or ways of managing/governing a relationship, and to acknowledge that our prime focus has been on one of these types – bilateral relationships. There are major opportunities for research in each quadrant of the matrix that move us away from generic labels even at a supra relationship level such as an alliance. We do acknowledge that the boundaries between types may not be fixed and there may be other types, but it becomes more difficult to differentiate among them as we move from one of the four categories to another.

Managing strategic market relationships is about making choices. The key decisions that have to be made include: whether or not to pursue collaboration as a strategy; which relationships offer the greatest value potential; what level of benefits should be provided to relationships; how should these benefits/resources be delivered. If relationships are considered strategic to a firm then a high value will be placed on them and on the contents of this book. Strategic market relationships were defined as the process of analysis and formulation of a relationship strategy

ACTION COMPONENT

		High	Low
		BILATERAL	RECURRENT
BELIEF COMPONENT	High		
	Low	HIERARCHICAL (One party dominant)	DISCRETE (Minimum relationship characteristics)

Figure 13.1   The relationship classification matrix.

for a firm. Relationship management is about implementing it. If relationships are deemed strategic then an organisation will have to embrace a relationship orientation. This requires managerial commitment and an internal culture appropriate to the relationship strategy. Relationships are processes and require organisational resources to be organised in this way, i.e. around processes not products. Relationships have ambiguous borders and multiple participants. We embraced the multi-layered fabric of a network as well as the concept of managed stakeholder relationships. Within an individual organisation, relationship do not recognise functions and may have many participants. Thus, the need to infuse the organisation in a culture appropriate to the relationship strategy chosen is all important.

Relationships have been presented in this book as a strategic resource. This view has been supported in most chapters but also from a theoretical standpoint. A quote from Barringer and Harrison (2000) illustrates the rich theoretical work completed on relationships:

> ...The fact that interorganisational relationships can be justified from such diverse theoretical backgrounds ... says a lot about the theoretical soundness of interorganisational relationships. As management researchers, we are hard pressed to think of another organisational practice that can be justified from such a broad range of traditions.
>
> Barringer and Harrison (2000, p. 395)

The question often asked of relationship is that are they appropriate to consumer markets? The work of Evert Gummesson and Christian Gronroos, part of the Nordic School of service business relationship among other things, would suggest that they are. However, in mass consumer relationship with little contact between the firm and its customers typical of most consumer products it is difficult to see how a relationship philosophy can be implemented (O' Malley and Tynan, 1999). We have suggested two strategic ways of investing in mass consumer relationships (i.e. outside the many tactics) – one is in adherence to the relationship philosophy which means listening and taking actions with the integrity and honesty needed to be a relational partner, and the second is through communication, especially, through long-term emotive brand relationships that are not one-to-one but do represents the beliefs in the relationship and act as a base line guarantee for relationship implementation at a further level down. Mass consumer relationships might be only evident in tactical short-term tactics but should be rooted in relationship brand values that last.

Relationship implementation

The second half of the book concentrated on relationship implementation. We organised our examination of relationship implementation around the 5-S framework – style, staff, structure, systems and schemes. The 5-S of relationship implementation were introduced in our chapter on relationship planning. Each of the 5-Ss is covered to varying degrees throughout this book mainly in the 2nd half. One of the best ways of getting into detail on implementation is to examine a specific implementation process. We do this with a focus on customer relationship management (CRM). However, this analysis also places CRM within an implementation domain rather than a strategic one. Many relationship authors argue that systems such as CRM or loyalty card schemes are strategic. We depart from this and argue that they can be part of implementing a relationship strategy but are not strategic in themselves. Often, when such systems and schemes are successful they are given strategic status. This may be to confuse successful implementation with strategy. Good implementation can disguise weak strategy but the two aligned are a powerful combination. Many fads of relationship management will come and go, but strategic foundations will be needed for sound relationship implementation in the long-term. We devoted a chapter to e-relationships. Making the decision to develop electronic business relationship is strategic, for example, the development of Ford and General Motors' electronic supply/trading systems but the ongoing management of these systems requires careful implementation.

Nowhere are underlying differences in relationship strategy so evident as in e-relationships. The technology is now readily available at relatively low costs but the levels of integration vary widely. Close relationships can exhibit a pattern of dense and rich electronic communication as well as allowing virtual cross-company electronic systems integration. Few other relationships would run the risks of such co-operation. One of the simplest technologies to use and one of the fastest to be adopted is electronic mail. Yet the content and density of e-mail exchange between partners can be illustrative of the way that relationship is managed. There are many areas for research in the e-relationship field as it is emergent. One interesting area for investigation is the development of virtual communities on the web and their interaction and effect on company policy. Can such e-groups be managed?

Whilst we provide a framework for relationship implementation we realise it is a very fluid concept. Relationships are embedded in a social structure that precludes absolute prescription. The need for flexibility in implementation is paramount, especially in close relationships. This responsiveness is delivered through people who are critical in inter-partner implementation interfaces. Strong relationship orientation acts as a guide for adaptation that may be needed at an implementation level as relationship responses at interfaces can be situational and therefore not capable of being planned. Yet, having systems that are planned is important from a consistency and control point of view to avoid partner confusion say, for example, with expected levels of service. Processes must be mapped using the 5-S but be flexible to respond to the relational need. Balancing the need for clear and standard processes with flexibility is a challenge for relationship management.

Two other opportunities for adding value in relationship implementation were presented in the 2nd half of the text – relationship innovation and internationalisation. The potential for new product/service/process development in collaborative relationships is immense. There are major benefits to such an approach including reductions in costs and risks in the process. Obviously, clear risk avoidance strategies are needed to prevent disputes over patents and innovation ownership in partnering scenarios, especially, where direct competitors are co-operating. Most collaboration happens in non-competitive relationships and the benefits of using relationships for generating and developing innovations goes without saying, regardless of how close the relationship. Bringing a relationship analysis to the internationalisation process also has clear benefits. Not to recognise the connectedness of international business would be a costly error. So often the choice of partner is critical to subsequent success. Using foreign relationships in a strategic way can bring big advantages but also cultural challenges not present in domestic relationships. Perhaps taking a relationship approach and getting to know your partners develops the home company's understanding in a way that alternative solo approaches do not.

We completed our analysis of implementation with relationship performance. This linked our presentation back to strategy as an analysis of relationship performance may drive future strategic choices. Measuring relationship performance can be specific to the type of business (service versus industrial) and to the type of relationship (bilateral versus hierarchical). Nonetheless, the calculation of a return on relationships is vital if relationships are to be used strategically. Suitable metrics will probably be situational but can be developed from among the sets presented in our chapter. Many measures such as satisfaction, loyalty and retention are appealing when applied to relationships and offer great potential when combined into overall metrics. Further performance research is necessary and there are loads of possible avenues in both measuring the process and outcomes of relationships. Indeed, developing a process performance audit for all key stakeholder relationship would be the ideal and could be used for board review of relationship governance.

Relationship ethics

Ethics plays a central role in much business practice. In relationships, ethical issues are often to the fore. Usually, ethical problems are prevalent where one party in the relationship is weaker relative to the other and the stronger party abuses its dominant position. It is not possible to give a full review of ethical relationship issues here but when one considers the potential ethical dilemmas in the multiple relationships and relationship interactions that any one company has, it is an area that warrants academic research and practice codes of conduct. In broader societal ethics (looking at relationships from the outside), co-operation that might cause collusion represented in price fixing, for example, is a competitive issue of some significance. Yet its very notion is against a real relationship philosophy that is concerned with all stakeholders.

One area for further research is in the area of customer relationship ethics. Fournier et al. (1998) in their research on relationship marketing argued that consumer can feel victimised and stressed by companies' self-interested attempts at relationship building. In particular, they questioned the use or non-use of consumer information by companies. Company-held customer records may be sold on by companies without their consent which makes consumers feel frustrated but they seem powerless to do anything about it. This type of situation leads to dissatisfaction and negative emotional responses to products and to companies. The authors argued for the need to regain trust through honest dealing and by being up-front about motives. Companies should consider the real costs of intimate relationships and whether it is possible to have these types of relationships with all consumers. Regaining an ethical balance in relationships is possible through genuine attempts at relationship building. LaBerge and Svendsen (2000) described how a forest products company re-built its relationships after the discovery by consumers and other interest groups of its intention to log old-growth forests. The company was forced by its stakeholders to change via the activism of these groups. Pressure was put on its customers and its share price dropped. The company turnaround was based on ethical values and led to the signing of a memorandum of understanding with interest groups 6 years after the problem surfaced. Being ethical in relationships requires a clear statement of relationship values and principles of conduct.

Researching relationship

Relationship researchers can use the vast array of qualitative and quantitative research methods available. We tend to favour the use of multiple methods from theory to the design of research instruments. However, there is a distinct divide among relationship researchers as the usefulness of quantitative versus qualitative methods. Many researchers prefer qualitative research due to relational and network complexity but researchers have used both methods – quantitative research tends to be more prevalent in the US research tradition.

At some stage in a research investigation it is probably germane to do some work that investigates both sides of a relationship (dyadic research). Obviously, if one accepts the process nature of relationships, dyadic research is a minimum necessary to get the full picture. Perhaps, one could go further and stress the need for longitudinal (over time) studies given that relationships are long-term. The easiest way to begin relationship research is to start with a particular focal relationship, for example, between a selling and a buying organisation. This can help anchor the researcher. However, micro relationship research of this type is often criticised as it may neglect the larger, more complex, network issues.

Networks can be extremely complex to research in their entirety, i.e. to take an holistic approach may be too challenging a task! One way out of this dilemma is to take, as a minimum, a triad – a focal relationship and another significant connection. We have already considered network research that begins at the level of the firm versus the broader macro or industry level in chapter 5.

The range of specific methodologies applied to relationships has been impressive and range from inductive approaches such as grounded theory to advanced statistical modelling. The Industrial Marketing and Purchasing Group (IMP) has tended to use multiple methods with a focus on a qualitative case framework (Hakansson, 1982). Multiple case study work has intuitive appeal in capturing complexity, allowing for comparison and in developing theory (see Easton, 1998, for a justification of the case method). Survey work (mail and structured interview) is also common but often only assesses a one-sided view with notable exceptions (see for exceptions, Anderson and Narus, 1990; Hallen et al., 1991; Ganesan, 1994).

Whichever method is used, new researchers to the field should have a firm grounding in relationship theory and in methodology. This means reading the original works and getting into theory and methodology early. At least, the language of these two fields is relatively comparable across research writings. Perhaps it is in theory and in method that we can begin to forge a common agenda for relationship research.

Future relationship scenarios

Throughout the text we raised many issues for future relationship research and practice. We do believe that relationships are going to continue to be a growing phenomenon in business and that companies may be forced to account for these relationships and their conduct in them. This does not mean that all relationships will be close but that companies will be accountable for their relationship actions. The accountability to different relationship stakeholder groups may even be forced by regulation as global markets are increasing national pressure on governments to counter balance the actions of large multinationals through legislation. Therefore, groups such as shareholders, employees and consumers are getting more rights. Globalisation is already leading to more cross-border strategic relationships. Few industries remain unmarked by international alliances and mergers. In this context, the need to manage relationships and have a framework for doing this becomes critical. One area where researcher co-operation could be of help is in agreeing a common lexicon and boundaries for the subject area. This might reduce confusion but also help build on what is already there.

The growing body of managerial and other models for studying relationships in theory and in practice points to the complexity of the subject area. Moller and Halinen (2000) examine the complexity of managing multiple models of relationships from a marketing perspective and draw a distinction between managerial approaches for relationships with high and low levels of complexity. The development and application of normative and theory models that address this range of complexity will be very helpful. Indeed, many of them are already there and presented in this text. The problem for managers is that they have to manage relationships that require quite distinct approaches. Relationships that are highly complex require an understanding and knowledge of an array of social and economic business processes. As the field develops the complexity will increase but so too will best practice diffuse and become part of every manager's and researcher's tool kit.

The book concentrates on a managerial approach to relationships. One future trend will be to an even greater focus on managerial issues and on the management of relationships. There can tend to be gaps in the academic literature between excellent theory and its link to practice, and between practice implications without adequate theory back-up. Bridging these translation gaps will be a feature of future work. For example, some of the relationship theory models will find their way into other disciplines and into the teaching of practitioners. One key avenue for further research is into the managerial style appropriate for different types of relationships. A generic heading might be 'the development of relationship managers'. What personal and procedural skills will managers need to be effective relationship practitioners? We identified style as a critical element in implementing strategic market relationships.

Relationships are best represented as processes. Sometimes we are not comfortable dealing with processes as they can be hard to visualise and may not be concrete. However, by attempting to map relationship processes, researchers and practitioners will find it easier to conceptualise relationships. Many processes have been mapped in related fields such as services and quality management but are often completed for non-interactive, less close relationship and can therefore be rigid in structure. Capturing the interactivity inherent in close relationship processes is difficult. The IMP's interaction model remains, in our opinion, a starting point for thinking about relationship processes.

Doing research on the performance of relationships will also be a future trend. It is already well advanced in some relationship types and sectors. Research into performance that is relationship-specific is necessary so that metrics become available for the main relationship types. If this is done then the value of relationships can be assessed. Combining financial and non-financial measures seems appropriate. In addition, developing measures of process performance, especially a stakeholder relationship audit, would be an extremely useful addition to the literature.

A final note

We set ourselves a difficult objective to bring together in a comprehensive way the diverse and rich research vein on business relationships. We believe we have achieved this. To do it we choose a strategic approach – placing relationships at the heart of business endeavour. We have also demonstrated the potential for research in the subject in each chapter. The relationship business model is not for everyone. But for organisations wishing to pursue it, it challenges the orthodoxy of independence with the tenant of co-operation. This book provides a route map from strategy to implementation for those who choose the collaborative alternative.

The typography of co-operation is detailed and complex and lost on many who view it as another tactic. We believe in the strategic potential of relationships and the need for this context to ensure realisation of the benefits of strong ties outlined in this book.

References

Chapter 1

Allen, J. (2001), Deal-maker wheeling his way up the grid, *Financial Times* 17 (Feb.), p. 22.

Blau, P.M. (1964), *Exchange and Power in Social Life*, Wiley, New York.

Boston Consulting Group (1999), *The B2B opportunity: creating advantage through E-marketplaces*, Boston Consulting Group, Boston, MA.

Boston Consulting Group (2001), *The next chapter in business to consumer E-commerce*, Boston Consulting Group, Boston, MA.

Bowen, L. (1999), The right formula SERIOUS RICHES, *Financial Times*, 11 (Nov.), p. 22.

Christopher, M., Payne, A. and Ballantyne, D. (1992), *Relationship Marketing: Bringing Quality, Customer Service and Marketing Together*, Butterworth-Heinemann, London.

Donaldson, B. (1996), Industrial marketing relationships and open-to-tender contracts: co-operation or competition? *Journal of Marketing Practice: Applied Marketing Science* 2 (2), pp. 22–33.

Doney, P.M. and Cannon, J.P. (1997), An examination of the nature of trust in buyer-seller relationships, *Journal of Marketing*, 61 (April), pp. 35–51.

Edwards, O. (1999), Detroit moves in to replace tobacco, Eurobusiness, 1 (1), (June), p. 23.

Gronroos, C. (1994), From marketing mix to relationship marketing: towards a paradigm shift in marketing, *Management Decision*, 32 (2), pp. 4–20.

Gundlach, G.T., Achrol, R.S. and Mentzer, J.T. (1995), The structure of commitment in exchange, *Journal of Marketing*, 59 (1), pp. 78–92.

Hakansson, H., ed. (1982), *International Marketing and Purchasing of Industrial Goods – An Interaction Approach*, Wiley, Chichester.

IGD Research (2000), Retail Market Overview, *IGD On-Line*, May 2000.

Jackson, B.B. (1985), Build customer relationships that last, *Harvard Business Review*, Nov.–Dec., pp. 120–128.

Keynote (2000), *Personal Banking*, Keynote Publications, London.

Lofthouse, R. (2000), Bespoke car making is upon us, *EuroBusiness*, Oct., p. 6.

Mazur, L. (2001), The direct approach, *Marketing Business*, (Feb.), pp. 20–24.

Meyer, J.P. and Allen, N.J. (1994), Testing the 'side-bet theory' of organisational commitment: some methodological considerations, *Journal of Applied Psychology*, 69 (3), pp. 372–378.

Morgan, R.M. and Hunt, S.D. (1994), The commitment-trust theory of relationship marketing, *Journal of Marketing*, 58 (3, July), pp. 20–38.

O'Toole, T. and Donaldson, B. (2000), Managing buyer-seller archetypes, *Irish Marketing Review*, 13 (1), pp. 12–20.

Peppers, D. and Rogers, M. (1997), *Enterprise One to One: Tools for Competing in the Interactive Age*, Doubleday, New York.

Rapp, S. and Collins, T.L. (1994), *Beyond Maximarketing*, McGraw Hill, New York.

Reicheld, F. (1996), *The Loyalty Effect: the Hidden Force Behind Growth, Profits and Lasting Value*, Harvard Business School Press, Boston, MA.

Sako, M. (1992), *Prices, Quality and Trust – Inter-firm Relations in Britain and Japan*, Cambridge University Press, London.

Sinclair, D., Hunter, L. and Beaumont, P. (1996), Models of customer-supplier relations, *Journal of General Management*, 22 (2), pp. 56–75.

Stone, M. and Woodcock, N. (1995), *Relationship Marketing*, Kogan Page, London.

Webster, F.E. (1992), The changing role of marketing in the corporation, *Journal of Marketing*, 56 (October), pp. 1–17.

Wilkstrom, S. (1996), The customer as co-producer, *European Journal of Marketing*, 30 (4), pp. 6–19.

Womack, J.P., Jones, T. and Roos, D. (1990), *The Machine that Changed the World*, MacMillan, New York.

Chapter 2

Barney, J.B. and Hansen, M.H. (1994), Trustworthiness as a source of competitive advantage, *Strategic Management Journal*, 15 (Special Issue), pp. 175–190.

Beckett-Camarata, E.J., Camarata, M.R. and Barker, R.T. (1998), Integrating internal and external customer relationships through relationship management: a strategic response to a changing global environment, *Journal of Business Research*, 12 (1–3), pp. 161–173.

Bleeke, J. and Ernst, D. (1993), *Collaborating to Compete*, Wiley, New York.

Dyer, J.H. and Singh, H. (1998), The relational view: cooperative strategy and sources of interorganisational competitive advantage, *Academy of Management Review*, 23 (4), pp. 660–679.

Ford, D. and McDowell, R. (1999), Managing business relationships by analysing the effects and value of different actions, *Industrial Marketing Management*, 28, pp. 429–442.

Freeman, R.E. and Reed, D.L. (1983), Stockholders and stakeholders: a new perspective on corporate governance, *California Management Review*, 25 (3), pp. 88–106.

Grant, R. (1988), *Contemporary Strategy Analysis*, 3rd edition, Blackwell Press, London.

Gummesson, E. (1994), Making relationship marketing operational, *Internal Journal of Services Industry Management*, 5 (5), pp. 5–20.

Gummesson, E. (1999), *Total Relationship Marketing*, Butterworth Heinemann, Oxford.

Heskett, J.L., Sasser, Jr., W.E. and Schlesinger, L.A. (1997), *The Service Profit Chain*, The Free Press, New York.

Hill, C.W.L. and Jones, G.R. (1999), *Strategic Management: An Integrated Approach*, Houghton Mifflin, Boston, MA.

Hunt, S.D. and Morgan, R.M. (1995), the comparative advantage theory of competition, *Journal of Marketing*, 59 (April), pp. 1–15.

Huxham, C., ed. (1996), *Creating Collaborative Advantage*, Sage, London.

Johnson, G. and Scholes K. (1997), *Exploring Corporate Strategy*, 3rd edition, Prentice Hall, Hertfordshire, UK.

Johnson, J.L. (1999), Strategic integration in industrial distribution channels: managing the interfirm relationship as a strategic assets, *Journal of the Academy of Marketing Sciences*, 27 (1), pp. 4–18.

Johnson, R. and Lawerence, P.R. (1998), Beyond vertical integration – the rise of value-adding partnerships, *Harvard Business Review*, 66 (July–August), pp. 94–101.

Kanter, R.M. (1994), Collaborative advantage, *Harvard Business Review*, 72 (4), pp. 96–108.

Kay, J. (1993a), *Foundations of Corporate Success: How Business Strategies Add Value*, Oxford University Press, Oxford.

Kay, J. (1993b), The structure of strategy, *Business Strategy Review*, 4 (2), pp. 17–37.

Kay, J. (1995), *Why Firms Succeed: Choosing Markets and Challenging Competitors to Add Value*, Oxford University Press, London.

Kumar, N. (1996), The power of trust in manufacturer-retailer relationships, *Harvard Business Review*, 74 (6), pp. 92–106.

Lorenzoni, G. and Lipparini, A. (1999), The leveraging of interfirm relationships as a distinctive organisational capability: a longitudinal study, *Strategic Management Journal*, 20), pp. 317–338.

Madhavan, R., Koka, B.R. and Prescott, J.E. (1998), Networks in transition: how industry events (re)shape interfirm relationships, *Strategic Management Journal*, 19 (5), pp. 439–459.

Morgan, R.M. and Hunt, S.D. (1994), The commitment-trust theory of relationship marketing, *Journal of Marketing*, 58 (July), pp. 20–38.

Peck, H., Payne, A., Christopher, M. and Clark, M. (1999), *Relationship Marketing*, Butterworth Heinemann, Oxford.

Porter, M.E. (1980), *Competitive Strategy*, The Free Press, New York.

Porter, M.E. (1985), *Competitive Advantage*, The Free Press, New York.

Porter, M.E. (1990), *The Competitive Advantage of Nations*, MacMillan Press, New York.

Ramirez, R. (1999), Value co-production: intellectual origins and implications for practice and research, *Strategic Management Journal*, 20, pp. 49–65.

Ravald, A. and Gronroos, C. (1996), The value concept and relationship marketing, *European Journal of Marketing*, 30 (2), pp. 19–30.

Stone, R.N. and Mason, J.B. (1997), Relationship management: strategic marketing's next source of competitive advantage, *Journal of Marketing Theory and Practice*, Spring, pp. 8–19.

Walton, S. and Huey, J. (1992), *Sam Walton, Made in America: My Story*, Doubleday, New York.

Wikstrom, S. and Normann, R. (1994), *Knowledge and Value: a New Perspective on Corporate Transformation*, Routledge, Oxford.

Wilkinson, I.F. and Young, L.C. (1994), Business dancing - the nature and role of interfirm relations in business strategy, *Asia-Australia Marketing Journal*, 2 (1), pp. 67–79.

Wilson, D.T. (1995), An integrated model of buyer-seller relationships, *Journal of the Academy of Marketing Sciences*, 23 (4), pp. 335–345.

Zajac, E. and Olsen, C.P. (1993), From transaction cost to transaction value analysis: implications for the study of interorganisational strategies, *Journal of Management Studies*, 30 (1), pp. 131–145.

Chapter 3

Anderson, J.C., Hakansson, H. and Johanson, J. (1994), Dyadic business relationships within a business network context, *Journal of Marketing*, 58, pp. 1–15.

Bergen, M., Dutta, S. and Walker, Jr., O.C. (1992), Agency relationships in marketing: a review of the implications and applications of agency and related theories, *Journal of Marketing*, 56, July, pp. 1–24.

Blau, P.M. (1964), *Exchange and Power in Social Life*, Wiley, New York.

Bradach, J.L. and Eccles, R.G. (1989), Price, authority and trust: from ideal types to plural forms, *Annual Review of Sociology*, 15, pp. 97–118.

Cook, K.S. and Emerson, R.M. (1978), Power, equity and commitment in exchange networks, *American Sociological Review*, 43, pp. 721–739.

Dant, S.P. and Wilson, D.T. (1988), Interorganisational exchange research: another share of paradigms, *AMA Conference Proceedings*, Chicago, IL, pp. 90–93.

Dataquest (1999), *The Worldwide Semiconductor Industry*, Gartner Group, California.

Dore, R. (1983), Goodwill and the spirit of capitalism, *British Journal of Sociology*, 34, pp. 459–482.

Dwyer, F.R., Schvar, P.H. and Oh, S. (1987), Developing buyer-seller relationships, *Journal of Marketing*, 51 (April), pp. 11–27.

Easton, G. (1998), Case research as a methodology for industrial networks: a realist apologia, In Naude, P. and Turnbull, P.W., eds., *Network Dynamics in International Marketing*, Pergamon, Oxford, pp. 73–87.

Eccles, R.G. (1991), The performance measurement manifesto, *Harvard Business Review*, Jan.–Feb., pp. 131–137.

Eisenhardt, K. (1989), Agency theory: an assessment and review, *Academy of Management Review*, 14 (1), pp. 57–74.

Ford, D., ed. (1990, 1997), *Understanding Business Markets - Interaction, Relationships and Networks*, Academic Press, London.

Frazier, G.L. (1983), Interorganisational exchange behaviour in marketing channels: a broadened perspective, *Journal of Marketing*, 47, pp. 68–78.

Frazier, G.L. (1999), Organising and managing channels of distribution, *Journal of the Academy of Marketing Science*, 27 (2), pp. 226–240.

Gassenheimer, J.B. and Calantone, R.J. (1994), Managing economic dependence and relational activities within a competitive environment, *Journal of Business Research*, 29 (3, March), pp. 189–197.

Gassenheimer, J.B., Calantone, R.J., Schmitz, J.M. and Robicheaux, R.A. (1994), Models of channel maintenance: what is the weaker party to do? *Journal of Business Research*, 30 (3), pp. 225–236.

Gemunden, H.G. (1985), Coping with inter-organisational conflicts. Efficient interaction strategies for buyer and seller organisation, *Journal of Business Research*; 13, pp. 405–420.

Granovetter, M. (1985), Economic action and social structure: the problem of embeddedness, *American Journal of Sociology*, 91 (3, November), pp. 481–510.

Granovetter, M. (1992), Problems of explanation in economic sociology, In Nohria, N. and Eccles, R.G., eds., *Networks and Organisations*, Vol. 1, Harvard Business School Press, Boston, MA, pp. 25–56.

Hakansson, H., ed. (1982), *International Marketing and Purchasing of Industrial Goods – An Interaction Approach*, Wiley, Chichester.

Hallen, L.J., Johanson, J. and Seyed-Mohamed, N. (1991), Interfirm adaptation in business relationships, *Journal of Marketing*, 55 (April), pp. 29–37.

Heide, J. (1994), Interorganisational governance in marketing channels, *Journal of Marketing*, 58 (Part 1), pp. 71–85.

Heide, J.B. and John, G. (1988), The role of dependence balancing in safeguarding transaction-specific assets in conventional channels, *Journal of Marketing*, 52 (January), pp. 20–35.

Hunt, S.D. (1983), *Marketing Theory: The Philosophy of Marketing Science*, Irwin, Homewood, IL.

Husted, B.W. (1994), Transaction Costs, Norms and Social Networks, *Business and Society*, 33 (1, April), pp. 30–57.

Jackson, B.B. (1985), Build customer relationships that last, *Harvard Business Review*, Nov.–Dec., pp. 120–128.

Kaplan, R.S. and Norton, D.P. (1996), *The Balanced Scorecard: Translating Strategy into Action*, Harvard Business School Press, Boston, MA.

Macneil, I.R. (1980), *The New Social Contract*, Yale University Press, New Haven, CT.

Miettila, A. and Moller, K. (1990), *Interaction Perspectives into Professional Business Services: a Conceptual Analysis*, 6th IMP Conference, Milan.

Moller, K. and Halinen, A.(2000), Relationship marketing theory: its roots and direction, *Journal of Marketing Management*, 16, pp. 29–54.

Pfeffer, J. and Salancik, G. (1978), *The External Control of Organisations: a Resource Dependence Perspective*, Harper & Row, New York.

Prahalad and Hamel, G. (1990), The core competence of the corporation, *Harvard Business Review*, May–June, pp. 79–91.

Reve, T. (1990), The firm as a mexus of internal and external contacts, In *The Firm as a Nexus of Treaties*, Sage Publications, London, pp. 133–161.

Stern, L W. and Reve, T. (1980), Distribution channels as political economies: a framework for comparative analysis, *Journal of Marketing*, 44 (Summer), pp. 52–64.

Timmers, P. (2000), *Electronic Commerce: Strategies and Models for Business to Business Trading*, Wiley, Chichester.

Wernerfelt, B. (1995), The resource-based view of the firm: ten years after, *Strategic Management Journal*, 16 (3), pp. 171–174.

Wikstrom, S. and Normann, R. (1994), *Knowledge and Value: a New Perspective on Corporate Transformation*, Routledge, London.

Williamson, O.E. (1979), *Markets and Heirarchies: Analysis and Anti-Trust Implications*, The Free Press, New York.

Williamson, O.E. (1985), *The Economic Institutions of Capitalism*, The Free Press, New York.

Yamaguchi, K. (1996), Power in networks of substitutable and complementary exchange relations: a rational-choice, model and an analysis of power centralization, *American Sociological Review*, 61 (2, April), pp. 308–332.

Zajac, E.J. and Olsen, C.P. (1993), From transaction cost to transaction value analysis: implications for the study of interorganisational strategies, *Journal of Management Studies*, 30 (1, January), pp. 131–145.

Chapter 4

Blau, P.M. (1964), *Exchange and Power in Social Life*, Wiley, New York.

Bonoma, T.V. (1985), *The Marketing Edge: Making Strategies Work*, The Free Press, New York.

Bowen, J.T. and Shoemaker, S. (1998), Loyalty: a strategic commitment, *Cornell Quarterly*, 39 (1), pp. 12–28.

Cardozo, R.N., Shipp, S.H. and Roering, K.J. (1992), Proactive strategic partnerships: a new business markets strategy, *Journal of Business and Industrial Marketing*, 7 (1), pp. 51–63.

Colgate, M.R. and Danaher, P.J. (2000), Implementing a customer relationship strategy: the asymmetric impact of poor versus excellent execution, *Journal of the Academy of Marketing Sciences*, 28 (3), pp. 375–387.

Davidow, W.H. and Malone, M.S. (1992), *The Virtual Corporation*, Harper and Row, New York.

Dwyer, F.R, Shurr, P.H. and Oh, S. (1987), Developing buyer-seller relationships, *Journal of Marketing*, 51 (2), pp. 11–27.

Grant, R. (1998), *Contemporary Strategy Analysis*, 3rd edition, Blackwell: Oxford.

Gronroos, C. (1990), *Service Management and Marketing: Managing Moments of Truth in Service Competition*, Lexington Books, New York.

Hakansson, H., ed. (1982), *International Marketing and Purchasing of Industrial Goods*, Wiley, New York.

Hakansson, H. and Wootz, B. (1979), A framework for industrial buying and selling, *Industrial Marketing Management*, 8, pp. 28-39.

Hallen, L., Johanson, J. and Seyed-Mohamed, N. (1991), Interfirm adaptation in business relationships, *Journal of Marketing*, 55, pp. 29–37.

Hill, C. and Jones, G.R. (1998*), Strategic Management: an Integrated Approach*, Haughton Miffin, Boston, MA.

Huckestein, D. and Duboff, R. (1999), Hilton Hotels: a comprehensive approach to delivering value for all stakeholders, *Cornell Quarterly*, 40 (4), pp. 28–38.

Johnson, G. and Scholes, K. (1997), *Exploring Corporate Strategy*, 3rd edition, Prentice Hall, Hertfordshire, UK.

Kanter, R.M. (1989), *When Giants Learn to Dance*, Simon and Schuster, New York.

Keep, W.W., Hollander, S.C. and Dickinson, R. (1998), Forces impinging on long-term business-to-business relationships in the united states: an historical perspective, *Journal of Marketing*, 62 (2), pp. 31–45.

Kothandaraman, P. and Wilson, D.T. (2000), Implementing relationship strategy, *Industrial Marketing Management*, 29 (4), pp. 339–349.

Lincoln, J.R. (1982), Intra- (and inter-), organisational networks, *Research in the Sociology of Organisations*, 1, pp. 1–38.

Macneil, I.R. (1980), *The New Social Contract*, Yale University Press, New Haven, CT.

Matthyssens, P. and Van den Bulte, C. (1994), Getting closer and nicer: partnerships in the supply chain, *Long Range Planning*, 27 (1), pp. 72–83.

Mintzberg, H., Quinn, J.B. and Ghoshal, S. (1998), *The Strategy Process*, revised European edition, Prentice Hall, Hertfordshire, UK.

O'Toole, T. and Donaldson, W.G. (1999), Making relationship assessments using the relationship strength construct, In McLoughlin, D. and Horan, C., eds., *Proceedings of The 15th Annual IMP Conference*, Dublin, pp. 1–12.

Provan, K.G. (1983), The federation as an interorganisational linkage network, *Academy of Management Review*, 8 (1), pp. 79–89.

Quinn, J.B. (1992), *The Intelligent Enterprise*, The Free Press, New York.

Ricard, L. and Perrien, J. (1999), Explaining and evaluating the implementation of organisational relationship marketing in the banking: clients, perception, *Journal of Business Research*, 45 (2), pp. 199–209.

Turnbull, P.W. and Wilson, D.T. (1989), Developing and protecting profitable customer relationships, *Industrial Marketing Management*, 18 (3), pp. 233–238.

Whetten, D.A. and Leung, T.K. (1979), The instrumental value of interorganisational relations: antecedents and consequences of linkage formation, *Academy of Management Journal*, 22 (2), pp. 325–344.

Whittington, R. (1993), *What is Strategy - and Does it Matter?* International Thomson, London.

Chapter 5

Anderson, J.C., Hakansson, H. and Johanson, J. (1994), Dyadic business relationships within a network context, *Journal of Marketing*, 58 (October), pp. 1–15.

Araujo, L. and Easton, G. (1996), Networks in socioeconomic systems: a critical review, In Iacobucci, D., ed., *Networks in Marketing*, Sage, Thousand Oaks, CA, pp. 63–107.

Axelsson, B. (1992), Corporate strategy models and networks – diverging perspectives, In Axelsson, B. and Easton, G., eds., *Industrial Networks: A New View of Reality*, Routledge, London, pp. 185–204.

Bolton, M.K., Malmrose, R. and Ouchi, W.G. (1994), The organisation of innovation in the us and japan: neoclassical and relational contracting, *Journal of Management Studies*, 31 (5), pp. 653–679.

Bryson, J., Wood, P. and Keeble, D. (1993), Business networks, small firm flexibility and regional development in UK business services, *Entrepreneurship and Regional Development*, 5, pp. 265–277.

Child, J. and Faulkner, D. (1998), *Strategies of Co-operation: Managing Alliances, Networks and Joint Ventures*, Oxford University Press, Oxford.

D'Cruz, J.R. and Rugman, A. (1994), The five partners model, *European Management Journal*, 12 (1), pp. 59–66.

Easton, G. (1992), Industrial networks: a review, In Axelsson, B. and Easton, G., eds., *Industrial Networks: a New View of Reality*, Routledge, London, pp. 3–27.

Grabher, G. (1993), Rediscovering the social in the economics of interfirm relations, In Grabher, G., ed., *The Embedded Firm: on the Socioeconomics of Industrial Networks*, Routledge, London, pp. 1–31.

Grandori, A., ed. (1999), *Interfirm Networks: Organisation and Industrial Competitiveness*, Routledge, London.

Grandori, A. and Soda, G. (1995), Inter-firm networks: antecedents, mechanism and forms, *Organisation Studies*, 16 (2), pp. 183–214.

Granovetter, M. (1985), Economic action and social structure: the problem of embeddedness, *American Journal of Sociology*, 91 (3), pp. 481–510.

Hakansson, H. and Johanson, J. (1992), A model of industrial networks, In Axelsson, B. and Easton G., eds., *Industrial Networks: a New View of Reality*, Routledge, London, pp. 28–34.

Halinen, A., Salmi, A. and Havila, V. (1999), From dyadic change to changing business networks: an analytical framework, *Journal of Management Studies*, 36 (6), pp. 779–794.

Harari, O. (1998), Transform your organisation into a web of relationships, *Management Review*, 87 (1), pp. 21–25.

Holm, D.B., Eriksson, K. and Johanson, J. (1999), Creating value through mutual commitment to business networks relationships, *Strategic Management Journal*, 20 (5), pp. 467–486.

Jarillo, J.C. (1993), *Strategic Networks: Creating the Borderless Organisation*, Butterworth Heinemann, Oxford.

Jones, C., Hesterly, W. and Borgatti, S.P. (1997), A general theory of network governance: exchange conditions and social mechanisms, *Academy of Management Review*, 22 (4), pp. 911–945.

Lincoln, J.R. (1982), Intra- (and Inter-), Organisational Networks, *Research in the Sociology of Organisations*, 1, pp. 1–38.

Madhavan, R., Koka, B.J. and Prescott, J.E. (1998), Networks in transition: how industry events (re)shape interfirm relationships, *Strategic Management Journal*, 19 (5), pp. 439–459.

Nohria, N. and Eccles, R.G., eds. (1992), *Networks and Organisations: Structure, Form and Action*, Harvard University Press, Boston, MA.

Oliver, A. and Ebers, M. (1998), Networking network studies: an analysis of longititude conceptual configurations in the study of inter-organisational relationships, *Organisation Studies*, 19 (4), pp. 549–583.

Oliver, C. (1991), Network relations and loss of organisational autonomy, *Human Relations*, 44 (9), pp. 943–961.

Powell, W.W. (1990), Neither market nor hierarchy: network forms of organisation, *Research in Organisational Behaviour*, 12, pp. 295–336.

Powell, W.W. (1998), Learning from collaboration: knowledge and networks in the biotechnology and pharmaceutical industries, *California Management Review*, 40 (3), pp. 228–240.

Provan, K.G. (1993), Embeddedness, interdependence and opportunism in organisational supplier-buyer networks, *Journal of Management*, 19 (4), pp. 841–856.

Ring, P.S. (1999), The costs of networked organisations, In Grandori, A., ed., *Interfirm Networks: Organisation and Industrial Competitiveness*, Routledge, London, pp. 237–277.

Thorelli, H.B. (1986), Networks: between markets and hierarchies, *Strategic Management Journal*, 7, pp. 37–51.

Uzzi, B. (1997), Social structure and competition in inter-firm networks: the paradox of embeddedness, *Administrative Science Quarterly*, 42 (1), pp. 35–67.

Chapter 6

Christopher, M., Payne, A. and Ballantyne, D. (1991), *Relationship Marketing: Bridging Quality, Customer Service and Marketing Together*, Butterworth Heinemann, Oxford.

Donaldson, W. and O'Toole, T. (2000), Classifying relationship structures: relationship strength in industrial markets, *Journal of Business and Industrial Marketing*, 15 (7), pp. 491–506.

Dwyer, F.R., Schurr, P.H. and Oh, S. (1987), Developing buyer-seller relationships, *Journal of Marketing*, 51 (2, April), pp. 11–27.

Dyer, J.H. (1996), Specialized supplier networks as a source of competitive advantage: evidence from the auto industry, *Strategic Management Journal*, 17 (4), pp. 271–291.

Financial Times (1998), Carmakers are feeling uneasy, 23/02/1998.

Ford, D., Hakansson, H., Lundgren, A., Snehota, I., Turnbull, P. and Wilson, D. (1998), *Managing Business Relationships*, Wiley, Chichester.

Harari, O. (1998), Transform your organisation into a web of relationships, *Management Review*, 87 (1), pp. 21–24.

Heide, J.B. (1994), Interorganisational governance in marketing channels, *Journal of Marketing*, 58 (1), pp. 71–85.

Hirschman, A. (1970), *Exit, Voice and Loyalty – Responses to Declines in Firms, Organisations and States*, Harvard University Press, Cambridge, MA.

Holm, D.B., Eriksson, K. and Johanson, J. (1999), Creating value through mutual commitment to business network relationships, *Strategic Management Journal*, 20 (5), pp. 467–486.

Jackson, B.B. (1985), *Winning and Keeping Industrial Customers*, Lexington Books, New York.

Krapfel, Jr., R.E., Salmond, D. and Spekman, R. (1991), A strategic approach to managing buyer-seller relationships, *European Journal of Marketing*, 25 (9), pp. 22–37.

Olsen, R.F. and Ellram, L.M. (1997), A portfolio approach to supplier relationships, *Industrial Marketing Management*, 26 (2), pp. 103–113.

O, Toole, T. and Donaldson, W. (2000), Managing buyer-supplier relationship archetypes, *Irish Marketing Review*, 13 (1), pp. 12–20.

Prokesch, S.E. (1993), Mastering chaos at the high-technology frontier: an interview with silicon graphics' Ed. McCracken, *Harvard Business Review*, 1 (6, Nov.–Dec.).

Sako, M. (1992), *Prices, Quality and Trust - inter-firm relations in Britain and Japan*, Cambridge University Press, London.

Shapiro, B.P., Rangan, V.K., Moriarty, R.T. and Ross, E.B. (1987), Manage customers for profits (not just sales), *Harvard Business Review*, Sep.–Oct., pp. 101–108.

Sinclair, D., Hunter, L. and Beaumont, P. (1996), Models of customer-supplier relations, *Journal of General Management*, 22 (2), pp. 56–75.

Steward, K. (1998), The customer exit process – a review and research agenda, *Journal of Marketing Management*, 14 (4), pp. 235–250.

Turnbull, P. and Zolkiewski, J. (1997), Profitability in customer portfolio planning, In Ford, D., ed., *Understanding Business Markets*, Dryden Press, London, pp. 305–325.

Chapter 7

Cespedes, F. (1996), *Managing Marketing Linkages*, Prentice Hall, Englewood Cliffs, NJ.

Christopher, M., Payne, A. and Ballantyne, D. (1991), *Relationship Marketing: Bringing Quality, Customer Service and Marketing Together*, Butterworth Heinemann, Oxford.

Dnes, A.W. (1992), *Franchising: A Case Study Approach*, Avebury, Aldershot, UK.

Donaldson, B. (1990), Internal problems with developing market responsive strategies in industrial markets, *Proceedings of the British Academy of Management*, Glasgow, September.

Donaldson, B. (1996), Industrial market relationships and open to tender contracts: cooperation or competition? *Journal of Marketing Practice*, 2 (2), pp. 23–34.

Duck, S. (1991), *Understanding Relationships* Guildford Press, New York.

Kaufmann, P.J. (1996), The state of research in franchising, *Franchising Research: An International Journal*, 1 (1), pp. 4–7.

McDonald, M., Millman, T. and Rogers, B. (1997), Key account management: theory, practice and challenges, *Journal of Marketing Management*, 13, pp. 737–757.

Mendleson, M. (1993), *Franchising in Europe*, Cassell, London.

Millman, T. and Wilson, K. (1996), developing key account management competencies, *Journal of Marketing Practice*, 2 (2), pp. 7–22.

Morgan, R.M. and Hunt, S.D. (1994), The commitment-trust theory of relationship marketing, *Journal of Marketing*, 58 (July), pp. 20–38.

Newsbyte (2000), Cisco in $200m alliance with Korea's Hanaro Telecom, *Newsbyte*, June 17.

Outsourcing Institute (1998), *Survey of Current and Potential Outsourcing End-users*, Outsourcing Institute www.outsourcing.com.

O'Toole, T. and Donaldson, W.G. (2000), relationship governance structures and performance, *Journal of Marketing Management*, 16, (4), pp. 327–341.

Peppers, D. and Rogers, M. (1997), *Enterprise One to One: Tools for Competing in the Interactive Age*, Doubleday, New York.

Price Waterhouse Coopers (1999), *Open Sky Retailing*, May, Price Waterhouse Coopers, London.

Reicheld, F. (1996), *The Loyalty Effect: the Hidden Force Behind Growth, Profits and Lasting Value*, Harvard Business School Press, Boston, MA.

Stone, M. and Woodcock, N. (1995), *Relationship Marketing*, Kogan Page, London.

Tzokas, N. and Donaldson, B., (2000), A research agenda for personal selling and sales management in the context of relationship marketing, *The Journal of Selling & Major Account Management*, 2 (2), pp. 13–30.

Timmers, P. (2000), *Electronic Commerce: Strategies and Models for Business-to-Business Trading*, Wiley, Chichester.

Chapter 8

Advertising Age (2000), *Polaroid Combo Cam Targets Teens*, July 17, Cara Beradi, Chigago, IL.

Christopher, M., Payne, A. and Ballantyne, D. (1991), *Relationship Marketing: Bringing Quality, Customer Service and Marketing Together*, Butterworth-Heinemann, Oxford.

Compeer (1999), *Private Client Stockbroking and Fund Management Survey for the Year 1998*, Published only to subscribing companies.

Deloitte & Touche (2000), *Retail Broking Survey, 1999*.

Donaldson, B. (1995), Customer service as a competitive strategy, *Journal of Strategic Marketing* 3, pp. 113–126.

Donaldson, B. (1995), Manufacturers need to show greater commitment to customer service, *Industrial Marketing Management*, 24, pp. 421–430.

Gummesson, E. (1999), *Total Relationship Marketing - Rethinking Marketing Mangement: from 4Ps to 30Rs*, Butterworth-Heinemann, Oxford.

Hennig-Thurau, T. (2000), Relationship quality and customer retention through strategic communication of customer skills, *Journal of Marketing Management* 16, 1–3, pp. 55–79.

Heskett, J.L., Jones, T.O., Lovemann, G.H., Sasser, W.E. and Schalesinger, L.A. (1994), Putting the service profit chain to work, *Harvard Business Review*, Mar.–Apr., pp. 164–174.

Jones, T.O. and Sasser, W.E. (1995), Why satisfied customers defect, *Harvard Business Review*, Nov.–Dec., pp. 88–99.

Keaveney, S. (1995), Customer switching behaviour in service industries: an exploratory study, *Journal of Marketing* 59 (Apr.), pp. 71–82.

Klein, A. (2000), On a roll: the techies grumbled but polaroid's pocket turned into a huge hit, *Wall Street Journal*, 5 (Feb.), pp. 22–24.

Naumann, E. and Jackson, D.W. (1999), One more time: how do you satisfy customers? *Business Horizons*, May–Jun., pp. 71–86.

O'Brien, L. and Jones, C. (1995), Do rewards really create loyalty? *Harvard Business Review*, May–Jun., pp. 75–82.

Parasuraman, A., Zeithaml, V. and Berry, L.L. (1985), A conceptual model of service quality and its implication for future research, *Journal of Marketing* 49 (Fall), pp. 41–50.

Peppers, D., Rogers, M. and Dorf, B. (1999), Is your company ready for one to one marketing? *Harvard Business Review*, Jan.–Feb., pp. 151–160.

Peters, T. (1992), *Liberation Management*, A.F. Knopf, New York.

Reichheld, F. (1996), *The Loyalty Effect: the Hidden Force Behind Growth, Profits and Lasting Value*, Harvard Business School Press, Boston, MA.

Chapter 9

Angehrn, A.A. (1998), Towards the high-tech, high touch web site, *New Marketing Media, Marketing Series*, Financial Times, London, Sep.–Nov., pp. 8–9.

Bakos, J.Y. and Brynjolfsson, E. (1993), Information technology, incentives and the optimal number of suppliers, *Journal of Management Information Systems*, 10 (2), pp. 37–53.

Banerjee, S. and Golhar, D.Y. (1993), EDI implementation in JIT and non-JIT manufacturing firms: a comparative study, *International Journal of Operations and Production Management*, 13 (3), pp. 25–37.

Benjamin, R.I., de Long, D.W. and Morton, M.S. (1990), Electronic data interchange: how much competitive advantage? *Long Range Planning*, 23 (1), pp. 29–40.

Benjamin, Robert I. and Blunt, J. (1992), Critical IT issues: the next ten years, *Sloan Management Review*, 33 (4), pp. 7–19.

Benjamin, Robert I. and Levinson, E. (1993), A framework for managing IT-enabled change, *Sloan Management Review*, Summer, pp. 23–33.

Bensaou, M. and Venkatraman, N. (1996), Interorganisational relationships and information technology: a conceptual synthesis and a research framework, *European Journal of Information Systems*, 5 (2), pp. 84–91.

Bitner, M.J., Brown, S.W. and Meuter, M.L. (2000), Technology infusion in service encounters, *Journal of the Academy of Marketing Science*, 28 (1), pp. 138–149.

Brady, M., Saren, M. and Tzokas, N. (2000), The impact of IT on marketing": An Evaluation, *Management Decision*, 37 (10), pp. 758–766.

Brynjolfsson, Erik (1994), Information assets, technology and organisation, *Management Science*, 40 (12), pp. 1645–1662.

Buzzell, R.D. and Ortmeyer, G. (1995), Channel Partnerships Streamline Distribution, *Sloan Management Review*, Spring, pp. 85–96.

Cash, J.I. and Konsynski, B.R. (1985), IS redraws competitive boundaries, *Harvard Business Review*, Mar.–Apr., pp. 134–142.

Clemons, E.K., Reddi, S.P. and Row, M.C. (1993), The impact of information technology on the organization of economic activity: the 'move to the middle' hypothesis, *Journal of Management Information Systems*, 10 (2), pp. 9–35.

Corbett, C.J., Blackburn, J.D. and Van Wassenhove, L.N. (1999), Partnerships to improve supply chain, *Sloan Management Review*, 40 (4), pp. 71–82.

Cunningham, C. and Tynan, C. (1993), Electronic trading, interorganisational systems and the nature of buyer-seller relationships: the need for a network perspective, *International Journal of Information Management*, 13, pp. 3–28.

Galliers, R.D. (1993), IT strategies: beyond competitive advantage, *Journal of Strategic Information Systems*, 2 (4), pp. 283–291.

Glazer, R. (1991), Marketing in and information intensive environment: strategic implications of knowledge as an asset, *Journal of Marketing*, 55 (Oct.), pp. 1–19.

Grover, V. (1990), An empirically derived model for the adoption of customer-based inter-organisational systems, *Decision Sciences*, 24 (3), pp. 603–640.

Gurbaxani, V. and Whang, S. (1991), The impact of information systems on organisations and markets, *Communications of the ACM*, 34 (1), pp. 59–73.

Hagel, III, J. and Armstrong, A.G. (1997), *Net Gain, Expanding Markets Through Virtual Communities*, Harvard Business School Press, Boston, MA.

Holland, C. and Lockett, G. (1993), Forms of association in business markets: the impact of inter-organisational information systems, *Advances in International Marketing*, 5, pp. 125–143.

Jarillo, J.C. (1993), *Strategic Networks: Creating the Borderless Organisation*, Butterworth-Heinemann, Oxford.

Johnston, R. and Lawrence, P.R. (1988), Beyond vertical integration – the rise of the value-adding partnership, *Harvard Business Review*, Jul.–Aug., pp. 94–120.

Johnson, R. and Vitale, M.R. (1988), Creating competitive advantage with interorganisational information systems, *MIS Quarterly*, June, pp. 153–165.

Khalil, O.E.M. and Harcar, T.D. (1999), Relationship marketing and data quality management, *SAM Advanced Management Journal*, 64 (2), pp. 26–33.

Konsynski, B.R. (1993), Strategic control in the extended enterprise, *IBM Systems Journal*, 32 (1), pp. 111–142.

Konsynski, B.R. and McFarlan, F.W. (1990), Information partnerships – shared data, shared scale, *Harvard Business Review*, Sep.–Oct., pp. 114–120.

Kozinets, R.V. (1999), E-trablised marketing? The strategic implications of virtual communities of consumption, *European Management Journal*, 17 (3), pp. 252–264.

Lorenzoni, G. and Lipparini, A. (1999), The leveraging of interfirm relationships as a distinctive organisational capability: a longitudinal study, *Strategic Management Journal*, 20, pp. 317–338.

Mata, F.J., Fuerst, W.L. and Barney, J.B. (1995), Information technology and sustained competitive advantage: a resource-based analysis, *MIS Quarterly*, 19 (4), pp. 487–504.

Nidumolu, S.R. (1995), Interorganisational information systems and the structure and content of seller-buyer relationships, *Information and Management*, 28, pp. 89–105.

Ogbonna, E. and Wilkinson, B. (1996), Information technology and power in the UK grocery distribution chain, *Journal of General Management*, 22 (2), pp. 20–35.

Parasuraman, A. and Grewal, D. (2000), The impact of technology on the quality-value-loyalty chain, *Journal of the Academy of Marketing Science*, 28 (1), pp.168–174.

Parsons, G.L. (1983), Information technology: a new competitive weapon, *Sloan Management Review*, 25), pp. 3–14.

Peppard, J., ed. (1993), *IT Strategy for Business*, Pitman Publishing, London.

Peppers, D. and Rogers, M. (1999), *Enterprise One-To-One – Tools for Competing in an Interactive Age*, Bantam Doubleday, New York.

Riggins, F.J., Kriebel, C.H. and Mukhopadhyay, T. (1994), The growth of interorganisational systems in the presence of network externalities, *Management Science*, 40 (8), pp. 984–998.

Senn, J.A. (1992), Electronic data interchange: the elements of implementation, *Information Systems Management*, Winter, pp. 45–53.

Stump, R.L. and Sriram, V. (1997), Employing information technology in purchasing, *Industrial Marketing Management*, 26 (2), pp. 127–136.

Suomi, R. (1991), Removing transaction costs with interorganisational systems, *Information and Software Technology*, 33 (3), pp. 205–211.

Suomi, R. (1992), On the concept of interorganizational information systems, *Journal of Strategic Information Systems*, 1 (2), pp. 93–100.

Suomi, R. (1994), What to take into account when building and interorganisation information system, *Information Processing and Management*, 30 (1), pp. 151–159.

Turner, J. (1998), The role of IT in organisational transformation, In Galliers, R.D. and Baets, W.R.J., eds., *Information Technology and Organisational Transformation: Innovation for the 21stt Century*, Wiley, Chichester, pp. 245–260.

Venkatraman, N. and Henderson, J.C. (1998), Real strategies for virtual organising, *Sloan Management Review*, 40 (1), pp. 33–48.

Venkatraman, N. and Loh, L. (1994), The shifting logic of the is organisation: from technical portfolio to relationship portfolio, *Information Strategy: The Executives Journal*, 10 (2), pp. 5–11.

Chapter 10

Achrol, R.S. and Kotler, P. (1999), Marketing in the network economy, *Journal of Marketing*, 63 (Special Issue), pp. 146–163.

Albach, H. et al (1993), *Culture and Technical Innovation*, Research Report 9, The Academy of Sciences and Technology, Berlin.

Benjamin, R. and Wigand, R. (1995), Electronic markets and virtual value chains on the information super highway, *Sloan Management Review*, Winter, pp. 62–72.

Biemans, W.G. (1991), *Innovative Networks*, Routledge, London.

Booz, Allen and Hamilton (1982), *New Products Management for the 1980s*, Booz, Allen and Hamilton, New York.

Cooper, R.G. (1998), Benchmarking new product performance: results of best practices study, *European Management Journal*, 16 (1), pp. 1–17.

Cooper, R.G. and Kleinschmidt, E.J. (1991), New product processes at leading industrial firms, *Industrial Marketing Management*, 10 (2), pp. 137–142.

Downes, L. and Mui, C. (1998), *Unleashing the Killer Application: Digital Strategies for Market Dominance*, Harvard Business School Press, Boston, MA.

Economist (US) (1997), *Big, boring, booming: business-to-business e-commerce is a revolution in a ball valve*, May 10, p. 16.

Eisenhardt, K.M. and Tabrizi, B.N. (1995), Accelarating adaptive processes: product innovation in the global computer industry, *Administrative Science Quarterly*, 40 (1, Mar.), pp. 84–111.

Ford, D., ed. (1998), *Managing Business Relationships*, Wiley, Chichester.

Ford, D. and Saren, M. (2000), *Technology Strategy for Business* International Thomson Business Press, London:.

Ghosh, S. (1998), Making sense of the internet, *Harvard Business Review,* Mar–Apr., pp. 127–135.

Griffin, A.J. and Hauser, J.R. (1993), The Voice of the Customer, *Marketing Science,* 12 (Winter), pp. 1–27.

Gupta, A.K. and Wilemon, D. (1988), the credibility-corporation connection at the R&D marketing interface, *Journal of Product Innovation Management,* 5 (1), pp. 20–31.

Hagel, J. and Rayport, J.F. (1997), The coming battle for customer information, *Harvard Business Review,* Jan.–Feb., pp. 53–65.

Hakansson, H., ed. (1987), *Industrial Technology Development: a Network Approach,* Croom Helm, London.

Hakansson, H. (1989), *Corporate Technological Behaviour: Cooperation and Networks,* Routledge, London.

Hart, S.J., ed. (1996), *New Product Development: a Reader,* Dryden Press, London.

Hoey, A. (1998), *The Computerised Lawyer: a Guide to Computers in the Legal Profession,* Spinger, New York.

Hutt, M.D. and Speh, T.W. (1998), *Business Marketing Management,* 6th edition, Dryden, Fort Worth, TX.

Kiani, G.R. (1998), Marketing opportunities in the digital world, *Internet Research: Electronic Networking Applications and Policy,* 8, p. 2.

Klein, A. (2000), Polaroid's latest development…, *Wall Street Journal,* February 5.

McKenna, R. (1991), *Relationship Marketing: Successful Strategies for the Age of the Customer,* Addison Wesley, New York.

Moore, G. (1995), *Inside the Tornado: Marketing Strategies from Silicon Valley's Cutting Edge,* Harper Business, New York.

O'Dwyer, M. and O'Toole, T. (1998), Marketing-R&D interface contexts in new product development, *Irish Marketing Review,* 11 (1), pp. 59–68.

Prince, G.M. (1970), *The Practice of Creativity,* Collier Books, New York.

Rayport and Sviokla (1994), Managing in the market space, *Harvard Business Review,* Nov.–Dec., pp. 141–150.

Rheinhardt, A. (1998), Extranets: log on, link up, save big, *Business Week,* June 26, p. 134.

Saren, M. and Tzokas, N. (1998), The nature of the product in market relationships: a plurisignified product concept, *Journal Of Marketing Management,* 14, pp. 445–464.

Urban, G.L. and Hauser (1993), *Design and Marketing of New Products,* 2nd edition, Prentice Hall, Englewood Cliffs, NJ.

Urban, G.L. and von Hippel, E. (1988), Lead user analysis for the development of new industrial products, *Management Science,* 34, (5, May), pp. 569–582.

Van der Heijden, K. (1997), *Scenarios: the Art of Strategic Conversation,* Wiley, Chichester.

Von Hippel, E. (1978), Successful industrial products from customer ideas, presentation of a new customer-active paradigm with evidence and implication, *Journal of Marketing,* 42 (1), pp. 39–49.

Von Hippel, E. (1988), *The Sources of Innovation,* Oxford University Press, New York.

Von Hippel, E., Thomke, S. and Sonnck, M. (1999), Creating breakthroughs at 3M, *Harvard Business Review,* Sep.–Oct., pp. 47–57.

Wikstrom, S. (1996), The customer as co-producer, *European Journal of Marketing,* 30 (4), pp. 6–19.

Chapter 11

Axelsson, B. and Johanson, J. (1992), Foreign marketing entry – the textbook versus the network view, In Axelsson, B. and Easton, G., eds., *Industrial Networks: A New View of Reality*, Routledge, London, Chapter 12, pp. 218–233.

Buckley, P.J. and Casson, M. (1979), A theory of international operations, In Buckley, P.J. and Ghauri, P., eds., *The Internationalisation of the Firm: A Reader*, Academic Press, London, pp. 45–63.

Ghauri, P.N. and Holstius, K. (1996), The role of matching in the foreign market entry process in the Baltic States, *European Journal of Marketing*, 30 (2), pp. 75–78.

Johanson, J. and Wiedersheim-Paul, F. (1975), The internationalisation of the firm – four Swedish cases, *Journal of Management Studies*, 3 (October), pp. 305–322.

Johanson, J. and Vahlne, J.-E. (1977), The internationalisation process of the firm – a model of knowledge development and increasing foreign market commitment, *Journal of International Business Studies*, 8 (1), pp. 23–32.

Johanson, J. and Mattsson, L.-G. (1988), Internationalisation in industrial systems – a network approach, In Hood, N. and Vahlne, J.E., eds., *Strategies in Global Competition*, Croom Helm, New York, pp. 287–314.

Hoecklin, L. (1994), *Managing Cultural Differences: Strategies for Competitive Advantage*, Addison-Wesley, Wokingham, UK.

Hofstede, G. (1991), *Culture and Organisations: Software of the Mind*, McGraw Hill, Maidenhead, UK.

Hollensen, S. (1998), *Global Marketing: A Market-Responsive Approach*, Prentice Hall, London.

Hyder, A.S. and Ghauri, P.N. (2000), Managing international joint venture relationships: a longitudinal perspective, *Industrial Marketing Management*, 29 (3), pp. 205–218.

Keeble, D., Lawson, C., Smith, H.L., Moore, B. and Wilkinson, F. (1998), Internationalisation processes, networking and local embeddedness in technology-intensive small firms, *Small Business Economics*, 11 (4), pp. 327–342.

Kiong, T.C. and Kee, Y.P. (1998), Guanxi bases, Xinyong and Chinese business networks, *British Journal of Sociology*, 49 (1), pp. 75–96.

Lovett, S., Simmons, L.C. and Kali, R. (1999), Guanxi versus the market: ethics and efficiency, *Journal of International Business Studies*, 30 (2), pp. 231–248.

Nohria, N. and Ghoshal, S. (1997), *The Differentiated Network*, Jossey-Bass Publishers, San Francisco, CA.

Root, F.R. (1994), *Entry Strategies for International Markets*, Lexington Books, New York.

Trompenaars, F. (1993), *Riding the Waves of Culture: Understanding Cultural Diversity in Business*, Economist Books, London.

Turnbull, P.W. and Valla, J.-P., eds. (1986), *Strategies for International Industrial Marketing*, Croom Helm, London.

Usunier, J.-C. (2000), *Marketing Across Cultures*, 3rd edition, Prentice Hall, Harrow, UK.

Yang, M. (1994), *Gifts, Favours and Banquets: the Art of Social Relationships in China*, Cornell University Press, New York.

Yeung, H.W.-c. (1998), *Transnational Corporations and Business Networks, Hong Kong Firms in the ASEAN Region*, Routledge, London.

Chapter 12

Anderson, J.C. and Narus, J.A. (1990), A model of distributor firm and manufacturing firm working partnership, *Journal of Marketing*, 54 (5), pp. 42–58.

Artz, K.W. (1999), buyer-supplier performance: the role of asset specificity, reciprocal investments and relational exchange, *British Journal of Management*, 10 (2), pp. 113–126.

Bergen, M., Dutta, S. and Walker, O. C. (1992), agency relationships in marketing: a review of the implications and applications of agency and related theories, *Journal of Marketing*, July (56), pp. 1–24.

Blau, P.M. (1964), *Exchange and Power in Social Life*, Wiley, New York.

Booz, Allen and Hamilton (1999), *Payment, The Battle Banks must win*, Booz, Allen and Hamilton, McLean, VA.

Boyle, B.A. and Dwyer, F.R. (1995), power, bureaucracy, influence and performance: their relationship in industrial distribution channels, *Journal of Business Research*, 32, (3), pp. 189–200.

Cook, K.S. and Emerson, R.M. (1978), Power, equity, communication in exchange networks, *American Sociological Review*, October (43), pp. 721–739.

Dalstrom, R., McNeilly, K.M. and Speh, T.W. (1996), Buyer-seller relationships in the procurement of logistical services, *Journal of the Academy of Marketing Science*, 24 (2), pp. 110–124.

Datamonitor (1998), *Consumer Trends in UK Retail Banking*, DMFS 0421, London.

Datamonitor (1999), *UK Retail Banking and Building Societies*, DMFS 0704, London.

Dawkins, P.M. and Reichheld, F.F. (1990), Customer retention as a competitive weapon, *Directors and Boards*, Summer, pp. 42–47.

Donaldson, B. (1995), Manufacturers need to show greater commitment to customer service, *Industrial Marketing Management* 24, pp. 421–430.

Donaldson, B. and O'Toole, T. (2000), Classifying relationship structures: relationship strength in industrial markets, *Journal of Business and Industrial Marketing* 15 (7), pp. 491–504.

Dwyer, F., Schurr, P.H. and Oh, S. (1987), Developing Buyer-Seller Relationships, *Journal of Marketing*, April, 51 (2), pp. 11-27.

Dyer, J.H. (1996), Specialized supplier networks as a source of competitive advantage: evidence from the auto industry, *Strategic Management Journal*, 17, (4), pp. 271–291.

Eccles, R.G. (1991), The performance measurement manifesto, *Harvard Business Review*, 69, (1), pp. 131-137.

Ernst and Young (1999), *E-commerce: Customer Relationship Management, Special Report on Technology in Financial Services*, Ernst & Young, New York.

Evans, J.R. and Laskin, R.L. (1994), The relationship marketing process: a conceptualisation and application, *Industrial Marketing Management*, 23, pp. 439–452.

Ganesan, S. (1994), Determinants of long-term orientation in buyer-seller relationships, *Journal of Marketing* 58 (2), pp. 1–19.

Goodman, J.A. (1995), Building a world-class service system and setting rational priorities, *Tarp Assistance Research Program*, June, p. 3.

Gummesson, E. (1999), *Total Relationship Marketing*, Butterworth Heinemann, Oxford.

Hakansson, Hakan, ed. (1982), *International Marketing and Purchasing of Industrial Goods*, Wiley, London.

Heide, J.B. and John, G. (1988), The role of dependence balancing in safeguarding transaction-specific assets in conventional channels, *Journal of Marketing*, 52 (1), pp. 20–35.

Heide, J.B. and Stump, R.L. (1995), Performance implications of buyer-supplier relationships in industrial marketing – a transaction cost explanation, *Journal of Business Research*, 32 (1), pp. 57–66.

Heskett, J.L., Sasser, Jr., E. and Schlesinger, L.A. (1997), *The Service Profit Chain*, The Free Press, New York.

Heskett,J.L., Jones, T.O., Loveman, W.G., Sasser, W.E. and Schlesinger, L.A. (1994), Putting the service profit chain to work, *Harvard Business Review*, Mar.–Apr., pp. 164–174.

Jackson, B.B. (1985), *Winning and Keeping Industrial Customers*, Lexington Books, New York.

Jones, T.O. and Sasser, W.E. (1995), Why satisfied customers defect, *Harvard Business Review*, Nov.–Dec., pp. 88–99.

Joseph, W.B., Gardner, J.T., Thach, S. and Vernon, F. (1995), How industrial distributors view distributor-supplier partnership arrangements, *Industrial Marketing Management*, January (24), pp. 27–36.

Kalwani, M.U. and Narayandas, N. (1995), Long-term manufacturer-supplier relationships: do they pay off for supplier firms? *Journal of Marketing*, January (59), pp. 1–16.

Kaplan, R.S. and Norton, D.P. (1996), *The Balanced Scorecard*, Harvard Business School Press, Boston, MA.

Ketchen, Jr., D.J., Thomas, J.B. and McDaniel, Jr., R.R. (1996), Process, content and context: synergistic effects on organisational performance, *Journal of Management*, 22 (2), pp. 231–257.

Knauer, V. (1992), *Increasing Customer Satisfaction*, U.S. Office of Consumer Affairs, Pueblo, CA.

Kumar, N., Stern, L.W. and Achrol, R.S. (1992), Assessing reseller performance from the perspective of the supplier, *Journal of Market Research*, May, 29 (2), pp. 238–253.

Leuthesser, L. and Ajay, K. (1995), Relational behaviour in business markets: implications for relationship management, *Journal of Business Research*, 34 (3), pp. 221–233.

Macneil, I.R. (1980), *The New Social Contract*, Yale University Press, New Haven, CT.

McNeilly, K.M. and Russ, F.A. (1992), Co-ordination in the marketing channel, In Frazier, Gary L., ed., *Advances in Distribution Channel Research,* Vol. 1, JAI Press, London, pp. 161–186.

Mintel (1998), *Customer Loyalty in Retailing*, Mintel, London.

Mohr, J. and Spekman, R. (1994), Characteristics of partnership success: partnership attributes, communication behaviour and conflict resolution, *Strategic Management Journal*, 15 (2, February), pp. 135–152.

Morgan, R.M. and Hunt, S.D. (1994), The commitment-trust theory of relationship marketing, *Journal of Marketing*, 58 (3, July), pp. 20–38.

Morgan Stanley Dean Witter (1999), *The Internet and Financial Services*, Morgan Stanley Dean Witter, New York.

Noordewier, T.G., John, G. and Nevin, J. R. (1990), Performance outcomes of purchasing arrangements in industrial buyer-vendor relationships, *Journal of Marketing*, 54 (4, October), pp. 80–93.

O'Toole, T. and Donaldson, W.G. (2000), Relationship governance structures and performance, *Journal of Marketing Management,* 16 (4), pp. 327–341.

Reicheld, F.F. (1996), *The Loyalty Effect: The Hidden Force Behind Growth, Profits and Lasting Value*, Harvard Business School Press, Boston, MA.

Reicheld, F.F. and Sasser, W.E. (1990), Zero defection: quality comes to services, *Harvard Business Review*, Sep.–Oct., pp. 105-111.

Ross, S.A. (1973), The economic theory of agency: the principal's problem, *American Economic Review,* 63 (2), pp. 134–139.

Sako, M. (1992), *Prices, Quality and Trust: Inter-firm Relations in Britain and Japan*, Cambridge University Press, Cambridge, MA.

Williamson, O.E. (1985), *The Economic Institutions of Capitalism*, The Free Press, New York.

Young J.A., Gilbert, F.W. and McIntyre, F.S. (1996), An investigation of relationalism across a range of marketing relationships and alliances, *Journal of Business Research*, 35 (2), pp. 139–151.

Chapter 13

Anderson, J.C. and Narus, J.A. (1990), A model of distributor firm and manufacturing firm working partnerships, *Journal of Marketing*, 54 (January), pp. 42–58.

Barringer, B.R. and Harrison, J.S. (2000), Walking a tightrope: creating value through inter-organisational relationships, *Journal of Management*, 26 (3), pp. 367–403.

Easton, G. (1998), Case research as a methodology for industrial networks: a realist apologia, In Naude, P. and Turnbull, P.W., eds., *Network Dynamics in International Marketing*, Pergamon, Oxford, pp. 73–87.

Fournier, S., Dobscha, S. and Mick, D.G. (1998), Preventing the premature death of relationship marketing, *Harvard Business Review*, 76 (1), pp. 42–51.

Ganesan, S. (1994), Determinants of long-term orientation in buyer-seller relationships, *Journal of Marketing*, 58 (April), pp. 1–19.

Hakansson, H., ed. (1982), *International Marketing and Purchasing of Industrial Goods – an Interaction Approach*, Wiley, Chichester.

Hallen, L., Johanson, J. and Seyed-Mohamed, N. (1991), Interfirm adaptation in business relationships, *Journal of Marketing*, 55 (April), pp. 29–37.

LaBerge, M. and Svendsen, A. (2000), New growth: fostering collaborative business relationships, *The Journal for Quality and Participation*, 10 (3), pp. 48–50.

Moller, K. and Halinen, A. (2000), Relationship marketing theory: its roots and direction, *Journal of Marketing Management*, 16 (1–3), pp. 29–54.

O'Malley, L. and Tynan, C. (1999), The utility of the relationship metaphor in consumer markets: a critical evaluation, *Journal of Marketing Management*, 15 (7), pp. 587–602.

Index